Learning to Teach in an Era of Privatization

Global Trends in Teacher Preparation

EDITED BY

Christopher A. Lubienski

T. Jameson Brewer

Foreword by Janelle Scott

TEACHERS COLLEGE PRESS
TEACHERS COLLEGE | COLUMBIA UNIVERSITY
NEW YORK AND LONDON

Published by Teachers College Press, 1234 Amsterdam Avenue, New York, NY 10027

Cover photo by Hero Images / Getty Images.

Library of Congress Cataloging-in-Publication Data is available at loc.gov

ISBN 978-0-8077-6159-5 (paper)
ISBN 978-0-8077-6180-9 (hardcover)
ISBN 978-0-8077-7767-1 (ebook)

Printed on acid-free paper
Manufactured in the United States of America

CAL*: For Jameson, and all my students, past, present, and future, who make mentoring so fulfilling.*

TJB*: For my mentors (Chris above all), my teachers past and present, and the generations of future teachers who, through their dedication and commitment to the common good, bring out the very best in their students.*

Contents

Foreword

Teachers on the Move

American teachers are joining together in broad public activism not seen for some time. The "Red for Ed" movement, an effort to generate public support for increased investment in public education, including better salaries and benefits for teachers and instructional aides, and a curtailment of austerity and privatization policies, has been spurred on by rank and file, progressive unionism, and by accumulated frustrations over more than a decade of fiscal austerity, and longstanding state disinvestment from public education. Massive teacher demonstrations in Oklahoma and West Virginia, South Carolina, and teacher strikes in Los Angeles, Denver, Chicago, and Oakland have joined issues of teacher salaries and benefits into a broader framework that is elevating the public nature and purpose of public education. This framework is critical of the growth and concentration of charter schools, school closures, ballooning class sizes, racial and social class segregation, the lack of school-based supports for students, including nurses, counselors, coaches, and librarians, and the uses of high-stakes testing and other summative accountability metrics to evaluate teacher performance. In Chicago, Washington, DC, and Los Angeles, charter school educators have also participated in strikes against their management organizations, thereby upending popular notions that charter school teachers and organized labor were always incongruent.

These teacher movements in traditional public schools and charter schools are far from simple labor actions. They represent many years of teachers organizing against what have become the commonsense hallmarks of the so-called "education reform" movement. For example, teacher labor actions in Oakland and Los Angeles have placed the growth and concentration of charter schools as central in their concerns, arguing that the concentration of charter schools has drained resources from traditional public schools, and that the charter schools' tendency to underserve students requiring special education supports, homeless students, or students in foster care has placed the onus of supporting and educating these students on public schools that are already under financial strain. And in Denver, in 2019, teachers went on strike in part to oppose the pay-for-performance plan, known as ProComp, that the union had previously supported in cooperation with reformers and philanthropic actors (Will, 2019).

Yet these strikes and mass actions also reflect a re-envisioning of the teacher profession itself. The rise and institutionalization of alternative pathways into teaching, most famously through programs like Teach For America, and also through related organizations that bypass schools of education to prepare teachers, reveals how some policymakers and advocates regard the practice of teaching: itinerant work, requiring technical skills that result in improved test scores or proficiency rates, but not necessarily calling for pedagogical, philosophical, or cultural expertise. Teacher educators have similarly raised questions about what they perceive to be a narrowing of teacher preparation to technical proficiency, often at the expense of helping teachers to understand and interrupt longstanding racial, gender, linguistic, and other forms of inequality in schools and school systems (Phillip et al., 2018).

In many school districts, a growing number of new teachers don't expect to remain in the classroom for more than a few years. In addition, many who hope to make teaching their long-term profession find that they cannot withstand the lack of resources, support, and investment in their professional development, and they leave the classroom permanently, often within 5 years of entering teaching. Those who stay find that they are unable to afford to live and thrive on their salaries, and take on work in the "gig" economy by subsidizing their pay with ride-share driving, tutoring, babysitting, and other service provisions. Teacher movements and strike actions are demanding that policymakers broaden and deepen their investments to revive and strengthen public supports for public education.

It is in this politically charged context that this essential volume emerges. Christopher Lubienski and T. Jameson Brewer have assembled a wonderful collection that examines the role of market-oriented education reforms in teaching and teacher preparation. The researchers have crafted careful, theoretically rich analyses that help us make sense of the fraught terrain in which teachers enter their profession, and further help us to understand who stays, who leaves, and why. Undergirding these important chapters is an understanding of the essential role that teachers play in fortifying robust, equitable, and high-quality public schools, but also in strengthening an increasingly fragile and fractured democratic society. The chapters grapple with core, critical questions about the present and future of teaching in light of the dominance of ideologies that support the privatization and marketization of education. Together, these chapters will help readers make sense of the current mass activism of teachers, as well as the forces that have come to shape teacher preparation, curriculum, and teacher evaluation policies. Ultimately, and perhaps most importantly, this book will help readers consider possibilities for democratic visions for the teaching profession and in public education, particularly in this time of intense political polarization when critical citizen engagement with our public institutions and policies is deeply needed.

—Janelle Scott, University of California, Berkeley

REFERENCES

Phillip, T., Souto-Manning, M., Anderson, L., Horn, I., Andrews, D. C., Stillman, J., & Varghese, M. (2018). Making justice peripheral by constructing practice as "core": How the increasing prominence of core practices challenges teacher education. *Journal of Teacher Education, 70*(3), 1–14.

Will, M. (2019). Denver teachers to strike over merit-pay system. *Education Week*. Retrieved from www.edweek.org/ew/articles/2019/02/06/denver-teachers-to-strike-over-merit-pay-system.html

Teaching as a Profession in an Age of Privatization

Issues, Advocacy, and Approaches

T. Jameson Brewer and Christopher A. Lubienski

Preparing teachers to educate the next generation is crucial for states and nations. But in an age of consumer choice, decentralization, and deregulation in education, policymakers sometimes demonstrate surprisingly little awareness of the impacts of such reforms on those doing the actual teaching, and especially on their preparation for the profession. While similar neglect is evident in other policy areas such as healthcare, geopolitics, and law (Nichols, 2017), this inattention, in education specifically, raises a number of questions: To what extent has the push for privatization and marketization of education in general shaped how we recruit and train the next generation of teachers? Who then goes into teaching? What are they taught and why? How do such policies impact the dispositions of colleges of education and alternative teacher certification organizations? And what are the implications of a move away from public control of the teaching profession for the larger (small d) democratic project of public education itself?

The growing tide of educational reforms that seek to inject competition into education often aims at education schools' "monopoly" on teacher training (Walberg & Bast, 2003), and finds its ideological antecedents in the push for deregulation in the 1980s and Milton Friedman's (1995) call to make public education a private endeavor (Ball, 1994, 2007, 2012; Harvey, 2005). This volume develops a more robust understanding of the nature of such reforms in teacher preparation—broadly conceived—as well as an in-depth appreciation of how these policies, practices, and ideologies have taken root in colleges of education and alternative certification programs domestically and internationally.

TEACHER PREPARATION IN THE UNITED STATES

Families in post-colonial United States used a range of what we would now consider to be non-public schooling options, from home-based education, to charity schools, to town "academies," to itinerant tutors to provide an education to children. Given the myriad forms of schooling, there was not much in the way of formalized teacher preparation or certification before the creation of the public school system. The development of normal schools to train teachers coincided with Horace Mann's general call for "common schools" as a vehicle for mass public education in the early 19th century. As most schools—overseen by local communities and towns—focused primarily on teaching the Bible (Fraser, 2014; Urban & Wagoner, 2009), individuals who were seen to be moral and upstanding and who possessed knowledge of the Bible were the ones hired to teach. The formal requirements for maintaining a job as a teacher were, in some instances, less being a good teacher and more being a good person, as evidenced even in the early 20th century by female teachers being prohibited from riding in cars with men other than a father or brother and not being allowed to spend time in downtown ice cream shops (Strauss, 2011).

Among the most notable early forms of a more formalized preparation for teachers can be found in Catharine Beecher's Hartford Female Seminary where she trained women for work in education. And while Beecher's ideology was one that also celebrated the traditional role of woman-at-home, she forged new understandings about the role of women outside of the home—predominantly as schoolteachers (Urban & Wagoner, 2009)—as she advocated for the United States to open "normal" schools that would train teachers the way France and Prussia did (the latter's form of schooling becoming the model upon which U.S. schools ultimately were modeled) (Beecher, 1835). Normal schools would, in time, become the modern colleges of education that oversee teacher preparation. To this day, these colleges of education and traditionally certified teachers are the mainstay of the teaching profession in the United States. Colleges of education have certainly evolved from Beecher's regulations and oversight, grounded in her theology, to oversight from the Council for the Accreditation of Educator Preparation (CAEP) that now regulates almost all traditional forms of teacher preparation. CAEP is a relatively recent consolidation of the National Council for the Accreditation of Teacher Education (NCATE) that began in 1954 with the goal of "rais[ing] the quality of preparation [of teachers]" and the Teacher Education Accreditation Council (TEAC) founded in 1997 to ensure evidence-based qualifications (Council for the Accreditation of Educator Preparation, n.d.).

While public schools have long required formal certification, private schools have historically set their own standards for what constitutes readiness or qualification to teach. Similarly, home schooling, on the rise in a political and legal environment conducive to privatization, has not brought with it oversight over who is qualified to teach; many states have no standard requirements. In fact, private schools and home schooling alike have no standardized requirements that teachers possess content-specific backgrounds or degrees in education (Brewer & Lubienski, 2017).

Juxtaposed to the traditional college of education and certified teacher are those alternative certification programs and organizations that circumvent the years of coursework, practicum experience, and in many cases, the pedagogical tenets of teacher preparation associated with colleges of education. The term "alternative" in the phrase *alternative teacher preparation* situates such teacher preparation outside the recent historical context of locating teacher preparation within education schools in higher education institutions. It equally situates teacher training outside of normal conceptions of professional training and credentialing—a point we take up further below. On the face of it, alternative certification programs operate under the premise of: (1) injecting competition into the "monopoly" of teacher preparation historically held largely by state universities, and/or (2) proposing that teacher preparation can be expedited and that extensive training in both methodology and practicum practice (i.e., student teaching) is not necessary for sufficient teacher preparation. Alternative certification processes and organizations have received increasing support for expansion given the purported difficulty of finding teachers for "hard-to-staff" schools—often urban schools that serve predominately non-White and non-affluent students. The combination of those assumptions works to justify the existence of alternative certification programs as a necessity to combat burdensome government and professional oversight and expenses at the state level (e.g., funding for colleges of education) in addition to offering individuals who aspire to be teachers a faster—and assuredly cheaper—entry into the field while seemingly serving as the best solution to a problem that traditional colleges of education have not been able to solve.

THE LANDSCAPE OF ALTERNATIVE CERTIFICATION

Alternative certification programs have taken on many shapes and sizes and have expanded their functions and agendas beyond teacher preparation. The most notable of nationwide programs include Teach For America (TFA), the New Teacher Project (TNTP), and the Relay Graduate School of Education (formerly known as "Teacher U"). (There are also city-specific programs like the New York City Teaching Fellows and state-specific programs for alternative licensing. However, such state-based licensing programs tend not to recruit candidates; rather, they provide coursework, often in partnership with a local university's college of education, for individuals who are seeking employment as a teacher but do not have a traditional background or training in education.) TFA recruits individuals with no background in education and gives them a 5-week crash course in training—including only 18 hours of student teaching—and places them in schools serving low-income students (Brewer, 2014). Additionally, the organization has informed or inspired a myriad of spin-off reform organizations. For example, TNTP was founded in 1997 by TFA alumna Michelle Rhee and functions in similar ways to that of TFA; an important aspect specific to TNTP has been the organization's production of original research that has argued that teacher unions are one of the main obstacles to education reform (Levin, Mulhern, & Schunck, 2005) and per the ongoing myth that public schools continue to fail students (The New Teacher Project, 2018). Within the hyper-focus on testing accountability, TNTP produced a study that concluded that current forms of teacher professional development are inadequate and that professional development should be more specific toward helping teachers increase metrics (e.g., test scores) (The New Teacher Project, 2015). TNTP founder Rhee became Chancellor of DC Public Schools in 2007 and resigned in 2010 following an election cycle that challenged her credibility and accusations of cheating that put her on the defensive. Following her resignation, Rhee established Students First, a lobbying organization that publishes a state-based grading scale each year in addition to providing political and financial support for anti-union activities. Students Matter (an organization that is supported by Rhee and Students First) was also involved in advancing the anti-teacher union case of *Vergara v California*, which made national headlines when a court found that teacher tenure laws were unconstitutional because they protected ineffective teachers at the expense of students' access to quality education (Students Matter, 2014).

The Relay Graduate School of Education ("Relay") was founded as a partnership between three large charter network providers: Uncommon Schools, Knowledge is Power Program (KIPP), and Achievement First. Heralded by then-Secretary of Education Arne Duncan (U.S. Department of Education, 2014), Relay has quickly become a mainstay for the alternative certification of charter school teachers in addition to providing credentialing for TFA corps members outside of traditional colleges of education. Relay has also become a source for districts seeking to attend to the present teacher shortage. Established at Hunter College by David Steiner and in conjunction with charter operators Norman Atkins (Uncommon Schools) and David Levin (KIPP), Relay is an initiative grounded on the assertion that teacher preparation should be characterized by more clinical practice or "training," and less on the theoretical or methodological preparation usually found in traditional colleges of education (Carey, 2009). Unlike TFA's training that consists of only five weeks in the summer, Relay was designed as a master's degree program where candidates spend the bulk of their time teaching. Relay and its founders assert that the course of study prescribed for preservice teachers at traditional colleges of education is antiquated and does not meet the demands of schooling in the 21st century—namely charter schools—and that "the existing university-based process of teacher training and licensure wasn't giving [charter schools] enough of the staff that they required" (Carey, 2009). For a more robust examination of Relay, see Chapter 4.

Market-oriented educational reforms fueled by venture philanthropic funding and spearheaded by intermediary organizations have spread through the United States (La Londe, Brewer, & Lubienski, 2015; Lubienski, Brewer, &

La Londe, 2015; Reckhow, 2013; Reckhow & Snyder, 2014; Scott, Jabbar, Goel, Debray, & Lubienski, 2015) and throughout the globe. Internationally, Teach First (TF) and Teach For All (TFAll) are examples of exporting the belief that what is needed most in education reform is easing entry into the teaching profession. TF, founded in 2002, and TFAll presuppose that limited pedagogical training is needed in the course of teacher preparation; instead, they favor selecting for certain traits that are deemed beneficial to the classroom. The quest for certainty in education affords alternative certification programs the opportunity to "plan backward" from high test scores to the purported individual characteristics of teachers that facilitate such academic growth. TF and TFAll have successfully exported TFA's disposition that teacher preparation need not adhere to the regulated traditional system of training and credentialing (Brewer, deMarrais, & McFaden, forthcoming; La Londe et al., 2015; Straubhaar & Friedrich, 2015).

THE (DE-)PROFESSIONALIZATION OF TEACHING

While there are jokes about incapable teachers, and the supposed low bar for people going into the field, parents and policymakers also want the best possible classroom experience for children. In an area where there is substantial tacit or arcane knowledge, such as medicine or the law, the non-expert public often has little way of evaluating the abilities or expertise of those providing services. Such fields, governed by professional models, put much stock in training and inculcation into a professional community, partly as a way of certifying and signaling the expertise of a service provider. After all, the average person might not understand much about neuroscience or bankruptcy law, but they do not want just anyone operating on them or representing them in court. Instead, they look to individuals who have devoted substantial amounts of time to training and preparation.

This raises the question: What constitutes a profession? What sets a profession apart from any other job? In contrast to a non-professional job, a "true profession . . . is an occupation that is regarded as a position of which a certain amount of authority, autonomy, and [a] formal body of knowledge is afforded to the individuals [within that group]" (Harness, 2012, p. 3), and that concentrated knowledge conveys a professional status and expertise that is not readily available to non-members (Nichols, 2017). Given the onerous task of acquiring such knowledge, entry into a professional field is heavily regulated and, consequently, "an autonomous profession proves its worth to society—within markets or political systems—as a result of the perceived value of its trademark skill, developed through intense training" (Purinton, 2012, p. 30). The designation of a professional status is arguably clear within the medical field (doctors and nurses), law (lawyers and judges), aviation, etc., but remains unclear within education.

The uncertainty over the status of teaching as a profession has become exacerbated as educational reforms have challenged professional autonomy through the exertion of external control and oversight of the teaching profession. External reforms have created an environment that challenges the expectation of autonomy within the teaching profession and, ultimately, has led to a constrained sense of professionalism (Willis & Sandholtz, 2009) that has driven many teachers out of the profession (Dworkin & Tobe, 2015; Riggs, 2013; Vandenberghe & Huberman, 1999). And while the past few decades have seen an increase in attempts to undermine autonomy within education, the teaching profession has long been confronted with assumptions surrounding the need for extensive training given that teaching in the United States has long been understood as a feminized job requiring little more than the skill of nurturing (Goldstein, 2014; Griffiths, 2006; Urban & Wagoner, 2009). The maintenance of this understanding has afforded the most recent wave of education reform the opportunity to attack teacher pay, unionization, and the idea of teaching as a profession. And, in fact, teaching positions in the United States remain largely occupied by females who are paid significantly less—up to 60% less (OECD, 2017; Strauss, 2017)—than their similarly college-educated peers (Allegretto, Corcoran, & Mishel, 2004; Will, 2018). Regarding teaching as women's work began with Beecher's campaign to recruit women into teaching as "missionary work" (Burstyn, 1974; Goldstein, 2014). Women teachers in the 1800s and for the greater part of the 1900s were expected to quit their jobs upon marriage and pregnancy, highlighting the understanding of teaching as a temporary position. Much in the same vein, alternative teacher certification programs like Teach For America, which establish the expectation that their teachers teach for only 2 years, bolster this conception of teaching as a temporary job (Brewer, 2014). Additionally, if teaching is understood as a feminized job requiring no training, knowledge, autonomy, or self-regulation, or viewed as a job that is temporary (i.e., not a profession), then it becomes easier to rationalize low salaries. These low salaries are justified through the myth of teaching being easy work or, by high-achieving individuals, through a belief that they can soon move into a higher-salaried position by capitalizing on the prestige of alternative certification programs like TFA on their curriculum vitae.

The debate surrounding whether or not teaching is a true profession, a "helper" profession, has any professional status at all is decidedly unsettled (Ginsburg & Megahed, 2011; Harness, 2012). Both true professions and helping professions have relatively high standards for entry. But the popular notion that teacher training and certification is not, or should not be, similar to the rigorous requirements found in other professions implies that nearly anyone can teach. This disposition is not necessarily an anti-professional or anti-expert stance, as it is seemingly unique to education. The common American adage of "those who can, do; those who can't, teach" is not a sentiment projected onto other professions such as medicine and law. Low salaries and access to teaching by way of fast-entry alternative programs reinforce the ideas that teaching is not a full profession and preservice teachers do not benefit from a multi-year training process—thus, it is not to be understood as a profession.

Even within traditional certification programs that require preservice teachers to complete a multi-year program, the manifestations of privatization, commercialization, and commodification have altered the experience for many students. Many traditional university programs have reduced the total amount of pedagogical and foundations courses in the course sequence in favor of more content-area coursework. The theory, as it were, is that teachers should have more expertise in their subject/content area and less on the softer skills of teaching such as understanding educational psychology or the philosophy, history, and politics of education, including the impact of race, class, and gender in education (Butin, 2007; Sirotnik, 1990; Swain, 2013; Tutwiler et al., 2012).

An essential part of the general anti-state, pro-market tendencies in policymaking that wish to see an end to the "monopoly" that government holds in education by way of alternative certification and the reimagining of traditional certification coursework is the strong belief that government-run schools and teachers have generally failed. While some reformers advocate for markets for the sake of markets, many education reformers advance from the position that public education in the United States has experienced a precipitous decline over the decades and, given the government "monopoly" of training teachers and overseeing schools, new non-governmental approaches must be employed (or, at the very least, tried). The myth of government failure in general, and the failed school and the bad teacher in particular, persists in popular and policy discourse (Berliner & Biddle, 1995; Berliner & Glass, 2014; Kumashiro, 2012) despite being debunked over and over again (Berliner & Glass, 2014; Lubienski & Lubienski, 2014; Ravitch, 2010, 2013). Teachers remain a primary scapegoat and target of the latest generation of education reform.

Deron Boyles (who authored Chapter 1) previously argued that the privatization of education requires, in part, that teaching not be understood as a soft service (holistically) but rather as a hard service (measurable minutiae) for the purpose of quantification. Accordingly, the "de-skill[ing] [of] teaching and learning such that the traditional 'soft' services become subsumed under the behavioristic, scientistic, economic logics of 'hard' services" in an effort to reduce teaching and learning down to "their most component parts for ease of accountancy" (Boyles, 2011, p. 359). Operating within business and market logic, teaching and teacher preparation should become subservient to market measurements, accountability, and consideration of return on investment. Indeed, under President Obama, the U.S. Department of Education went so far as to suggest that colleges of education be evaluated based, in part, on how well the students of their graduates did on some test at some point in the distant future (Kumashiro, 2015). The logic is that the outcome of teaching and the preparation of teachers can be—and more to the point, should be—quantified into measurable and comparable units of measurement to determine value in the same way that shareholders might evaluate actions taken by the company and the consequent impact on share prices. This corporate-style approach to teacher preparation and the teaching profession situates teachers as being subjected to accountability, some would say. But others see this approach as positioning teachers as the target of skepticism and not as trusted professionals. What is clear is that this shift from organic or professional trust to contractual arrangements (Dworkin & Tobe, 2015) has eroded control over how teachers are trained, what that training looks like, who oversees that training, and who ultimately enters the teaching profession. Privatization requires deregulation and, as market factors overtake training, de-skilling is a necessary outcome. Ted Purinton (2012) notes that,

> De-skilling, then, is the natural consequence of neoliberalism, which seeks occupational deregulation in favor of flexible employment. A profession controls employment through training, *credentialing*, and performance monitoring and then obtains certification granting rights from the state. Flexible employment markets allow for quicker introduction into a field, as well as simpler firings by managers and fewer certification constraints from the state. (p. 30, emphasis added)

The efforts to privatize or deregulate teacher preparation have not been undertaken in a silo. On the contrary, the drive to deregulate colleges of education, to force them into more market-like institutional environments and to end their "monopoly" by allowing corporate competition, fits squarely within the broader agenda of privatization and deregulation affecting education as a whole along with many other sectors (healthcare, military endeavors, etc.). Parallel to the arguments set out by Friedman, many reformers have set out to dismantle public schools, through the capture and reorientation of the charter school movement, the creation and expansion of private school voucher systems, and the standardization, for accountability and profit, of school curriculum. Despite emerging research showing that school choice models exacerbate racial and economic segregation (Frankenberg, 2011; Frankenberg & Siegel-Hawley, 2011; Vasquez Heilig, Brewer, & Williams, in press), often producing educational outcomes that are no better and all too often worse than their public school counterparts (Lubienski & Lubienski, 2014), reformers have embraced choice models as a viable remedy to the perceived failing state of American public schools. It is important to point out that a growing number of reformers have accepted the downsides of choice since they seek choice not as a means to other ends, such as better learning, but for its own sake. In this logic, racial segregation and stagnant achievement are acceptable side effects of an educational market landscape (Hatfield & Malkus, 2017; Persson, 2015). This effort, however, is best understood as a solution that ignores the on-the-ground realities, since the majority of American parents are largely satisfied with their local public schools (deMarrais, Brewer, Atkinson, Herron, & Lewis, 2019; Lopez, 2010).

This volume is based on the idea that these momentous social and policy trends of moving toward competition and markets, while evident across many sectors and institutions in our society, remain particularly underexamined around teaching and teacher preparation. Teaching has consistently been a poor cousin to other professions, as reflected in the constant criticism leveled against traditional teacher preparation programs and used to bolster the argument for alternatives. While there has been research on the impact of teacher credentials and the relative effectiveness of alternative teacher preparation (much of which is discussed in this volume), too often that research has not been situated within the broader social and policy trend of moving toward market models based on competition and deregulation. In that regard, there is much more to learn. We do not know how changes in teacher preparation will reshape public schools, for instance. How will global shifts toward privatization and de-skilling of teacher preparation and the teaching profession manifest across international contexts? Are such moves rooted in, or in opposition to, popular control of public education? Are potential costs associated with a move toward a more competitive model worth the (potential) benefits? These are just some of the critical issues addressed in this volume.

ABOUT THIS BOOK

This book began in the spring of 2015 as many of the authors in this volume attended a 2-day working conference, The Privatization of Teacher Preparation and the Teaching Profession in the Age of Markets, at the University of Illinois at Urbana–Champaign, hosted by the Forum on the Future of Public Education. The goal of the working conference was to bring authors together to share papers in progress, engage in rich conversation and debate, and discuss the work with other faculty and students who attended the conference. After the conference, we set out to curate additional chapters in an effort to provide the reader with a nuanced, complex, and balanced view. We have been intentional about compiling a compelling and authoritative group of chapters from across the United States and around the globe, representing not only different areas of geographical focus, but also drawing on a diverse set of often quite distinct disciplinary perspectives. The authors offer varying views on marketization and alternative teacher training and a broad range of insights into the profound changes being experienced in teaching and teacher preparation.

The chapters in the first section of this volume lay out the philosophical foundations that provide the context and justification for (and against) the privatization of teacher preparation and the deprofessionalization of teaching. They explore how corporate ideology and commodification have shaped the educational policymaking landscape. This landscape has supported the implementation of the Common Core State Standards within the teaching profession and edTPA as a mechanism to evaluate teacher preparation under a corporate model. In Chapter 1, Deron Boyles offers a more philosophical exploration of the ways in which corporate ideology and ethical egoism have launched a joint assault to redefine the teaching profession. He argues that this aligns teaching with pro-business and pro-capitalist ideologies that have not only shifted teachers' pedagogical practices but have forced colleges of education to reimagine what it means to prepare educators. The commodification of education, teaching, and learning has, as Christopher Tienken and Dario Sforza explore in Chapter 2, been made manifest through the Common Core State Standards. Tienken and Sforza explicate the ways in which educational policies that align with the broader assault on education have a detrimental impact on creativity, often orienting conceptions of creativity toward pro-market dispositions. Similarly, pro-market reforms have redefined notions of accountability—specifically those directed at measuring preservice teachers and their ability to conform to a standardized landscape, as Westry Whitaker and Jim Burns take up in Chapter 3.

The chapters in the second section lay out specific domestic and international examples of how these broad dispositions of reform have impacted teacher preparation at a more local or focused level. In Chapter 4, Jamie Atkinson and Brian Dotts contend that the push for marketization and privatization within the educational landscape of teacher preparation has facilitated the rise of alternative training programs such as the Relay Graduate School. As they note, Relay not only represents the privatization of teacher training but reinforces the belief that educational practices (training and teaching) should be oriented toward marketization. The landscape of educational policy reform over the past two decades has, without a doubt, had a lasting impact on the teaching force. In Chapter 5, Anthony Cody draws on his more than 2 decades of experience working in K–12 schools to raise concerns about how the privatization, standardization, and hyper-accountability that are indicative of marketization have impacted teacher morale and damaged recruitment into the teaching profession. Chapter 6, written by Priya Goel La Londe and Warren Mark Liew, considers how the ideologies of marketization have taken shape in Singapore, with particular attention to shifts in policy and practice as they relate to teacher recruitment and training against the backdrop of social efficiency.

Noting that we are in an age of declining enrollment in teacher preparation programs, Hilary Conklin, Lauren Gatti, and Kavita Kapadia Matsko write in Chapter 7 that many traditional certification programs may be pressured to partner with non-traditional training programs, but this can result in partnerships that are incongruent with one another, causing negative impacts on teacher candidates and, in turn, their students. Chile has been a testing ground for most of the marketization reforms targeted at education. In Chapter 8, Carmen Montecinos and Beatriz Fernández argue that the many public–private arrangements across the educational landscape have not addressed the concerns of inequality and the impact such realities have for teacher candidates and students. As a result, neoliberalism in Chile has diminished the overall quality of teacher education programs across the country. Much like their partner organization Relay, Teach For America (TFA) operates as a considerable jurisdictional challenger within teacher preparation. In Chapter 9, Kerry Kretchmar, Beth Sondel, and Joseph Ferrare draw on social network analysis to highlight the ways in which TFA has situated itself within the broader network of organizations seeking to privatize teacher education and schooling. Not only do they point out the ways in which TFA represents the privatization of teacher preparation, they also show how the organization and its alumni go on to shape the public perception of schools (that is, that public schools have failed and traditionally certified teachers are to blame) through their policy advocacy. Chapter 10 stands in juxtaposition to that viewpoint as Denise Whitford, Dake Zhang, and Antonis Katsiyannis point to programs like TFA as a viable mechanism to address the growing teacher shortage that Anthony Cody explores in Chapter 5, while advocating for a balance between stricter admissions into the teaching profession and ameliorating a growing desire among Americans to enter the teaching profession.

As the reader will see, this volume offers a range of perspectives on a complex issue. We sought to compile chapters that, individually and in the aggregate, would help shape policy conversations around the critical issue of teaching and teacher preparation, particularly by offering deeper insights than what is typically the case with such discussions. Therefore, we want to express our gratitude to the authors and to participants in the discussions surrounding the development of this volume.

REFERENCES

Allegretto, S. A., Corcoran, S. P., & Mishel, L. (2004). *How does teacher pay compare? Methodological challenges and answers*. Economic Policy Institute: Washington, DC. Available at www.epi.org/files/page/-/old/books/teacher_pay-intro.pdf

Ball, S. (1994). *Education reform: A critical and post-structural approach*. Bristol, PA: Open University Press.

Ball, S. (2007). *Education plc: Understanding private sector participation in public sector education.* New York, NY: Routledge.

Ball, S. (2012). *Global education inc.: New policy networks and the neo-liberal imaginary.* New York, NY: Routledge.

Beecher, C. (1835). *An essay on the education of female teachers.* New York, NY: Van Nostrand & Dwight.

Berliner, D. C., & Biddle, B. J. (1995). *The manufactured crisis: Myths, fraud, and the attack on America's public schools.* Reading, MA: Addison-Wesley.

Berliner, D. C., & Glass, G. V. (2014). *50 myths and lies that threaten America's public schools: The real crisis in education.* New York, NY: Teachers College Press.

Boyles, D. (2011). "Public" schools, privatization, and the public/private distinction. In S. Tozer, B. P. Gallegos, A. M. Henry, M. B. Greiner, & P. G. Price (Eds.), *Handbook of research in the social foundations of education* (pp. 358–366). New York, NY: Routledge.

Brewer, T. J. (2014). Accelerated burnout: How Teach For America's academic impact model and theoretical framework can foster disillusionment among its corps members. *Educational Studies, 50*(3), 246–263.

Brewer, T. J., deMarrais, K., & McFaden, K. (Eds.). (forthcoming). *Teach for all counter-narratives: International perspectives on a global reform movement*. New York, NY: Peter Lang.

Brewer, T. J., & Lubienski, C. (2017). Homeschooling in the United States: Examining the rationales for individualizing education. *Pro-Posições, 28*(2), 21–38.

Burstyn, J. N. (1974). Catharine Beecher and the education of American women. *The New England Quarterly, 47*(3), 386–403.

Butin, D. W. (2007). Dark times indeed: NCATE, social justice, and the marginalization of multicultural foundations. *Journal of Educational Controversy, 2*(2), 1–17.

Carey, K. (2009). "Teacher U": A new model in employer-led higher education. Available at chronicle.com/article/Teacher-U-A-New-Model-in/49442/

Council for the Accreditation of Educator Preparation. (n.d.). History. Available at caepnet.org/about/history/

deMarrais, K., Brewer, T. J., Atkinson, J. C., Herron, B., & Lewis, J. (2019). *Philanthropy, hidden strategy, and collective resistance: A primer for concerned educators*. Borham, ME: Myers Education Press.

Dworkin, A. G., & Tobe, P. E. (2015). Does school accountability alter teacher trust and promote burnout? In J. H. Ballantine & J. Z. Spade (Eds.), *School and society: A sociological approach* (5th ed., pp. 183–192). Los Angeles, CA: Sage.

Frankenberg, E. (2011, Spring). Charter schools: A civil rights mirage? *Kappa Delti Pi Record, 47,* 100–105.

Frankenberg, E., & Siegel-Hawley., G (2011). Choice without equity: Charter school segregation and the need for civil rights standards. *Education Digest, 76*(5), 44–47.

Fraser, J. (2014). *The school in the United States: A documented history.* New York, NY: Routledge.

Friedman, M. (1995, June 25). *Public schools: Make them private* (Briefing Paper 23). Available at www.cato.org/publications/briefing-paper/public-schools-make-them-private

Ginsburg, M., & Megahed, N. M. (2011). Comparative perspectives on teachers and professionalism. In S. Tozer, B. P. Gallegos, A. M. Henry, M. B. Greiner, & P. G. Price (Eds.), *Handbook of research in the social foundations of education* (pp. 662–671). New York, NY: Routledge.

Goldstein, D. (2014). *The teacher wars: A history of America's most embattled profession.* New York, NY: Doubleday.

Griffiths, M. (2006). The feminization of teaching and the practice of teaching: Threat or opportunity? *Educational Theory, 56*(4), 387–406.

Harness, M. A. (2012). *Pretending teaching is a profession: Why public school teaching will never be considered a true profession.* (Master's thesis.) University of Tennessee, Knoxville. Available at trace.tennessee.edu/utk_gradthes/1243/

Harvey, D. (2005). *A brief history of neoliberalism*. Oxford, UK: Oxford University Press.

Hatfield, J., & Malkus, N. (2017). *Differences by design? Student composition in charter schools with different academic models.* Washington, DC: American Enterprise Institute.

Kumashiro, K. (2012). *Bad teacher! How blaming teachers distorts the bigger picture.* New York, NY: Teachers College Press.

Kumashiro, K. (2015). *Review of proposed 2015 federal teacher preparation regulations.* Boulder, CO: National Education Policy Center. Available at nepc.colorado.edu/thinktank/review-proposed-teacher-preparation

La Londe, P., Brewer, T. J., & Lubienski, C. (2015). Teach For America and teach for all: Creating an intermediary organization network for global education reform. *Education Policy Analysis Archives, 23*(47), 1–28.

Levin, J., Mulhern, J., & Schunck, J. (2005). *Unintended consequences: The case for reforming the staffing rules in urban teachers union contracts.* Brooklyn, NY: The New Teacher Project.

Lopez, S. J. (2010). America's views of public schools still far worse than parents'. *Gallup News*. Retrieved from news.gallup.com/poll/142658/americans-views-public-schools-far-worse-parents.aspx

Lubienski, C., Brewer, T. J., & La Londe, P. (2015). Orchestrating policy ideas: Philanthropies and think tanks in us education policy advocacy networks. *Australian Educational Researcher, 43*(1), 55–73.

Lubienski, C., & Lubienski, S. (2014). *The public school advantage: Why public schools outperform private schools.* Chicago, IL: The University of Chicago Press.

Nichols, T. (2017). *The death of expertise: The campaign against established knowledge and why it matters.* New York, NY: Oxford University Press.

OECD. (2017). *Education at a glance 2017: OECD indicators*. Paris, France: OECD. Retrieved from www.oecd-ilibrary.org/education/education-at-a-glance-2017_eag-2017-en

Persson, J. (2015, July 22). ALEC admits school vouchers are for kids in suburbia. *PR Watch*. Retrieved from www.prwatch.org/news/2015/07/12869/alec-school-vouchers-are-kids-suburbia

Purinton, T. (2012). Teachers as professionals: Owning instructional means and negotiating curricular ends. In J. A. Gorlewski, B. J. Porfilio, & D. A. Gorlewski (Eds.), *Using standards and high-stakes testing for students: Exploiting power with critical pedagogy* (pp. 27–44). New York, NY: Peter Lang.

Ravitch, D. (2010). *The death and life of the great American school system: How testing and choice are undermining education.* New York, NY: Basic Books.

Ravitch, D. (2013). *Reign of error: The hoax of the privatization movement and the danger to America's public schools*. New York, NY: Knopf.

Reckhow, S. (2013). *Follow the money: How foundation dollars change public school politics.* Oxford, UK: Oxford University Press.

Reckhow, S., & Snyder, J. (2014). The expanding role of philanthropy in education politics. *Educational Researcher, 43*(186), 186–195.

Riggs, L. (2013, October 18). Why do teachers quit? *The Atlantic.* Retrieved from www.theatlantic.com/education/archive/2013/10/why-do-teachers-quit/280699/

Scott, J., Jabbar, H., Goel, P., Debray, E. H., & Lubienski, C. (2015). Evidence use and advocacy coalitions: Intermediary organizations and philanthropies in Denver, Colorado. *Educational Policy Analysis Archives, 23*(124), 1–23.

Sirotnik, K. A. (1990). On the eroding foundations of teacher education. *Phi Delta Kappan, 71*(9), 710–716.

Straubhaar, R., & Friedrich, D. (2015). Theorizing and documenting the spread of Teach For All and its impact on global education reform. *Education Policy Analysis Archives, 23*(44), 1–11.

Strauss, V. (2011). Rules for teachers in 1872: No marriage for women or barber shops for men. Retrieved April 1, 2019 from www.washingtonpost.com/blogs/

answer-sheet/post/rules-for-teachers-in-1872-no-marriage-for-women-or-barber-shops-for-men/2011/06/01/AGTSSpGH_blog.html?utm_term=.2a5b9ce01910

Strauss, V. (2017). *Teachers in U.S. paid far less than similarly educated professionals, report finds.* Available at www.washingtonpost.com/news/answer-sheet/wp/2017/09/14/teachers-in-u-s-paid-nearly-60-percent-less-than-other-professionals-report-finds/?utm_term=.38043cce2438

Students Matter. (2014). *Vergara v. California* case summary. Retrieved from studentsmatter.org/our-case/vergara-v-california-case-summary/

Swain, A. (2013). The problem with "nuts and bolts:" How the emphasis on "highly qualified professionals" is undermining education. *Educational Studies, 49*(2), 119–133.

The New Teacher Project. (2015). *The mirage: Confronting the hard truth about our quest for teacher development.* Brooklyn, NY: The New Teacher Project.

The New Teacher Project. (2018). *The opportunity myth.* Brooklyn, NY: The New Teacher Project. Retrieved from tntp.org/assets/documents/TNTP_The-Opportunity-Myth_Web.pdf

Tutwiler, S. W., deMarrais, K., Gabbard, D., Hyde, A., Konkol, P., Li, H.-l., . . . Swain, A. (2012). Standards for academic and professional instruction in foundations of education, educational studies, and educational policy studies. *Educational Studies, 49*(2), 107–118.

Urban, W. J., & Wagoner, J. L. (2009). *American education: A history* (4th ed.). New York, NY: Routledge.

U.S. Department of Education. (2014). U.S. Department of Education proposes plan to strengthen teacher preparation. Retrieved from www.ed.gov/news/press-releases/us-department-education-proposes-plan-strengthen-teacher-preparation

Vandenberghe, R., & Huberman, A. M. (Eds.). (1999). *Understanding and preventing teacher burnout: A sourcebook of international research and practice.* Cambridge, UK: Cambridge University Press.

Vasquez Heilig, J., Brewer, T. J., & Williams, Y. (in press). Choice without inclusion? Comparing the intensity of racial segregation in charters and public schools at the local, state, and national levels. *Journal of Education Sciences.*

Vergara v. California (*Superior Court of the State of California* 2014).

Walberg, H. J., & Bast, J. L. (2003). *Education and capitalism: How overcoming our fear of markets and economics can improve America's schools.* Stanford, CA: Hoover Institution Press.

Will, M. (2018). Teachers are paid almost 20 percent less than similar professionals, analysis finds [Blog post]. *Education Week.* Retrieved from blogs.edweek.org/edweek/teacherbeat/2018/09/teachers_wage_penalty.html

Willis, J., & Sandholtz, J. (2009). Constrained professionalism: Dilemmas of teaching in the face of test-based accountability. *Teachers College Record, 111*(4), 1065–1114.

Part I

DISPOSITIONS, IDEOLOGY, AND PHILOSOPHY DRIVING EDUCATIONAL REFORMS

CHAPTER 1

Countering the Continued Corporate Assault on Schools

Endorsing *Public* Education, Ethical Altruism, and Critical Policy Studies

Deron Boyles

> Why do not the rich states use their wealth and solve their educational problems? They do not for several reasons. First, they encounter a clever tactic whereby one state is played against another by that segment of our population which chronically considers profits first and the education of children second, or not at all. (Norton, 1957, pp. 386–387)

Norton's concern is actually multifaceted: He laments that states, and their schools, have fallen prey to a logic of competition, greed, and selfishness. The result is dehumanizing to both teachers and students via the reproduction of corporate culture imposed on schools.

Nearly 20 years prior to Norton's article, the National Association of Manufacturers (NAM) circulated a memo making the case that the average American needed to be "sold" on the idea that the United States was the best country in the world and that industry, specifically high wages earned in what one billboard called "United States, Inc.," should be at the center of their initiative to "manufacture consent" (see Ewen, 1996, p. 303; Lippmann, 1922; Spring, 2003). NAM's campaign was titled "The American Way" and featured billboards across the country proclaiming "World's Highest Wages—There's No Way Like the American Way" (Ewen, 1996, p. 323). If there is any doubt about the role corporations play in influencing school culture, one need only be reminded of NAM's role in ridding schools of Harold Rugg's critical and influential social studies textbook series from the 1920s, "Man in His Changing Society" (Winters, 1967). Tarring it "un-American" and "subversive," NAM mounted a campaign to rid U.S. History of critique and argued that America's exceptionalism should be central to teaching social studies (Evans, 2007; Spring, 2003, 125–153). While Rugg's case was in the early 1940s, the recent arguments in Georgia, Oklahoma, and other states over the content of Advanced

Placement U.S. History (APUSH) is strikingly similar (Jacobs, 2015). Conservatives, overwhelmingly aligned with business interests, are shrill in claiming that the content of APUSH is "radically revisionist" and that it focuses far too much on themes like oppression and marginalization and not enough on free markets, Founding Fathers, and love of country. The economics curriculum in Texas was changed in 2010 so that "capitalism" would be replaced with "free market economics." The Republican members of the board feared that "capitalism" was subject to epithets like "capitalist pig" and believed that "free markets" could not be so tarnished along the same lines (McKinley, 2010). They also limited references to Thomas Jefferson (who advocated for the separation of church and state) and added Milton Friedman and Friedrich von Hayek in an effort to make the curriculum more pro-business (Weissert, 2018). I mention these historical morsels to remind us that corporate logic has been active in infiltrating or preying on schools for over a hundred years—and it continues today (Molnar, 2005; Saltman, 2012).

Carl Glickman (2009) also gestures toward this history in a wonderfully pithy *Phi Delta Kappan* article that helps me set the stage for the bulk of my initial comments on the future of public education in the United States. For the "Backtalk" section of the *Kappan*, he wrote a piece titled "Educators Tell Business How to Stop Ruining America." His commentary is informed by decades of economic discourse from the business world asserting that schools are failing, businesses are succeeding, and, thus, business people know what is best for schools, teachers, and students. Glickman mimics and mocks the idea that businesses should be telling schools how to operate in light of the corporate failures that led to the 2007 start of the Great Recession. Using language from *A Nation at Risk*, he writes that "the business and financial foundations of our society are currently being eroded by a rising tide of mediocrity that threatens our very future as a Nation and a people." He goes on:

> The hubris of high rollers on the top floors of America's giant companies permitting unfettered profit-making at the expense of others has no limit. To be blunt, the business community has become an industry at risk of implosion. To help our colleagues in the business community, we educators hereby recommend a new guiding and mentoring organization for business and financial institutions. The Education Roundtable will gather a team of the country's top educators, whose charge will be to set business standards, goals, and accountability structures for all corporations and financial institutions. (p. 392)

Given the theme of this book, Glickman's not-so-tongue-in-cheek evisceration of corporate culture and business influences provides me the opportunity to examine the nexus between the theme and business influences in light of both ethics and education policy. To do so, I clarify and situate two forms of ethics as part of my main argument. I then briefly outline the neoclassical economic foundation upon which most of education policy rests, provide examples of this policy's practical effects on teachers, and offer an appraisal of the consequences of corporate influences on teacher education policy specifically, and teaching in public education generally. I conclude the chapter with arguments in favor of critical policy studies (CPS) that reflect heterodox theories of economics and a commitment to social justice. By endorsing CPS in this way, I focus attention on the importance of ethical altruism and criticality for the future of public education in the United States.

My central claim is that education policy in the United States is inexorably linked to business interests and, therefore, promotes ethical egoism over ethical altruism. While I am tempted to declare that business ethics is an oxymoron, a more careful analysis reveals that the ethic of corporate America is egoism. The primary problem with applying business ethics to schools is that the goals and purposes of corporations are fundamentally *different in kind from,* and *antithetical to,* those of education. (Here I distinguish education, schooling, and training. Education is far broader in scope than either schooling [*qua* mechanisms for learning] or training [narrow expertise].) Business operates under the imperative of self-interest, manifest in profit-making, and is, in terms of ethics, a form of egoism. Milton Friedman (1970) summed it up in one sentence: "There is *one and only one* social responsibility of business . . . to use resources designed to increase profits."[1] When business logic drives the thinking and pervades the construction of education policy, the assumptions inherent in ethical egoism (be they rationalist or normative) become reified and other forms of ethics, in this case ethical altruism, are either marginalized or negated by neoclassical economic orthodoxy. In other words, to the degree that U.S. public schools function as businesses or extensions of businesses, they jettison altruism in favor of selfishness defined by and tied to "free market" rationality. Accordingly, they abdicate their altruistic ethical responsibility for *educating* in favor of the self-interest of ethical egoism and the narrow *training* it entails. This applies directly to teacher education insofar as certification requirements increasingly shift the focus away from courses that explore the history, philosophy, and sociology of teaching and learning. In their place are courses that de-professionalize teachers by imposing overly-detailed rubrics, models, and "best methods" technicalities that do not engage critical questions about how these rubrics, models, and methods undercut teacher autonomy and teacher intellect. This chapter explores education policy, teacher education policy, and the implications of corporate logic on both. I argue that education policy and teacher education policy are not separable because the overriding logic of business in education policy, writ large, directly influences teacher education policy and teacher practice. By exploring ethics, economics, and the implications of corporate influences on and in schools, this chapter demonstrates how nefarious neoclassic economics is to teacher education policy and practice.

ETHICS: EGOISM AND ALTRUISM

Ethicists make it clear that it is exceptionally hard to agree on a single definition of egoism (or altruism, for that matter). Ethical egoism manifests as descriptive or psychological egoism as well as normative egoism—under which rational and ethical egoism exist. The central questions include "Do I act for myself, a deity, or the good of the planet?" "Can I ever act with a complete disregard for my own interests?" "Is there any other reason, except self-interest, for considering the interests of others?" Descriptive or psychological egoism asserts that it is human nature to be wholly self-motivated and self-interested. Our motivation as human beings is to take care of ourselves. Normative egoism requires that we consider what we *ought* to do. Self-preservation is still sacrosanct here, but two distinct forms of normative egoism answer the "ought question" differently. Rational egoists, best represented by Ayn Rand, maintain that selfishness is a virtue and promoting our own interests is necessarily and always reasonable. Put another way, it is irrational not to pursue your own interests. Further, any emotional elements that might enter decisionmaking are anathema to rational egoists. Ethical egoists claim self-interest, too, but they are broader than rational egoists in that judgments made regarding what will benefit an individual most will, at least sometimes, entail sentiment or emotion (Glasgow, 1968; Glickman, 2009; Regis, 1980). In short, there are multiple forms of egoism. The one I think best describes corporations is ethical egoism. This does not mean that the people who populate businesses are evil or unethical. It also does not mean that many of those same people are cognizant of the theory they enact and enact upon others. It means that ethical egoism actively structures the metanarratives that influence the purpose of schools in the United States. Accordingly, democracy is replaced by privatization, "not simply because so many government functions are hired out to private firms, but, more importantly, because many citizens' attitude toward their government and their sense of public responsibility are shrinking so as to include only themselves and those intimates who form their private life" (Clohesy, 2000).

For the purpose of this chapter, neoclassical economics recasts egoism as reasoned choice—regarding human nature as dedicated to single-minded pursuit of self-interest. As Clohesy (2000) puts it,

> Neoclassical economics presumes rational individuals seeking to maximize their utility, the single-minded pursuit of self-interest, or *egoism*. The market, it is presumed, operates successfully because all entering it display rational, self-interested behavior. Although Adam Smith had taken the market to be an institution of self-interest contained within a larger society directed by moral sentiments such as benevolence, many contemporary economists seek to expand the market mechanism into a universal principle governing all practices so that all of life takes on market characteristics. (p. 238)

Set against ethical egoism is ethical altruism, the view that we are morally obliged to serve and help others so *they* may benefit. Altruism, as a form of consequentialism, means that an action is ethically correct if it results in the betterment of the welfare of others. In short, it is not about the individual, but supra-individual others. Teachers feature prominently here when their work yields increased knowledge, self-efficacy, and the well-being of their students. The problem is that teaching is increasingly non-altruistic insofar as "teaching" instantiates test-prep, scripted curriculum, and accountability schemes like pay-for-performance. That teaching, and by extension public education, is under attack from ethical egoism impels construction of a counternarrative to challenge the prevailing assumptions and enactments of neoclassical economic rationality.

ECONOMIC AND BUSINESS RATIONALITY OVER EDUCATION POLICY: BRIEF SURVEY OF NEOCLASSICAL ECONOMICS

According to Gordon Bigelow (2005), neoclassical economics is another way of articulating the logic of business. It is currently the overwhelming economic view propagated in free-market cultures and is being imposed on what we are calling public schools in the United States. Bigelow noted that

> neoclassical economics downplays the importance of human institutions, seeing instead a system of flows and exchanges that are governed by an inherent equilibrium. Predicated on the belief that markets operate in a scientifically knowable fashion, it sees them as self-regulating mathematical miracles, as delicate ecosystems best left alone. (p. 34; see also Fisher, 1980; Fullbrook, 2007)

Consequently, neoclassical economics positions itself as a science and claims objectivity in order to reify its standing and exert its power. When William Jevons made the case, in 1871, that economics was akin to physics, he elevated economics to a field that was supposed to be perceived as objective and value-free. The problem, as Bigelow points out, is that "the laws of Newtonian mechanics, like any basic law of science, depend on the assumption of ideal conditions—e.g., the frictionless plane. In conceiving their discipline as a search for mathematical laws, [neoclassical] economists have abstracted to their own ideal conditions, which for the most part consist of an utterly denuded vision of [humanity]" (Bigelow, 2005, p. 37). This underscores a central fallacy of corporatization: that there *is* a free market—objectively standing—within which organizations (like schools) not only function but perpetuate assumptions as to why we exist as *homo economicus*. When objectivism and value-neutrality are presupposed, questionable premises and debatable assertions can only be questioned and debated by those who are least likely to find them so—those who take the view that what they are debating are law-like propositions within a "scientific" realm.

Schools in general suffer from discourse mired in neoclassical economics because "production" and "provision" are commodified such that the evaluative criteria for judging schools in the first place (e.g., in determining whether they are "failing," "succeeding," "excellent," "accountable") are restricted to measurement standards that favor neoclassical analyses and thus business rationales. Teacher education, as a result, devolves into teacher training and tends to be reduced to processes of production and provision that must meet market goals of transfer efficiency and quality control (think edTPA [Education Teacher Performance Assessment] and Pearson). Such training necessarily favors corporate interests and privatization efforts, because the form of the measurements of learning ("standardized," "scientific," "objective") are the same measurements used on durable goods and "hard" services like manufacturing and shipping. One problem is that when education is reduced to the techniques and procedures that embrace market logics of this kind, teaching, learning, leading, etc., are turned into a proceduralism that is both mechanistic and reductive. As to the all-too-often used term "accountability," I suggest, consistent with the overall point of this chapter, that "accountability" is, itself, part of the problem. It reifies the very corporate logic that reduces teaching and teacher education to a set of deliverable, observable "goods": mere procedures to show what work has been done. In place of accountancy and its corporate logic, we should think about teaching and teacher education in terms of trust and responsibility.

Are we not faced with the strange reality that what we call public schools are actually and already venues for future private capital production? Where in public schools are students (and teachers and leaders) encouraged to consider the idea of schooling itself in any way that is not caught up in the bait-and-switch of neoclassical, reductionist thinking? Where do teachers reject listing goals and objectives on the prescribed left side of their white boards? When are "word walls" subversively populated with terms that critique the idea of a word wall in the first place? I suppose that these sorts of actions happen once in a while, but their rarity is a function of the dominance of neoclassical economic orthodoxy on and in schools. To wit, who in the United States is unaware of the reason for going to school? In catechistic chant, join in: "We go to school to learn the necessary skills we will need to get a job and compete in a global economy." Such neoclassical, reductionist, accountancy-oriented, preparation-for-the-"real world" ideology is not only already in evidence in public schools, it is their *modus operandi*.

When it comes to education policy, does it matter that 51% of the current members of Congress are millionaires—that is, they are among those benefitting from and promoting the neoclassical economic structure? What about state legislatures that are inordinately pro-business? Are not the policies they sanction a logical extension of neoclassical economic thinking? Consider the American Legislative Exchange Council (ALEC). According to its website, ALEC has a staff of 30, boasts 2,400 national memberships of state legislators from both parties, has more than 300 private-sector members (including

ExxonMobil, Pfizer, Walmart, and R.J. Reynolds Tobacco), and a $9 million yearly budget to push "decidedly pro-business bills through state legislatures" (ALEC, 2019).[2] Given the connection between ALEC, legislators, and private business and given that legislators are responsible for school funding and school policy, could schools be anything other than ethically egoist corporatized spheres? Even when schools are not wholly or formally privatized, they are still subsumed under neoclassical economic rationality and repeatedly enact and reinforce it.

ILLUSTRATIONS OF PRIVATIZATION LOGIC IN EDUCATION POLICY AND PRACTICE

Part of my interest is to trace out how deep in history and social perception lie the forces that reduce schooling to neoclassical economic exchanges. Recall Joseph Mayer Rice who, in the late 1800s, went around the country trying to find the best schools. His goal was to point out to the bad schools what the good schools were doing. His view was a precursor to the recent phenomenon of Finland-envy. Establishing an early form of reductionism or overgeneralization, whereby the vicissitudes of human learning were condensed to a 19th-century version of "what works" or "best practices," Rice was setting the foundation for the social efficiency advocates of the early 20th century (Kliebard, 2004, pp. 17, 51–77; see also Labaree, 1987; for a critique of "what-works" logic, see Biesta, 2007). These corporate promoters saw schools as Ford factories: Break the curriculum down into its most component parts, then sequentially lay out the information students would need for future occupations. Teachers would then bolt the specifics onto the product *qua* student and, at the end of the assembly line (graduation), you get a complete piece of merchandise.

For those who may wish to argue that this point is an oversimplification or extreme interpretation, consider the direct parallel to teacher education in Georgia. In my adopted state, there is a law that colleges of education have to guarantee the quality of their graduates (University System of Georgia, 2007; see, also, Zigo & Moore, 2002). If a graduate of my college goes out to teach and is deemed by the school district to be "defective," that person, like a faulty washing machine, can be returned to the factory, the college, to be fixed—and for free. Schools and colleges are factories, teachers and professors are assembly-line workers, and students are widgets.

The law did not come out of the ether. It is situated in a state, a culture, and a country that seemingly vaunt business logic over all. Moreover, the curricula that arise from corporatized logic de-skill teachers and school leaders, turning them into script-readers or policy-policing bureaucrats. Such corporatized logic is another form of reductionism that restricts and narrows inquiry and undermines trust between teachers and student and that is fomented by social conservatives and corporate lobbyists who want to consolidate their influence by seeing public schools privatized and colleges and universities gutted of public support. (Thus the sharp turn toward grant-writing and external funding; Bok, 2003; Geiger, 2004; Washburn, 2005.) In addition to the "manufacturer's guarantee" example from above, I would like to consider three more illustrations: (a) Georgia's Growth Model; (b) Value-added measurements; and (c) Pearson's burgeoning, monopolist control of all things education. Each of these illustrations represent reactions to or proposals for a particular kind of thinking that privileges economic rationality and corporate encroachment in teachers' lives. As such, they clarify the flawed logic and provide insight into its function and limitations.

Georgia's Growth Model uses Student Growth Percentiles to categorize students within three percentage parameters: the lowest 33%, the middle 33%, and the upper 33% (Georgia Department of Education, 2015). (I presume the missing 1% is symbolic of the manifestation of wealth in the broader society, but that is another paper.) Growth models in general are supposed to show individual changes over time. As Ann Martin (2014) sees it, the problem is not the general definition, because growth models recognize individual improvements. The problem she points out is at least two-fold: (a) students are grouped with other students who received the same score on the previous year's standardized test, ostensibly to avoid correlational issues, and (b) the structure of percentage groups precludes students from achieving "high" growth. For instance, a 3rd-grader who scored an 800 on the Criterion-Referenced Competency Test (CRCT) goes on to score 850 as a 4th-grader. This looks like growth; but the scores are still codified as low, middle, or high, so even though the 3rd-grader improved, if her improvement did not exceed the boundaries of her 33% bracket, she did not grow according to this system. Growth models tied to teacher evaluations appear to be a logical extension, but I have to wonder about the pressures placed on teachers (and their students) to score higher and higher when, in fact, higher scores may not be high enough to show "growth."

Relatedly, as Nick Eastman (2014) notes, value-added assessments are all the rage. AERA's *Educational Researcher* produced a special issue dedicated to the topic of valued-added measurement and issues related to it (Harris & Herrington, 2015). The topic gained prominence given that the Bill & Melinda Gates Foundation funded the $45 million project they called Measures of Effective Teaching or MET, a form of value-added measurement. Eastman offers a provocative point regarding value-added assessment in a paper he delivered at the Council for Professors of Instructional Supervision (COPIS), whose conference theme was the question "How does supervision support teachers and learners in a hostile policy environment?" Eastman (2014) wrote that the conference theme contains a number of interesting assumptions. "Foremost is that instructional supervision does, in practice, *support* teachers and learners in a hostile policy environment rather than *reinforce* 'hostile' policies of accountability and standardization by adopting the same (or similar) view of student achievement" (p. 1). At least part of this similar view is the logic of value-added assessment. Value-added measurement uses hierarchical linear modeling to predict the score for a given student in a given classroom in a given school. This prediction is based on aggregated results of all students. Each student's predicted score takes student data (past performance, socioeconomic status, race/ethnicity), teacher data (certification, years of experience, highest degree earned, teaching practices, instructional materials, curriculum), and school data (size, type, setting) as variables to consider. The variables included depend on the particular assessment model.

Eastman charges that a key problem with value-added measurement is that it isolates teacher behaviors for reification. He argues,

> Once these behaviors are isolated, they can be packaged as "best practices" and disseminated to public school systems throughout the country, which with the help of the Common Core State Standards and their accompanying assessment consortia (Partnership for Assessment of Readiness for College and Careers [PARCC] and Smarter Balanced Assessment Consortium [SBAC]) will be using the same or similar measurement tools. The extent to which this conceptual problem becomes ingrained in public school classrooms is influenced by the administrators' willingness and ability to resist reductive standardized curricula and the high stakes, norm-referenced assessments that govern them. (Eastman, 2014, p. 4; see also Milner, 2013)

Instead of focusing attention on humane interaction, value-added measurement is another example of turning professional judgment into one of materialistic, objectified targets—as easily carried out by technicians or by robots as by caring, autonomous professionals. Following another of Eastman's points, how many public school teachers and leaders will succumb to this logic as *they* are subjected to similar measurement schemes? It is as though "professional development" has become a stand-in for more top-down indoctrination of the neoclassical economic mindset. As another illustration of the metanarrative, I turn to the recent growth of Pearson.

Pearson was founded as an engineering and construction company in London in the mid-1800s.[3] Existing as a successful construction supply company throughout the 19th century, the company began a period of aggressive growth and acquisition throughout the early 20th century. Pearson's first forays into publishing came in the 1920s with the purchase of several newspapers in London that the company consolidated into the *Westminster Times*. In the 1950s, Pearson continued its growth by buying both the *Financial Times* and a controlling stake in *The Economist*. Throughout the latter half of the 20th century, Pearson continued to strengthen its place in publishing by acquiring Penguin Books and Simon & Schuster (Attick & Boyles, 2016; Pearson, 2015).

Pearson Education was formally created in 1998 when Pearson PLC purchased the education division of Simon & Schuster from Viacom and merged it with its own education division, Addison-Wesley and Longman, thus marking the beginning of Pearson's commitment to dominating the education materials market. Pearson Education was rebranded Pearson Learning in 2011 and, in that same year, won the contract to develop and administer mathematics and English language arts tests for grades 3 through 8 in New York. The contract, worth $32 million, ran until 2015. This may sound like a lot of money, but its contract with the Texas Education Agency is worth nearly 500 million dollars, and its $254 million contract with the Florida Board of Education to provide testing and accountability measures in that state is part of a profiteering motive about which I fear many may know little to nothing.

In fact, Pearson spent $5 billion acquiring 25 smaller education publishing companies between 2007 and 2012, resulting in its being three times larger than its closest competitor. Pearson also aims to dominate content delivery online by creating courses that tout flexibility and choice via online academies and virtual charter schools. Pearson's third growth strategy relies on online learning modules customizable for individual students yet standardizing teacher education certification via edTPA. To this end, nearly every teacher and every student in the United States will be a Pearson customer and, ironically for neoclassical economics, not by choice. If there are still doubts as to the mercantile goal of Pearson, consider an email I received on Wednesday, October 15, 2014. The email was sent by a Pearson representative to a long list of professors in order to promote Pearson products. The salutation portion of the computerized "merge" function apparently failed to kick in my last name, but the symbolism is apt: "Dear Professor $Last Names$."[4] Professors are not considered intellectuals who should question Pearson, but consumers of their products who are also symbolically, and in the illustration literally, commodified.

These illustrations are only indicative of the many efforts to manipulate teachers' roles regarding assessment and entry into the field. Accordingly, these efforts to influence teacher education policy and practice are part of the larger push to corporatize schools. They are important illustrations because they allow us to see how market logic is used to build monopolies and alter what it means to participate in teacher education/training and what is required to become a teacher in 2019. The language of crisis repeats calls for accountability and assessments that prove that strategies work (Lipman, 2013). Do we really think more Interstate School Leadership Licensure Consortium (ISLLC) standards are the answer? Does the Common Core benefit students' critical thinking? Can we see no way around perpetual self-study reports to top-down bureaucracies like professional standards commissions or the Council for the Accreditation of Educator Preparation (CAEP)? How many more bullet points and rubrics must exist before we see ourselves as what we have become under neoclassical economic theory: human *resources*? That is, what will it take to realize that what we do is inordinately related to direct threats to our livelihoods—livelihoods that now have less to do with living, by the way, and more to do with writing up yet another set of reports that spell out facetious learning objectives and fake goals? It seems to be a twist on Ronald Reagan's adoption of the Russian proverb "Trust, but verify." We are, instead, faced with "don't trust, quantify." It's reductionism. It's corporatism. It's the proletarianization of teachers—and it's bereft of ethical altruism—*by design*. To counter the ethical egoism of corporatism and its hold over education policy, I now turn to a more detailed exploration of the contrasts between traditional policy analysis and critical policy studies. In doing so, I want to make clear that much education policy work is undertaken in departments of economics or public policy, where researchers have backgrounds in economics and public policy, but rarely in education. Accordingly, and as I detail below, the research produced in those fields is overwhelmingly neoclassical in its economic assumptions and actions. It is also replete with ethical egoism.

TOWARD ETHICAL ALTRUISM IN SCHOOLS: CRITICAL POLICY STUDIES

The idea of policy is traceable to the ancient development of city-states, to the development of "police sciences" in 18th-century Europe, and public policy debates after World War II (Simons, Olssen, & Peters, 2009). There are numerous distinctions within and among policy scholars. While an exhaustive listing is beyond the scope of this chapter, I will outline a series of different schools of thought related to policy and policy studies. This background will clarify and situate what I take to be critical policy studies in education and how CPS might promote a robust understanding of ethical altruism in public education. Please note that the origins and emphases within CPS are also diverse and thus defy easy categorization. Variably linked to the Frankfurt School, Karl Marx, Thorstein Veblen, John Dewey, and others, CPS might itself be too general in conveying what I think might help resurrect—or bring about for the first time—*truly* public education in the United States.[5] As a starting point, articulating what is necessary for CPS, and the critical scholarship and teaching it entails, is the next move. Part of that articulation is comparative and challenges traditional policy analyses (see, e.g., Cohn & Geske, 1990; McCool, 1995; Weimer & Vining, 1992).

Traditional policy analysis from the 20th and 21st centuries in the United States is characterized by a reliance on enlightenment rationality, scientism, and appeals to objectivity (Hammersley, 1994; Marshall & Gerstl-Pepin, 2005; Whittrock, Wagner, & Wollman, 1991). Policy analysis was more formally developed in the United States in the 1960s and 1970s and, applied to education issues, advanced a rationality of systemic analysis to achieve effective and efficient planning that is, according to P. H. Coombs (1970), "ideologically neutral." As Simons, Olssen, and Peters (2009) noted, "[P]olicy analysis focused on improving decision making and applying quantitative, functionalist, and policy-directed approaches" (p. 6; see also Parsons, 1995). These sorts of characterizations, however generally accurate, hide important distinctions among and between traditional policy analyses.

Dualistic thinking posits the quantitative versus the qualitative, conservative versus liberal, men versus women, even egoism versus altruism. Such binaries often hide more than they reveal. Instead, there has been a continuum of thought regarding traditional policy analysis, particularly from the 1960s and into the 1990s. From critical rationalists (like Amitai Etzioni, 1993) who added moral and communitarian dimensions to otherwise "cold, efficient logic" through political rationalists (like Charles Lindblom [Lindblom & Woodhouse, 1992]) who objected to policy analysts talking among themselves at the expense of an informed public, to business-centered managerialists (like Peter Drucker, 1954, 1964; John Chubb & Terry Moe, 1990) who argued for replacing rational models with analytic techniques from the management and corporate sector, policy analyses varied (see also Pollitt, 1991).

To extend this very brief overview of policy, I borrow from the work of Simons, Olssen, and Peters (2009) in which they outline four broad areas to connect the background sketch of policy analysis to the central issues from which critical policy studies emerged: the context of policy and advocacy; reliance on political science, economics, and sociology; concern for education and public policy; and criticality toward knowledge–policy alliances. Firstly, they distinguish the "analysis of the policy process" from the "analysis for and in the policy processes" (p. 9). For the former, it constitutes the general overview of "understanding policy, policy making, and its content." For the latter, it means being concerned about "improving policies, decision making, and problem-solving." As they make clear, however, CPS thinkers "do not share a rigid positivist and instrumental distinction between on the one hand policy analysis (focusing on means and optimal allocation with a neutral stance toward aims or goals) and on the other hand policy advocacy (where the focus is on the sphere of values and goals)" (p. 9). Because CPS is committed to ethics and social issues and because it acknowledges and embraces the political and cultural dimensions of power, critical policy studies combine analysis *and* advocacy.

Simons, Olssen, and Peters (2009) also point out, secondly, that education policy was not historically, nor is it currently, ranked highly as a research focus for political scientists. They quote Charles Raab (1994) as follows:

> . . . a certain academic disdain has left research on education, and perhaps particularly on schooling, mainly to the "mere" teachers and their educators who were steeped in its practice, placing it out of contention as a "serious" political science. Although education is now an issue area of the first rank on government and party agendas, and in public debate, it remains the case that few political scientists with an inclination to policy studies have it clearly in their sites. (pp. 19–20, in Simons et al., p. 9)

Those analysts who do have education in their sights overwhelmingly apply statistical analyses that reinforce the primacy of calculations—arguably reducing very complex human interactions to algorithms and formulae. Because schooling has been so closely connected to economic productivity and global competition, at least since the late 1970s, scholars in general may have missed an opportunity to engage in education policy. If so, the opportunity was taken up by public policy analysts and those working in the field of economics who have colonized departments like political science, sociology, and public policy. Accordingly, it has become commonplace for policy scholars in schools of business, economics, and public policy to provide analyses that reify logical—sequential reasoning, mathematical—statistical reductionism, and neoclassical economics logic (see Sass, Semykina, & Harris, 2014; for critique, see Marshall & Gerstl-Pepin, 2005). This sort of approach to policy analysis reinforces the idea that such analyses are value-free, objective, and, thus, accurate descriptions of the world. As I argue below, CPS rejects as invalid the claims to neutrality and accuracy of descriptions that traditional policy analyses repeatedly assume or assert. In this way, and addressing the third point from above, CPS rejects traditional policy analyses because of their fundamental positivism and their link to controlling economic interests.

To further this point and extend it to the fourth and final issue noted above, traditional policy analyses' methods of analysis and the assumptions built into them (namely, utilitarian questions validated by utilitarian studies) lead to the circularity of replication and generalizability as the litmus tests for what is real and what is true. CPS challenges the assumptions built into typical or standard policy studies themselves. As Simons, Olssen, and Peters (2009) put it, "the alliances between rational policy research on the one hand and education policy making on the other hand become themselves the object of critical studies" (p. 10).

In order to avoid falling into the trap of the very reductionism I am criticizing, I want to list and briefly explain, again following Simons and colleagues (2009),[6] a series of frameworks that have been used in policy analysis. They list the principal frameworks as

- Welfare economics
- Public choice
- Information processing
- Comparative politics
- Social Structure
- Political process
- Political philosophy
- Management

The point is to highlight some of the differences and similarities of these frameworks and to tease out the key distinctions that critical policy studies represent. While it is true that some experts merge frameworks, I agree with Simons and his colleagues that it is helpful to understand the distinctions among the frameworks as part of the project of accurately describing the traditional policy analyses.

Largely representing work dating at least to the 1960s but arguably clearly evidenced in 2008, *welfare economics* holds that market failures require political intervention. This framework uses efficiency and cost-benefit analyses to determine the knowledge that advances welfare policies in an economic manner. More specifically, welfare economics relies on economic algorithms to support theoretical arguments (see, e.g., Besley & Coate, 1997; Brennan & Buchanan, 1980; Feldman, 1980; Herbener, 1997). Like "J. Evans Pritchard, PhD" in the movie *The Dead Poets' Society*, who was used by Robin Williams's character to show the absurdity of plotting graphs to determine the value of poetry, welfare economists appear eager to plot points on graphs to determine equity and efficiency in economics—and, by extension, education and schooling.

The *social structure* framework is where sociology is most clearly represented. That vast field allows the framework to extend from analyses of social problems and of power in society and organizations to the sociology of knowledge. In the United States, functionalist sociology has been most influential on the research done on policy processes. This framework considers "the social dimension of policies and policy making, and to explain and/or understand policies, their making and their effects in relation to social structures" (Simons et al., 2009, p. 12). Even here, however, what constitutes "the social dimension" is often operationalized and subsumed under market logic.

Perhaps broader than sociology, there are at least six variations on the *political process* framework. Relying primarily on D. Wayne Parsons's work, Simons et al. (2009) list the approaches as follows:

> - Stagist approaches: the analysis of policy as a process with different stages, from agenda to evaluation.
> - Pluralist–elitist approaches: the analysis of the distribution of power among (elite) groups and how they influence or make policy.
> - Neo-Marxist approaches: the analysis of ideology, hegemony, repression, and contradictions in policymaking, and the link between different levels in the political/policy system.
> - Subsystem approaches: the analysis of policymaking at the level of networks, communities, and the influence of subsystems and their institutions.
> - Policy discourse approaches: the analysis of policymaking at the level of language, discourse, and communication.
> - Institutionalism (economic, sociological, or political): analysis of the constitutional and institutional spaces and arrangements in which policy takes place, and relying on economics (e.g., transaction cost economics, agency theory), organizational sociology, or political theory and historical accounts. (p. 12; see also Parsons, 1995)

The spectrum covered by *political philosophy* is also vast and ranges all the way back to Plato, Niccolò Machiavelli, and Francis Bacon. Other political philosophers include Jeremy Bentham, John Stuart Mill, Karl Marx, William James, Hannah Arendt, John Dewey, Ayn Rand, and Friedrich Hayek. More recent connections include Patricia Hill Collins, Martha Nussbaum, Cornel West, John Rawls, and Robert Nozick. There is not enough space to detail the various ethical, normative, methodological, and theoretical issues represented in this (incomplete) spectrum. What is significant about this range in terms of policy studies is that "the empirical policy sciences typically proclaim themselves as emancipated from these speculative theories and philosophies" (Simons et al., 2009, p. 13). CPS considers such emancipation impossible.

Finally, the largest influence on policy studies is the *managerial framework*. The application of managerial thought and techniques to public administration occurred during the financial crisis in the late 1970s. The private, for-profit sector was largely influenced by Peter Drucker (1954, 1964) and Milton Friedman (1966), as well as David Osborne and Ted Gaebler (1993), becoming the model for "entrepreneurial government." Management by Objectives and New Public Management meant that applying techniques like "written contracts and performance agreements, short term employment contracts, new and multiple forms of accountability [like "learning outcomes"], client and customer orientations, and so on" (Simons et al., 2009, p. 13) became the norm. The overwhelming dominance of this approach to policy may provide the most justification for advancing CPS for education.

Borrowing from the foregoing sketch of traditional policy analyses and linking his critique of it to CPS in education, consider Carlos Alberto Torres's (1989) characterization of traditional policy analyses in education and what they lack. Torres provides a rationale for moving from traditional policy analyses toward CPS in education. He is worth quoting at length:

> Policy making . . . has been commonly analyzed as: (1) the production of interaction between political controllers and professional providers of services (Saran, 1973); (2) the focus on timing and feasibility as crucial elements in policy making (David, 1977): (3) research such as Wirt & Kirst (1982) which, by assuming that schools are miniature political systems, falls into the contradiction of accepting a pluralist power structure in the United States, but ends up portraying schools as a world of harmony and consensus; (4) research that deals with local state policy making, and the development of educational policies taxonomies, especially basic control mechanisms available to state-level policymakers, in which the independent (explanatory) variable would be the political culture and educational assumptions of policymakers (*Peabody Journal of Education*, 1985); or (5) an Eastonian-system analysis perspective that focuses on education units as parapolitical subsystems that include the processing of demands, the generation of support by authorities, regime and the political community, and the feedback response factor. (p. 82)

In Torres's view, the common theme missing from all of these conventional approaches is what he calls "an understanding of the state" and "critical conceptualization of issues such as domination, power, rules, and political representation in analyzing policy making" (p. 82). Implied here is ethical altruism. Domination is an important issue for Torres in terms not of content, but effect. The consequences of domination yield misery and marginalization, and any discourse that valorizes domination is one-sided, ill-informed, and either ethically bereft or egoist.

Differently, though consistent with the previous depictions, Michelle Young (1999) summarizes the positivist characteristics of traditional education policy studies as follows:

- Concerned with the process of educational changes or reforms (planning, implementation, examination, and/or evaluating); they assume reforms are deliberate processes that can be planned and managed (sequential, incremental, and/or political);
- Assume that action is driven by goals or preferences (and actually equate this with what rationality is about);
- Assumes that knowledge for decisions and for implementation is obtainable, cumulative, and communicable to others; and
- Holds to the idea that policies and their results can be evaluated; that in evaluation problems can be identified and that, accordingly, solutions can be given. (See also Humes & Price, 2003; Pring, 2001.)

All of these descriptions, taken together, provide a backdrop for comparison. Part of that comparison investigates the key differences between traditional policy analyses and CPS. Might it be the case that situating *power* as a central feature of policy analyses would let us justifiably articulate a different—and important—contribution to education policy studies? This question forms the bridge to the final section of this paper. In what follows, I characterize and provide examples of CPS and suggest how we might tangibly further CPS in order to focus on the possibilities of altruistic ethics for the future of public education.

COMPARISON FOR CLARIFICATION: CRITICAL POLICY STUDIES

CPS developed, in part, as a response to the neoliberal and neoconservative governments in the United States, United Kingdom, Australia, and New Zealand. By focusing on the contexts and consequences of education policy reforms (*A Nation at Risk*, *America 2000*, *Race to the Top*, etc.), education theorists and sociologists of education developed, as John Prunty (1984, 1985) puts it, a "unique policy orientation" (see also Ball, 1994; Harvey, 1990; Popkewitz, 1991). He goes further when he articulates the positionality of the critical policy analyst:

> A critical analysis would be overtly political. The personal values and political commitment of the critical policy analyst would be anchored in the vision of a moral order in which justice, equality, and individual freedom uncompromised by the avarice of a few. The critical analyst would endorse a political, social, and economic arrangement where persons are never treated as a means to an end, but treated as ends in their own right. (Prunty, 1985, p. 136)

Such critical analyses were, as Jenny Ozga (1987) noted, "rooted in the social science tradition, historically informed, and draw[ing] on qualitative and illuminative techniques" (p. 144). Even with these characteristics, the term "critical" is not understood monolithically. Consider Simons et al. (2009) again:

> . . . policy research should not merely be research for policy but research into policy, and more specifically on the consequences of policy, on issues of power and politics surrounding education and on social justice, equality, and individual freedom. However, a critical concern can also be more implicit, that is, part of the research process itself. Critical research can show for instance that what is taken for granted is part of a very particular configuration of power and knowledge. (p. 19)

As Popkewitz (2008) argues, "to make the naturalness of the present strange and contingent is a political strategy of change; to make visible the internments and enclosures of the commonsense of schooling is to make them contestable" (p. xv). What this approach to inquiry does is break down the distinction in traditional policy analysis between politics and policy. Politics is understood, traditionally, as the messy arena where debates over purposes and interests are muddled. Policy, differently, is the rational approach to smoothing out the irrationality that describes politics. CPS, in brief, denies the separation between the two and recognizes that the rational agenda of policy analysis is misguided in that it fails to recognize the positive centrality of "messiness" to human existence (see Codd, 1988). Such messiness is also a way to understand ethical altruism's needed role in education. Because life is filled with so many risks and opportunities, teachers demonstrating ethical altruism supervene in students' interactions, *not* as apolitical monoliths dutifully applying sterile methods onto their charges, but as caring others whose selflessness is shown in humane interaction.

Importantly, as with traditional policy analysis, CPS has a range of differences within and among its adherents. Henry Giroux (1983), for example, disagrees with Louis Althusser's determinism, Michael Apple (1982) emphasizes the role of the state (differently from Michel Foucault and Thomas Popkewitz), and Pierre Bourdieu (Bourdieu & Passeron, 1977/2000) denies that policy can change society and education. These differences and distinctions are not understood as a weakness but a strength because the intricacies of the theoretical and practical differences require a deep understanding of the disparate meanings being articulated. Understanding the variations and the arguments that describe and characterize those variations constitutes much of the point of CPS itself: critical reflection on the meaning and consequences of power.

Even with these differences, Bob Lingard and Jenny Ozga (2007) provide a list of descriptors to clarify the domain of study that constitutes CPS:

- as a field, in respect to schooling at least, CPS deals with all texts and seeks to frame, constitute, and change educational practices toward social justice . . .
- includes all sectors of education . . . it includes policy produced in parts of the state other than education departments or ministries of education . . .
- argues that the totally pedagogized society demands the extension and refocusing of its policy research gaze . . .
- includes the processes involved in the production of policy text and those involved in its practice . . .
- recognizes that contestation is usually involved at all stages of production and implementation, as well as in relation to the discourses that frame the actual written text . . .
- understands that policy texts are heteroglossic in character, discursively suturing together different interests to achieve apparent consensus and legitimacy . . .
- articulates a broad definition of politics as practices and discourses to do with power (in its structural sense, i.e., as concentrated and congealed, as well as in its poststructural sense, i.e., as dispersed, relational, and practical forms) . . .
- questions who benefits [most] from particular social arrangements . . .
- asserts that education policy is inherently political. (p. 2; see also Scott, 2011)

Taken together, and open to revision, these characteristics provide a glimpse of the possibilities CPS offers. Such characteristics also necessarily deny ethical egoism. Questioning who benefits most from specific social arrangements is not questioning how any *individual* benefits, but whether beneficiaries are in positions of privilege because economic structures ensure they are (and others are not). It is the others that are not to whom ethical altruism attends.

Far from being limited to a few instances, neoclassical economics and the continuing corporate assault on public education are increasing in number and variety and represent a larger agenda. The agenda is a pro-business, pro-capitalist, pro-careerist one that excludes questions about whether business exploits workers and schools, whether capitalism is the only or best economic theory, and whether elementary school students should be forced to consider their future selves as occupational job titles. The problem is that we are increasingly subsumed in a market logic that, in part because of its pervasiveness, appears impervious to critique (see Bettis, 2000; Feuerstein, 2000; Giroux, 2005).

To combat this pervasiveness, students, teachers, and leaders should use illustrative examples of corporate over-reach as object lessons for critique. This critique requires de-limiting the discourse and embracing the vicissitudes of inquiry (Laclau & Mouffe, 1985/2001, p. 192).[7] Students, teachers, and leaders are *all* engaged in CPS such that the restrictive structure of traditional curricula and schooling writ large give way to more wide-open opportunities for altruistic ethical growth and understanding. This means that schools and colleges must reconstitute themselves as spaces for the development of ethics. Rather than training teachers to follow edicts, educating teachers for humane ethical interaction with their students shifts power away from centralized bureaucratic power and requires teachers to grapple with literatures and ideas currently marginalized (or extinct) in current teacher preparation. My argument supports increased attention to the history, philosophy, sociology, politics, and economics of education (which I acknowledge as self-serving, but nonetheless important), through courses in what is generally termed the social and cultural foundations of education. The field of foundations has been diminishing in direct proportion to the domination of corporatized and monetized schools (see Baez & Boyles, 2009; Bok, 2003; Geiger, 2004; Schrecker, 2010; Slaughter & Rhoades, 2004; Washburn, 2005). Academics who do not directly train Common Core or EdTPA technicians or bring in external grants are facing serious threats to academic freedom, tenure, and employment.

For colleges and departments of education, the crisis to which I allude has practical ramifications for whether future teachers will be trained or educated. Currently, we are forced to create curricula that are little concerned that future teachers are well-read (in the many and varied ways this can be interpreted), inquisitive, and critical. We are concerned instead about completion rates and job placement percentages. This concern is not a vestige of ethical altruism, actually caring about our students' learning and futures, but an economistic ratings comparison to show purported "success."

Perhaps the largest problem facing the future of public education in the United States is the decreasing number of future teachers who identify or understand the degree to which school and society are saturated by neoclassical economic rationality. Recall that neoclassical orthodoxy asserts four main claims:

1. Economics is a science and as such demands belief in ways similar to modern physics;
2. Market outcomes reflect freedom of choice;
3. Humans enact rational choice; and
4. The major purpose of economic theory is to promote economic efficiency and economic growth via competition. (Cohen, 2003; see also Calnitsky & Dupuy-Spencer, 2013; Jennings, 2012; Nachane, 2008; Nussbaum, 1997; Postel, 2011; Sobel, 2013; Van den Berg, 2014; Whalen, 1987)

In their various iterations, the foregoing axioms of neoclassical economics structured the majority of the discourse of economics from the 1870s onward. While Thorstein Veblen (in the 1910s to 1930s) and John Maynard Keynes mounted challenges to neoclassical orthodoxy (in the 1930s and 1940s), in what came to be known as institutional economics, it was not until 2000 that a major public confrontation occurred regarding neoclassical economics. Future teachers in colleges of education in the United States might learn something from this important event that happened not that long ago. In 2000, French graduate students of economics drafted a petition attacking the curriculum to which they were subjected. Their complaint included the charge that neoclassical economic theory has no grounding in empirical fact, denies the possibility of plural understanding, and, thus, narrowly and invidiously precludes questions about realism and context (Fullbrook, 2007, pp. 471–472). As Fullbrook explains, "[T]he students were making a major epistemological point. . . . They identified a situation in which one theory illuminates a few facets of a domain, while its practitioners suppress other theories that illuminate some of the many facts that their theory leaves in the dark. In such a situation, the solution is not abandonment of a theory or a research programme, or a paradigm shift, but pluralism" (Fullbrook, 2007, p. 19; see also Brosio, 1994; Carey, 1995). We should all long for and participate in a similar uprising in colleges and departments of education in the United States. It would surely increase the hope for a legitimate future for teachers in a truly *public* education.

NOTES

1. See also Duska (2000). Duska ultimately concludes that business ethics is not oxymoronic because he defines egoism as the principle that "one ought always pursue one's self-interest" (p. 128). I disagree. That one ought to pursue one's self-interest, in this case a business's self-interest, is enough to meet the criteria of ethical egoism. The universal expectation of "always" is simply too high a bar to reach, thus giving businesses the kind of ethical wiggle room that allows them to carry on reaping enormous profits while gaps in wealth continue to expand.

2. For a critical examination of ALEC, see Scola, 2012.

3. This section of the paper is adapted from Attick & Boyles, 2016.

4. Email from Krista Clark to Deron Boyles, October 15, 2014. In author's possession.

5. Here I allude to the concern that a nostalgic understanding of public education is problematic. I do not believe there was a "golden age" of education in U.S. public schools. There is historical evidence, however, for schools' attempting what CPS requires. See Evans, 2007.

6. I reorder their list, but otherwise follow very closely their narrative.

7. As Laclau and Mouffe (2001) put it, "the educational system, labour relations, the discourses of the resistance of marginal populations construct original and irreducible forms of social protest, and thereby contribute all the discursive complexity and richness on which the programme of a [comparatively] radical democracy should be founded."

REFERENCES

American Legislative Exchange Council. (2019). About ALEC. Retrieved from www.alec.org/about/

Apple, M. (1982). *Education and power.* New York, NY: Routledge & Kegan Paul Ltd. Publishers.

Attick, D., & Boyles, D. (2016). Pearson Learning and the ongoing corporatization of public education. *Journal of Thought, 50*(1–2), 5–19.

Baez, B., & Boyles, D. (2009). *The politics of inquiry: Education research and the "Culture of Science."* Albany, NY: SUNY Press.

Ball, S. (1994). *Education reform: A critical and post-structural approach.* Buckingham, UK: Open University Press.

Besley, T., & Coate, S. (1997). An economic model of representative democracy. *Quarterly Journal of Economics, 112*(1), 85–114.

Bettis, P. (2000, Winter). Corporate discourses in school: Adapting to the prevailing economic climate. *Educational Foundations 14*(1), 3–49.

Biesta, G. (2007). Why what works won't work: Evidence-based practice and democratic deficit in educational research. *Educational Theory, 57*(1), 1–22.

Bigelow, G. (2005). Let there be markets: The evangelical roots of economics. *Harper's Magazine.* Retrieved from harpers.org/archive/2005/05/let-there-be-markets/

Bok, D. (2003). *Universities in the marketplace: The commercialization of higher education.* Princeton, NJ: Princeton University Press.

Bourdieu, P., & Passeron, J.-C. (2000). *Reproduction in education, society, and culture.* New York, NY: Sage. (Original work published 1977)

Brennan, J., & Buchanan, J. M. (1980). *The power to tax: Analytical foundations of a fiscal constitution.* Cambridge, UK: Cambridge University Press.

Brosio, R. A. (1994). *A radical democratic critique of capitalist education.* New York, NY: Peter Lang.

Calnitsky, D., & Dupuy-Spencer, A. (2013). The economic consequences of *Homo Economicus*: Neoclassical economic theory and the fallacy of market optimality. *The Journal of Philosophical Economics, VI*(2). Retrieved from jpe.ro/poze/articole/94.pdf

Carey, A. (1995). *Taking the risk out of democracy: Corporate propaganda versus freedom and liberty.* Urbana, IL: University of Illinois Press.

Chubb, J. E., & Moe, T. M. (1990). *Politics, markets, and America's schools.* Washington, DC: The Brookings Institution Press.

Clohesy, W. W. (2000). Altruism and the endurance of the good. *Voluntas: International Journal of Voluntary and Nonprofit Organizations, 11*(3), 237–253.

Codd, J. (1988). The construction and deconstruction of education policy documents. *Journal of Educational Policy, 3*(3), 235–247.

Cohen, S. (2003, February 4). Common ground critiques of neoclassical principles texts. *Post-Autistic Economics Review, 18,* Article 3. Retrieved from www.paecon.net/PAEReview/ issue18/Cohn18.htm

Cohn, E., & Geske, T. (1990). *The economics of education.* New York, NY: Pergamon Press.

Coombs, P. H. (1970). *What is educational planning? Fundamentals of educational planning.* Paris, France: UNESCO International Institute for Educational Planning.

Drucker, P. (1954). *The principles of management.* New York, NY: Harper & Row.

Drucker, P. (1964). *Managing for results: Economic tasks and risk-taking decisions.* New York, NY: Harper & Row.

Duska, R. (2000). Business ethics: Oxymoron or good business? *Business Ethics Quarterly, 10*(1), 111–129.

Eastman, N. J. (2014, Oct. 17–19). *Instructional supervision in the age of value-added measurements.* Paper presented at the COPIS Conference, Atlanta, GA.

Etzioni, A. (1993). *Public policy in a new key.* Piscataway, NJ: Transaction Press.

Evans, R. W. (2007). *This happened in America: Harold Rugg and the censure of social studies.* Charlotte, NC: Information Age Publishing.

Ewen, S. (1996). *PR! A social history of spin.* New York, NY: Basic Books.

Feldman, A. M. (1980). *Welfare economics and social choice theory.* Dordrecht, The Netherlands: Kluwer.

Feuerstein, A. (2000, November 1–5). *Selling our schools? Principals' views on schoolhouse commercialism and school business interactions.* Paper presented at the annual conference of the American Educational Studies Association, Vancouver, Canada.

Fisher, F. (1980). *Politics, values, and public policy: The problem of methodology.* Boulder, CO: Westview Press.

Friedman, M. (1966). *Essays in positive economics.* Chicago, IL: University of Chicago Press.

Friedman, M. (1970, Sept. 30). The social responsibility of business is to increase its profits. *New York Times Magazine, CXIX*(41,140), Sect. 5, pp. 32–33, 122, 124, 126.

Fullbrook, E. (2007). Appendix I: The French Students' Petition. In E. Fullbrook (Ed.), *Real world economics: A post-autistic economics reader* (pp. 471–472). London, UK: Anthem Press.

Geiger, R. L. (2004). *Knowledge and money: Research universities and the paradox of the marketplace.* Stanford, CA: Stanford University Press.

Georgia Department of Education. (2015). Georgia student growth model. Retrieved from www.gadoe.org/Curriculum-Instruction-and-Assessment/Assessment/Pages/Georgia-Student-Growth-Model.aspx

Giroux, H. A. (1983). *Theory and resistance in education: A pedagogy for the opposition.* Westport, CT: Bergin & Garvey.

Giroux, H. A. (2005, Winter). The terror of Neoliberalism: Rethinking the significance of cultural politics. *College Literature, 32*(1), 1–19.

Glasgow, W. D. (1968). The contradiction in ethical egoism. *Philosophical Studies: An International Journal for Philosophy in the Analytic Tradition, 19*(6), 81–85.

Glickman, C. (2009, January). Educators tell businesses how to stop ruining America. *Phi Delta Kappan, 90*(5), 392.

Hammersley, M. (1994). Ethnography, policy making, and practice in education. In D. Halpin & B. Troyna (Eds.), *Researching education policy: Ethical and methodological issues* (pp. 139–153). London, UK: Falmer Press.

Harris, D. N., & Herrington, C. D. (Eds.). (2015, March). Value added meets the schools: The effects of using test-based teacher evaluation on the work of teachers and leaders. *Educational Researcher, 44*(2).

Harvey, L. (1990). *Critical social research.* London, UK: Allen & Unwin.

Herbener, J. M. (1997). The Pareto Rule and welfare economics. *Review of Austrian Economics, 10*(1), 76–106.

Humes, W., & Price, D. (2003). Post-structuralism and policy research in education. *Journal of Education Policy, 18*(2), 175–187.

Jacobs, P. (2015, February 20). Here's how AP US History became one of the most controversial classes in America. *Business Insider [online].* Retrieved from www.businessinsider.com/heres-how-ap-us-history-became-controversial-2015-2

Jennings, F. B., Jr. (2012). A theory of planning horizons (2): The foundation for an ethical economics. *The Journal of Philosophical Economics, VI*(1). Retrieved from jpe.ro/pdf.php?id=2921

Kliebard, H. (2004). *The struggle for the American curriculum, 1893–1958.* New York, NY: RoutledgeFalmer.

Labaree, D. F. (1987). Public goods, private goods: The American struggle over educational goals. *American Educational Research Journal, 34*(1), 39–81.

Laclau, E., & Mouffe, C. (2001). *Hegemony and social strategy: Towards a radical democratic politics.* New York, NY: Verso. (Original work published in 1985)

Lindblom, C. E., & Woodhouse, E. J. (1992). *The policy making process.* Upper Saddle River, NJ: Prentice-Hall.

Lingard, B., & Ozga, J. (2007). Introduction: Reading education policy and politics. In B. Lingard & J. Ozga (Eds.), *The Routledge Falmer reader in education policy and politics* (pp. 1–8). London, UK: Routledge.

Lipman, P. (2013). Economic crisis, accountability, and the state's coercive assault on public education in the USA. *Journal of Education Policy 28*(5), 557, 573.

Lippmann, W. (1922). *Public opinion*. New York, NY: Harcourt, Brace, and Co.

Marshall, C., & Gerstl-Pepin, C. (2005). *Re-framing educational politics for social justice.* Boston, MA: Allyn & Bacon.

Martin, A. (2014, Oct. 17–19). *Georgia's growth model.* Paper presented at the COPIS Conference, Atlanta, GA.

McCool, D. C. (1995). *Public policy theories, models, and concepts: An anthology.* Englewood Cliffs, NJ: Prentice-Hall.

McKinley, J. C., Jr. (2010, March 12). Texas conservatives win curriculum change. *The New York Times.* Retrieved from www.nytimes.com/2010/03/13/education/13texas.html

Milner, H. R., IV. (2013). *Policy reforms and de-professionalization of teaching.* Boulder, CO: National Education Policy Center. Retrieved from nepc.colorado.edu/publication/policy-reforms-deprofessionalization

Molnar, A. (2005). *School commercialism: From democratic ideal to market commodity.* New York, NY: Routledge.

Nachane, D. M. (2008). The Unity of Science principle and the 'unreasonable effectiveness' of neoclassical economics. *Economic and Political Weekly, 43*(12 &13), 79–88.

Norton, J. K. (1957, May). The future of education in the United States. *Journal of Educational Sociology, 30*(9), 385–389.

Nussbaum, M. (1997). Flawed foundations: The philosophical critique of (a particular type of) economics. *The University of Chicago Law Review, 64*(4), 1197–1214.

Osborne, D., & Gaebler, T. (1993). *Reinventing government: How the entrepreneurial spirit is transforming the public sector.* New York, NY: Plume.

Ozga, J. (1987). Studying education through the lives of policymakers: An attempt to close the micro-macro gap. In S. Walker & L. Barton (Eds.), *Changing policies: Changing teachers* (pp. 138–150). Milton Keynes, UK: Open University Press.

Parsons, D. W. (1995). *Public policy: An introduction to the theory and practice of policy analysis.* Cheltenham, UK: Edward Elgar.

Pearson (2015). *Pearson annual report and accounts 2014.* Retrieved from www.pearson.com/content/dam/corporate/global/pearson-dot-com/files/annual-reports/ar2014/03%20PearsonAR_FinancialPerformance.pdf

Pollitt, C. (1991). *Managerialism and the public services: The Anglo-American experience.* Oxford, UK: Blackwell.

Popkewitz, T. (1991). *A political sociology of educational reform: Power/knowledge in teaching, teacher education, and research.* New York, NY: Teachers College Press.

Popkewitz, T. (2008). *Cosmopolitanism and the age of school reform: Science, education, and making society by making the child.* New York, NY: Routledge.

Postel, N. (2011). From the search for natural laws to the discovery of contingent rules in economics. *The Journal of Philosophical Economics, V*(1). Retrieved from jpe.ro/pdf.php?id=2902

Pring, R. (2001). *Philosophy of education research.* New York, NY: Continuum.

Prunty, J. J. (1984). *A critical reformulation of educational policy analysis.* Geelong, Victoria, Australia: Deakin University Press.

Prunty, J. J. (1985). Signposts for a critical educational policy analysis. *Australian Journal of Education, 29*(2), 133–140.

Raab, C. D. (1994). Where we are now: Reflections on the sociology of education policy. In D. Halpin & B. Troyna (Eds.), *Researching education policy: Ethical and methodological issues* (pp. 17–29). London, UK: Falmer Press.

Regis, E., Jr. (1980, Oct.). What is ethical egoism? *Ethics, 91*, 50–62.

Saltman, K. J. (2012). *The failure of corporate school reform*. Boulder, CO: Paradigm.

Sass, T. R., Semykina, A., and Harris, D. N. (2014) Value-added models and the measurement of teacher productivity. *Economics of Education Review, 38*, 9–23.

Schrecker, E. (2010). *The lost soul of higher education: Corporatization, the assault on academic freedom, and the end of the American university.* New York, NY: The New Press.

Scola, N. (2012, April 14). Exposing ALEC: How conservative-backed state laws are all connected. *The Atlantic.* Retrieved from www.theatlantic.com/politics/archive/2012/04/exposing-alec-how-conservative-backed-state-laws-are-all-connected/ 255869/

Scott, J. T. (2011). Market driven education reform and the radical politics of advocacy. *Peabody Journal of Education, 86*, 580–599.

Simons, M., Olssen, M., & Peters, M. A. (Eds.). (2009). *Re-reading educational policies: A handbook studying the policy agenda of the 21st century.* Rotterdam, The Netherlands: Sense Publishers.

Slaughter, S., & Rhoades, G. (2004). *Academic capitalism and the new economy: Markets, state, and higher education.* Baltimore, MD: Johns Hopkins University Press.

Sobel, R. (2013). The "desire for money": Aristotelian blind spot in the field of economics? A French heterodox point of view. *The Journal of Philosophical Economics, VI*(2). Retrieved from https://jpe.ro/poze/articole/90.pdf

Spring, J. (2003) *Educating the consumer citizen: A history of the marriage of schools, advertising, and media.* Mahwah, NJ: Lawrence Erlbaum Associates.

Torres, C. A. (1989). The capitalist state and public policy formation: Framework for a political sociology of educational policy making. *British Journal of Sociology of Education, 10*(1), 81–102.

University System of Georgia. (2007). USG teachers prepared to meet state's high demands. Preparation of New Teachers by University System of Georgia Institutions: 2007 Report on the Production, Hiring, and Retention of Teachers [Report Brief], pp. 2-3. Retrieved from http://www.usg.edu/assets/academic_affairs_and_policy/documents/2007_report_brief.pdf

Van den Berg, H. (2014). Growth theory after Keynes, Part II: 75 years of obstruction by the mainstream economics culture. *The Journal of Philosophical Economics, VII*(2). Retrieved from jpe.ro/pdf.php?id=6300

Washburn, J. (2005). *University Inc.: The corporate corruption of higher education.* New York, NY: Basic Books.

Weimer, D., & Vining, A. (1992). *Policy analysis: Concepts and practice.* Upper Saddle River, NJ: Prentice-Hall.

Weissert, W. (2018, February 25). Ideology tops facts in Texas history curriculum, experts say. *(Austin-American) Statesman*. Available at www.statesman.com/news/20180225/ideology-tops-facts-in-texas-history-curriculum-experts-say

Whalen, C. J. (1987). A reason to look beyond neoclassical economics: Some major shortcomings of orthodox theory. *Journal of Economic Issues, 21*(1), 259–280.

Whittrock, B., Wagner, P., & Wollman, H. (1991). Social science and the modern state. In P. Wagner, C. Weiss, B. Whittrock, & H. Wollman (Eds.), *Social sciences and modern states: National experiences and theoretical crossroads* (pp. 28–85). Cambridge, UK: Cambridge University Press.

Winters, E.A. (1967). Man and his changing society: The textbooks of Harold Rugg. *History of Education Quarterly* 7(1), 493–514.

Young, M. D. (1999). Multifocal educational policy research: Toward a method for enhancing traditional educational policy studies. *American Educational Research Journal, 36*(4), 677–714.

Zigo, D., & Moore, M.T. (2002). Accountability and teacher education: Just like everyone else: Teaching to the test? *English Education, 34*(2), 137–155.

CHAPTER 2

Common Core Creativity

What Are Preservice Teachers Learning?

Christopher H. Tienken and Dario Sforza

The notion that pre-K–12 public school graduates must possess skills such as creative and strategic thinking to succeed in what Drucker (1969) termed the knowledge economy has gained renewed traction in education policymaking circles since the release of the *A Nation at Risk* report (NCEE, 1983). Neither Drucker nor the authors of *Risk* invented the idea that creative and strategic thinking have value to an individual or a capitalistic society. Nonetheless, the focus on those skills by some in the corporate and education policymaking arenas increased with the release of the empirically vapid, yet politically influential, report.

One might argue that Spencer's (1883) seemingly utilitarian, eternal question of what knowledge is of most worth lies at the heart of the curricular debates about creativity and strategic thinking. Dewey's (1917) notions of free inquiry and critical reflection and Greene's (1995) concept of social imagination and the "ability to invent visions of what should be and what might be in our deficit society" (p. 5) expand the curricular debates. Their ideas of creativity and strategic thinking should cause educators and the broader society to consider the potential benefits to humanity of socially conscious versions of creative and strategic thinking beyond the economically utilitarian versions put forward by some policymakers and the authors of *Risk*. Much ink has been spilled about the need to increase creativity and strategic thinking in graduates of the United States public school system and tension exists about the best ways to do it (Duncan, 2013).

CORPORATE CREATIVITY CONCERNS

The drumbeat from portions of America's corporate sector about the need for teachers to provide businesses with a qualified labor pool continues almost unabated (National Council on Teacher Quality, 2014; Zheng, 2015). Business leaders request that their future workforce possesses skills and dispositions such as creativity, strategizing, critical thinking, and adaptability (Adobe, 2012; American

Society for Training and Development, 2010). *The Competitiveness and Innovative Capacity Report* (U.S. Department of Commerce, 2012) included the claim that "[G]iven the pace of change in today's global economy, investments to promote innovation deserve more emphasis than at any time in the past" (pp. 2–3). The K–12 education system has been identified as one target of such investment.

The economic, utilitarian camp of proponents for greater standardization of education processes and products increasingly frets that there is a void of skills in today's workforce and that it is the responsibility of public school teachers and college faculty to remedy the alleged situation by effectively delivering programs and practices based on standardization aimed at filling the alleged void (Belkin, 2015). Authors at the testing corporation, Educational Testing Services, identified several important skills they believe are missing from public school graduates: "Competency in domains such as reading literacy, numeracy, and problem solving are critical for success in the increasingly complex economies and societies of the 21st century" (ETS, 2015, pp. 7–8). The American Society for Training and Development (2010) identified "innovative thinking and action; the ability to think creatively and to generate new ideas and solutions to challenges at work" as one of the most important competencies and skills students will need to succeed in the 21st-century global economy (p. 13). Even the country's largest teacher association, the National Education Association, has told its members that students will not be able to face the demands of a 21st-century workforce if schools do not prepare them with the skills to "create and innovate" (NEA, 2012, p. 24).

It is obvious that teachers will be the main conduits for the transmission of the opportunities for creative and strategic thinking. University teacher preparation programs are one way teachers gain the expertise to deliver those skills. If instructional programs used in public schools and colleges of education are aligned to a curricular product that crowds out creativity and strategic thinking, then the prospects of increasing those types of skills in the future will be lessened.

COMMON CORE ARRIVES

Programs and policies built on altruistic claims that they are developed and implemented to increase creativity and strategic thinking to secure a positive economic future now dominate curriculum and assessment policymaking at the federal, state, and local levels. The Common Core State Standards (CCSS) for grades K–12 and national standardized testing consortia programs for grades 3–11, the Partnership for Assessment of Readiness for College and Careers (PARCC) and the Smarter Balanced Assessment Consortium (SBAC) are examples of the colonization in public schools by the standardized, utilitarian, economic conceptions of creativity and strategic thinking claimed to secure that positive future.

The Common Core State Standards are described by the National Governors Association (NGA) and the Council of Chief State School Offices (CCSSO) as a set of curriculum standards for grades K–12 in mathematics and language arts. More precisely, they are a set of performance-guarantee expectations for each grade level in those two subjects. The focus on economic utility is clear in the description of the standards:

> High standards that are consistent across states provide teachers, parents, and students with a set of clear expectations to ensure that all students have the skills and knowledge necessary to succeed in college, career, and life upon graduation from high school, regardless of where they live. These standards are aligned to the expectations of colleges, workforce training programs, and employers. The standards promote equity by ensuring all students are well prepared to collaborate and compete with their peers in the United States and abroad. (NGA & CCSSO, 2010)

Inherent in the brief description is the belief that one set of standards can prepare all students to succeed in any college, in any career, and in life regardless of geography, demographics, or other social impediments. The Standards are alleged to prepare students to simultaneously collaborate and compete in the economy of the future, as if collaboration and competition were complementary functions.

The descriptions of the Standards, their purpose, and their recommended use seem to fall short of Dewey's (1917) conceptions of creativity as part of the natural process in which humans reimagine the natural world and modify, remake, and reflect in reciprocity with the world around them for socially conscious purposes. Similarly, we have not read or seen any official communication or information about the Standards to suggest Greene's (1995) ideas of social imagination are at the core of the Common Core. However, in our view, we see the vendors of the Common Core answering Spencer's question about what knowledge is of most worth, and that knowledge seems to be: content in mathematics and English language arts that can be standardized, delivered efficiently to the masses, and measured in a mechanized way that quantifies a child's mastery of the content.

INFLUENCING HIGHER EDUCATION

Public school classrooms in the K–12 realm have not been the only venue influenced by the rhetoric calling for the standardization of creative and strategic thinking. Professors in some schools of education have been increasingly challenged to prepare preservice teacher candidates to deliver the Common Core in their future classrooms as part of the K–16 drive to secure an economically dominant future (Kyllonen, 2012). Depending on the state, some teacher education programs have been mandated to integrate explicit training on Common Core into their programs. For example, Arkansas, Massachusetts, and Washington aligned, or are in the process of aligning, their professional standards for teachers to synchronize with knowledge of teaching the Common Core. States including New York, Arizona, and Oregon have linked or are linking licensure procedures in part to knowledge of and competency in teaching Common Core (Poliokas, 2014). State education bureaucrats have worked with accreditation bodies like the Council for the Accreditation on Educator Preparation (CAEP) to embed the collection of evidence of Common Core teaching competencies into accreditation approvals (Poliokas, 2014). Over 900 teacher education certification programs in the United States fall under the accreditation of CAEP.

The notion that one set of curriculum standards in mathematics and English language arts and a collection of "core shifts" (Achieve, Inc., 2015) in instruction aligned to the Common Core can increase the creativity and strategic thinking of the approximately 50 million public school students educated in Common Core states is simplistic at best, and harmful at worst. Previous attempts to standardize educational outputs and processes did not produce the higher achievement and efficiencies promised. The Lancastrian system, the Gary Plan, intensive direct instruction, scientific management, mental discipline, and the mass movement of curriculum standards and standardized testing imposed by regulations found within the No Child Left Behind Act did not achieve their stated aims (Tienken & Orlich, 2013).

The mass standardization of education outcomes and teaching practices embedded in the Core seem eerily akin to some of Tyack's (1974) descriptions of the "systemization of schools" (p. 41) through standardized practices that some policy and education elites applied to impoverished children in urban public schools over 100 years ago. The assumptions and conceptions of creativity and strategic thinking advanced by the authors and proponents of Common Core are based on principles of factory-like mass production and standardization. This corporatized, mechanized, and economically utilitarian hijacking of the soul of creative and strategic thinking offered by the Common Core is a conception that we label *standardized creativity*. It stands in stark contrast to the unpredictable, divergent, humane, liberating, and deeply personal conceptions of creativity and strategic thinking forwarded by Greene, Dewey, and others.

A DIFFERENT VIEW OF CREATIVITY

We accept the assertion that opportunity for students to engage in activities that foster creative and strategic thinking in some way is an important part of the educative process. Although the appropriate purposes and time allotted to opportunities for such thinking are open for debate, we agree that creative and strategic thinking have a place in education. We even accept the idea that a utilitarian economic view of creativity and strategic thinking has a place in a much larger conception of the topics. However, we do not accept the utilitarian economic view of standardized creativity as the ultimate goal of education. Our view of creativity resides with conceptions like those provided by Dewey and Greene. Therefore, we reject the notion that creativity can be standardized, which we acknowledge as a bias that we have against one of the underlying conceptual frameworks of the CCSS.

For the purposes of this chapter we remain open to the notion that the Common Core might provide more opportunities for teachers to design learning activities that foster creative and strategic thinking in ways that are beneficial to the individual and society, economically and progressively, than were previously available in earlier versions of state mathematics and English language arts standards. If the CCSS are superior to previous state standards in facilitating some forms of creative and strategic thinking, even a standardized, economic utilitarian form, then state education bureaucrats and accreditation entities might be justified by imposing enhanced requirements for teacher education programs to include competencies with the CCSS in their preparation curricula and expectations.

However, if the CCSS do not contain more standards related to creative and strategic thinking than previous state curriculum standards, then preservice teachers might find themselves being prepared to teach a set of skills that do not lead to greater levels of higher-order thinking. In that case, state education bureaucrats and accreditation agency members that develop policies that require alignment to the Core might actually impede the long-term development of creativity and strategic thinking in students.

We argue that the Common Core State Standards might not be better than some previous state standards in terms of opportunities to develop creative and strategic thinking. We use the results from several existing analyses of the Common Core and results from a case study analysis of the New Jersey Core Curriculum Content Standards in mathematics and language arts as evidence that there might not be one best set of standards to develop creativity and strategic thinking. New Jersey was one of the first states to sign on to the Common Core. The New Jersey State Board of Education pledged its support before the final draft of the Common Core was completed and formally adopted the Core as its state curriculum less than two months after the final drafts were completed. New Jersey immediately changed its teacher education policies to require all candidates to learn how to implement the Common Core.

CORPORATELY CREATIVE TEACHING AND THE COMMON CORE

Although supporters of the Common Core State Standards (CCSS) claim they were conceived as a state-led initiative (National Governors Association &

Council of Chief State School Officers, 2010), they were born from portions of the larger multinational corporate world, with one of the main conduits for the corporate idea of mass standardization being Achieve, Inc. (2008). Achieve, Inc. was founded by the National Governors Association (NGA), a quasi-public organization, and various business leaders from some of the nation's largest corporations, during the National Education Summit held by President Bill Clinton in 1996 (Achieve, Inc., 2004a). In 2004, Achieve, Inc., along with partners from the Education Trust and the Thomas B. Fordham Institute, released the report *Ready or Not: Creating a High School Diploma that Counts* and launched the American Diploma Project, which some have called the precursor to the CCSS (Achieve, Inc., 2004b; Vander Hart, 2014).

Karp (2013) captured the essence of the main participants of the final versions of the CCSS when he wrote that "The standards were drafted largely behind closed doors by academics and assessment experts, many with ties to testing companies" (p. 13). Anthony Cody (2013) found similar links between the CCSS and the corporate world:

> a "confidential" process was under way, involving 27 people on two Work Groups, including a significant number from the testing industry. Here are the affiliations of those 27: ACT (6), the College Board (6), Achieve Inc. (8), Student Achievement Partners (2), America's Choice (2). Only three participants were outside of these five organizations. Only one classroom teacher was involved—on the committee to review the math standards. (p. 1)

Karp (2013) and Cody (2013) noted that not one of the participants on the standards development committees represented the K–3 teaching spectrum, and K–12 educators were brought into the process at the end to act as a rubber stamp and endorse the completed standards. The corporate bias suggested by the lack of K–12 educator input into the actual development of the Standards is reinforced by the amount of private money used to market the standards. For example, the Gates Foundation reportedly has spent over 160 million dollars to promote the Common Core, with other, smaller foundations also spending funds to do the same (Simon & Shah, 2013; Tienken, 2017).

The work of Karp (2013) and Cody (2013) represents some of the general concerns raised in the education research community and blogosphere regarding the corporate ties and interests surrounding the development of the Common Core. Couple those concerns with the fact that professors in colleges of education across the country are teaching preservice teachers to implement the CCSS, and we see that the standardizing influence of the CCSS and its corporate education ecosystem have begun to take root in the professional upbringing of the nation's future teaching force (Tienken, 2017).

It is not our concern that only one teacher was involved in the development of the CCSS. It is possible that even if more teachers were involved in the development of the Common Core there would have been widespread agreement to move forward with it, because the majority of teachers in 2010 had already experienced 10 to 15 years of standardization and standards-based curricula and might have come to accept standardization or taken it for granted. However, we do think that more teacher voices might have provided more insights into issues of developmental appropriateness at the K–3 grade levels. Furthermore, we believe that more teacher voices might have resulted in uncovering issues of implementation, one of which is the historical effect of standardization to narrow the curriculum and push out opportunities for creative and strategic thinking in favor of procedural skills and declarative knowledge using imitative pedagogy for the sake of efficiency due to the constraints of time (Tienken & Zhao, 2013).

CULT OF SPECIFICITY

Policy initiatives that result in the standardization of knowledge at the pre-K–12 levels of education—in particular, the use of grade-level, state-mandated, performance output curriculum standards—seem to flow from the traditionalists' view of education, born out of perennialist and essentialist philosophical streams. Some examples of traditionalist conceptions of curriculum include demonstrated mastery of discipline-centered subject matter isolated from authentic contexts, stated expectations for teacher instruction to guarantee student mastery, predictability and specificity of outcomes, and the transmission of a fixed set of knowledges (Tanner & Tanner, 2007, p. 120).

Curriculum standards built on perennialist and essentialist conceptions expect output of the intended curriculum specified in detail. There is an underlying belief that greater specificity leads to higher levels of student output and less variance in student output. Take, for example, Common Core grade 7 literacy standard RL.7.6: "Determine an author's point of view or purpose in a text and analyze how the author distinguishes his or her position from that of others" (NGA & CCSSO, 2010). The verbs "determine" and "analyze" specify the expected output actions to be performed by the student in order to demonstrate mastery of the standard. In this example, actions that require subjective evaluation, such as to critique, evaluate, create, or reimagine, would not be acceptable demonstrations of mastery.

The grade-by-grade specificity of the CCSS creates *de facto* pacing expectations for student mastery and teaching. The Common Core State Standards were designed as mastery standards. Students are expected to demonstrate mastery of every standard at every grade level (Tienken, 2017). Further, the CCSS include appendices in which specific examples of English language arts texts, mathematical representations, and student outcomes are presented to further define what is considered acceptable student demonstration of mastery.

The implied message of the standards is that there exist certain specific student behaviors and demonstrations that represent achievement of the standards. That message has the covert effect of reducing teaching to imitation or following a recipe or set of rules to achieve a standardized outcome. Dewey (1929) noted an insidious influence of standardized specificity on teaching when he wrote:

> In this situation there is a strong tendency to identify teaching ability with the use of procedures that yield immediately successful results, success being measured by such things as order in the classroom, correct recitations by pupils in assigned lessons, passing of examinations, promotion of pupils to a higher grade, etc. (p. 15)

Thus, not only is the content of the CCSS tightly specified, the corresponding teaching methods tend to become mechanical and based more on "how to do things" (Dewey, 1929, p. 15). Over time, teachers learn to imitate the examples and content found in the standards and they begin to "want recipes" (Dewey, 1929, p.15) for pre-packaged standardized outcomes.

The constricting influence of specificity becomes an antagonist to creativity and strategic thinking, especially if those ways of thinking are not specified in the expected curriculum standards. In effect, too much specificity and standardization might actually hinder creative and strategic thinking, unless great care is taken to include multiple opportunities within the curriculum standards for teachers to teach creatively and students to have consistent practice exploring and using creative and strategic thinking.

THE COMMON TEACHING SOLUTION

CCSS supporters advertise the Standards as the solution for the perceived need for greater global competitiveness on the part of students. For example, Craig Barrett (2010), the former CEO of Intel, stated, "I know that common education standards are essential for producing the educated work force America needs to remain globally competitive" (p. 1). Vander Ark (2013) proclaimed, "It's exciting to see 45 states voluntarily adopting common college and career ready expectations for students—it makes the U.S globally competitive, is embraced by teachers, and is unleashing an avalanche of innovation" (p. 1).

The widespread adoption of the CCSS among state education agencies has caused changes to teacher education programs across the country. One specific change can be seen in instructing teacher-education candidates in the CCSS and how to teach the Standards to their future students (Conference Board of Mathematical Sciences, 2012). Authors at the Association of Public and Land-Grant Universities (APLU, n.d.-b) working with the Science and Mathematics Teacher Imperative (SMTI), called for the alignment of the higher education curriculum with the Common Core State Standards at the K–12 level. The authors wrote,

> In particular, an emphasis needs to be placed on the Standards for Mathematical Practice, described in the CCSS, which paint a very different view of mathematics learning than is common in many content courses for teachers. Just as the CCSS outlines the knowledge and skills that will be expected of K–12 students, we will also need standards for teachers that outline the knowledge of mathematics and sciences that teachers will need in order to effectively teach the CCSS content. (p. 4)

The comments made by SMTI program officials seem to suggest that teachers should conform to ever-increasing edicts imposed by external policy-making bodies that reside far from the classroom. Would teaching standards help increase creative and strategic thinking among the K–12 public school student population?

One intent of SMTI program administrators is to align teacher education instruction to the teaching of Common Core. By default, some standardization of teaching will occur. With the standardization of teaching come fidelity of implementation and less discrepancy between the enacted curriculum and the intended curriculum. If the intended curriculum of the Common Core offers more opportunities for creative and strategic thinking, then perhaps fidelity of implementation is a positive outcome of SMTI work on the enacted curricula in classrooms. The reach of the SMTI on preservice teacher preparation in the area of mathematics cannot be overstated. SMTI-associated programs prepare upwards of 8,000 mathematics and science teachers per year, and the influence of SMTI on teacher education curricula is real (APLU, n.d.-a).

Another example of a project aimed at changing teacher-education preparation to be more aligned to the Common Core is the Mathematics Teacher Education Partnership, also convened by the SMTI, comprised of teams of faculty from 38 universities and community colleges and K–12 teachers from 30 states. The partnership has been involved in developing ways to enhance the preparation of teacher education candidates and current teachers to more effectively deliver the CCSS in order for America's youth to reach higher levels of creativity, strategic thinking, and global competitiveness (Sawchuck, 2014). Authors from the APLU (n.d.-b) associated with the Mathematics Teacher Education Partnership explained their focus on fidelity of implementation and the influence of their work:

> Developing communities of practice, including both practicing and prospective teachers, in schools focused on teaching the CCSS with fidelity provides opportunities for higher education faculty to simultaneously engage in improving practice in schools and nurturing the next generation of teachers, as has already occurred in many of the Math and Science Partnerships funded by the National Science Foundation. (p. 5)

Once again, with such a strong focus on fidelity of implementation, it becomes important that the program implemented is of a certain level of quality, or at least better than what existed previously.

CONCEPTIONS OF CREATIVITY

It is difficult to arrive at a single definition of creativity in the education context because creatively complex thinking does not have one manifestation, and implies various ways of arriving at the definition or conclusion of a problem. We suggest the essence of the large body of literature through examining the work of some of the prominent writers on the topic of creativity in education.

Sternberg (1998) explained that creativity is "the aptitude to generate work that is unique and original as well as suitable for the specific task or problem one is attempting to solve" (Sternberg, 1998, p. 3). Sternberg's conception places the relationship between creativity and education within the context of a purpose, similar to Greene's *social imagination* (1995). But Sternberg's conception of creative purpose can also be embraced by those with an economic, utilitarian view of creativity. For example, leaders of for-profit, publically traded corporations have specific purposes based on their mission to return shareholder value above all else and they expect the application of creativity to serve those purposes. Whereas Greene's (1995) social imagination points toward socially conscious remaking of social conditions, Sternberg's (1998) conception can be interpreted in many ways.

Albert and Runco (1998) enlarged Sternberg's conception of the study of creativity by introducing a humanizing function as part of the purpose:

> The early conceptualizations of creativity and research were in themselves exceptional creative acts, as was the eventual bridging of these concepts through deliberately applying research methods. These methods were essential not only to the meaning and significance of creativity in human experience, but to why and how historical events were set in motion. Understanding this should help us appreciate . . . creativity within history. (p. 16)

In this sense, Albert and Runco's conception situated creativity as an important aspect of human development and societal progress and not just an economic tool, much like Dewey's (1958) and Greene's (1995) conceptions. Runco and Jaeger (2012) synthesized from the extent research that the early conceptions of creativity were not enough to deem someone or something creative and offered that "original things must be effective to be creative" (p. 92). Hence, based on Runco and Jaeger's synthesis, creative thinking would mean nothing if it did not lead to some kind of progress for life or something productive or effective.

Creative thinking is not exclusively reserved for the individual. Padget (2013) extended the conception of creativity beyond the individual with the contention that creativity and creative thinking should be thought of as a collaborative effort and argued that "most modern human achievements are the result of teamwork; groups of individuals, like jigsaw puzzles of different coordinated talents and aptitudes, experiences and enthusiasms" (p. 22).

The existing conceptions present an overall humanistic view of creativity as a tool for advancing the greater good and societal progress. Due to changing economic conditions in the United States and increasing fascination with global economic competiveness, there has been a renewed interest in infusing a utilitarian form of creativity and strategic thinking into public education reforms as a way to prepare students for an economic landscape increasingly influenced by innovation (Craft, 2005).

TEACHING FOR ECONOMIC CREATIVITY

In the mainstream, armchair business literature and media, one hears or sees the term *innovation* used synonymously with creativity. Whether by coincidence or on purpose, the synonymous use of the terms creativity and innovation covertly moves the conception of creativity into an economic context as a strategic tool to generate profits, and away from a humanistic and educational context used to develop human beings with critical intelligence and a social imagination.

Creativity and innovation, and by association strategic thinking, are often associated with ideas that that are purposeful and profitable. For example, Craft (2005) defined innovation as the "implementation of new ideas to create something of value," increasing its attention in today's global marketplace (Craft, 2005, p. 16). Business leaders seek innovators and individuals who can think creatively and in complex new ways; this requires acquired creative thought and skills. Some commentators in the business world (e.g., George, 2012; IBM, 2012) identified risk-taking, creativity, innovation, and entrepreneurship on the part of business leaders and employees as key factors for the U.S. to increase its global competitiveness. The authors of the World Competitiveness Center's 2013 report echoed the need for creative, innovative, and entrepreneurial skills for the United States to maintain its top ranking on the World Competitiveness Index.

The results from the 2012 Global Chief Executive Officer Study (IBM, 2012) identified a group of skills necessary to compete in the global economy (Tienken & Mullen, 2014). The recommendations are similar to characteristics of creativity found in the social sciences literature but situates them in an economic context. According to the 1,700 CEOs surveyed, who represented 64 countries and 18 major industries, leaders and employees in the global economy must be able to (a) innovate, (b) collaborate and cooperate (globally amongst themselves and with their customer bases), (c) be creative, (d) seek opportunity, (e) use complexity to a strategic advantage, and (f) be communicative (pp. 21–24).

As in the IBM (2012) survey, more than a decade of reports from the U.S. Council on Competitiveness (USCOC, 2007, 2018) have listed innovation, entrepreneurship, flexibility, and creativity as important factors that are needed to keep the U.S. economy and its employees competitive in the future. Zhao (2012) identified creativity and entrepreneurial spirit as two important aspects children will need to remain competitive in a global economy. He warned that education policies that standardize curriculum content and learning output place a premium on the development and demonstration of routine academic skills, which suggests a kind of thinking easily offshored to countries where people work for much lower wages.

The for-profit corporate community's utilitarian concern about the economically oriented development of creativity and strategic thinking is supported in the business and social sciences literature. Creativity and strategic thinking "fuels all areas of our country's economy and prosperity" (Turnipseed, 2012, par. 3). Creativity is cognitively complex and often involves many different internal and external processes (Runco, 2007). Jackson (2003) contended that the United States' strength, economic success, and technological superiority depend on the creativity of our science and engineering workforce.

As competencies lauded by the business community are seen to be driving today's knowledge economy, creativity and strategic thinking are said to have the potential to build confidence in future leaders while allowing them to be competent despite economic uncertainty, leading them to make new and innovative business decisions (Bronson & Merryman, 2010; IBM, 2012). It is claimed that the ingenuity and creative capacity of the youth is critical to (re)building our economy and keeping U.S. employees globally competitive in the economic arena (Adobe, 2012; Kyllonen, 2012; NEA, 2010).

Cisco Systems Incorporated, Intel Corporation, Microsoft Corporation, and the University of Melbourne (2010) organized a report called *The Assessing and Teaching of 21st Century Skills* (ATC21S) to define more clearly the skills needed in the corporate environment. The ATC21S report categorized the skills into four categories:

- Ways of thinking: creativity, critical thinking, problem solving, decisionmaking, and learning
- Ways of working: communication and collaboration
- Tools for working: information and communications technology (ICT) and information literacy
- Skills for living in the world: citizenship, life and career, and personal and social responsibility.

The context of the ATC21S report was economic in nature, driven and funded mostly by for-profit corporate sources, and thus creativity and strategic thinking are aimed first at achieving corporate economic aims. How are the skills identified by the corporate community supposed to find their way into the public school education system? Enter the Common Core State Standards in the K–12 environment and teacher education preparation in higher education.

COMMON CORE CREATIVITY

One of the stated aims of the Common Core State Standards was to provide a foundation for creative and strategic thinking so that students could be globally economically competitive (NGA & CCSSO, 2010). However, no large-scale pilot testing was ever conducted on the CCSS and its influence on learning in general, or its influence on creative thinking or strategic thinking (Mathis, 2010; Tienken, 2011). Furthermore, no research was conducted on the influence of the CCSS on preservice teachers' ability to increase creative and strategic thinking in public school students. So the teacher preparation community finds itself in a situation in which preservice teachers in some states are being inculcated into a teaching environment in which a pre-packaged set of corporately developed curriculum standards are imposed under the banner of increasing creativity, critical thinking, and innovation; yet there is little empirical evidence that the language used in the CCSS encourages more creative thinking in mathematics and language arts than their states' previous standards.

CRITIQUING CREATIVITY

Although no research was conducted to assess the creativity of the Common Core in relation to previous state curriculum standards in mathematics and language arts, there have been studies that used Webb's framework to measure Depth of Knowledge (DOK), a proxy for creativity and critical thinking within the Common Core State Standards. For example, Florida State University's CPALMS (2012) standards categorization project assigned DOK levels for each of the CCSS, including the anchor standards that repeat in every grade level for math and ELA. Assigning an overall DOK to each anchor standard provides an exaggerated picture of the true overall creativity aspects of the Common Core because the anchor standards are more often open ended and more creative in nature than the specific standards. Because the same anchor standards appear in grades K–12, it seems as if there is more creativity in the CCSS, but in actuality, the same anchor standards are simply being counted 13 times instead of one time. Our more in-depth study assigned a DOK rating to the anchor standards only once, and then categorized all the substandards in each grade level in an attempt to provide a clearer picture of creativity among the standards.

Results from other studies on the difficulty of the Core seemed to indicate a "slight increase in emphasis on higher order content, a shift that is larger in English language arts than in mathematics" when compared to some states' previous standards (Porter, McMaken, Hwang, & Yang, 2011, p. 186). Cobb and Jackson (2011) noted a modest increase in some cognitive complexity within the Core but could not determine how much the Core differed from existing state standards. However, those previous studies did not examine the Core specifically for levels of creativity or strategic thinking, nor do they address how the Core aligned with technology-enriched learning environments (Beach, 2011).

ON-THE-GROUND IMPACTS OF COMMON CORE

We became concerned whether the Common Core provided a better foundation for creative and strategic thinking than the state's previous state standards. We suspended our bias against standardization and looked past the possibility that the conceptions of creativity and strategic thinking embedded in the CCSS are overly limited when compared against the range of definitions considered earlier. We proceeded with a pilot study under the idea that creative and strategic thinking are generally beneficial skills for students to learn, even if they are narrowly focused for the ultimate purpose of economic utility. As a rule, we would rather have students exposed more to creation of knowledge than to imitation of it.

We, along with another researcher, developed a focused qualitative case study to investigate our concern at the high school level (Sforza, Tienken, & Kim, 2016). The study was guided by the overarching question: What percentage of the high school CCSS in mathematics and language requires creative and strategic thinking compared to existing state standards? We chose to conduct a single-state pilot case study as our initial foray into the topic.

We selected the high school standards because New Jersey is a state that still uses high school exit exams to determine if a student is eligible to graduate from high school. Officials at the New Jersey Department of Education have gone so far as to state that the results of the exams, aligned to the Common Core State Standards, will determine whether students are college and career ready (NJDOE, 2014). Hence, the implication is that students must be learning the skills needed for successful careers, including creativity and strategic thinking.

We compared the levels of creativity found in the high school Common Core to those found in the New Jersey Core Curriculum Content Standards (NJCCCS) for high school math and language arts. We drew upon Webb's Depth of Knowledge levels as our conceptual framework to analyze the levels of curricular creativity found in the CCSS for mathematics and language arts and to the New Jersey Core Curriculum Content Standards in mathematics and language arts from 2009, prior to the state's adoption of the Core in 2010.

Webb defined four levels of cognitive complexity as Depth of Knowledge (DOK) levels. Webb's conception of creative and strategic thinking is pliable enough to include the utilitarian economic conception but also more expansive conceptions like those of Dewey and Greene. Therefore, we found it a useful platform from which to explore the types of opportunities present in the high school sets of CCSS in mathematics and English language arts.

Webb's DOK is ideally suited to provide an analysis of the general creative potential of curriculum standards because it clearly delineates between skills and concepts necessary for creative and strategic thinking and those suited to lower level cognitive complexity. The Depth of Knowledge framework includes more convergent forms of knowledge like declarative knowledge, based on facts, and procedural knowledge, which represents the "know-how" and procedures for creative and (Runco & Chand, 1995, p. 245). Declarative knowledge is directly linked to procedural knowledge, and together they can promote creative thinking if the appropriate opportunities are provided. If the "know-how" of standards is understood during their creation, then the standards, which could be intended to provide and assess procedural knowledge, can potentially increase "originality and flexibility," some of the critical ingredients of creativity and innovation (Runco & Chand, 1995, p. 245). The cognitive potential of procedural and declarative knowledge is necessary, but limited.

Procedural and declarative knowledge provide only the foundation needed to reach complex and extended forms of thinking but are more convergent in nature. Learning tasks and assessment questions based on procedural and declarative knowledge generally require the student to demonstrate very specific behaviors and determine one correct answer. Although these kinds of knowledge are important in the development of higher-level thinking, curriculum standards dominated by them can restrict learning to imitation. If deeper levels of cognitive demand are absent and curriculum content standards imply repetition of bits of information, then complex efforts to help students be creative and original can be marginalized (Runco & Chand, 1995, p. 245).

On the one hand, if the CCSS are laden overwhelmingly with procedural and declarative knowledge demands, then the potential effectiveness of teachers trained to implement the CCSS to enhance creativity and critical thinking could be compromised. An intended curriculum that is low in complexity and depth of knowledge will make it difficult for students to develop essential 21st-century skills that lead to creative and original thought (Gardiner, 1972, p. 327). On the other hand, an intended curriculum high in complexity and depth of knowledge will enhance a student's creative and extended levels of thinking by requiring them to "make multiple connections between several different key and complex concepts" (Gardiner, 1972, p. 327).

LEVELS OF THINKING

Webb's Level 1 Depth of Knowledge represents recall, and Level 2 represents imitative skills and concepts. Together, Levels 1 and 2 require basic knowledge recitation and comprehension. Creative and strategic thinking are not developed through curriculum standards dominated by DOK Levels 1 and 2 skills and concepts. Webb's Depth of Knowledge Level 3, strategic thinking and complex reasoning, and Level 4, extended levels of thinking, are levels that support opportunities for students to reach creative, analytical, and strategic levels of thinking and complex reasoning.

The cognition involved in Webb's DOK Levels 3 and 4 are where researchers argue that creative and strategic thinking begin (Hess, Jones, Carlock, and Walkup, 2009; Porter et al., 2011; Ward, Smith, & Finke, 2010; Webb, Alt, Ely, & Versperman, 2005). If the curriculum standards do not have the necessary flexibility for teachers to develop the learning activities and objectives necessary for creative and strategic thinking, students will be unable to break through the fixed and rigid objectives in the corresponding curriculum in order to make the complex connections needed to reach a Webb DOK 3 and 4 level of cognition. If there is no flexibility to the standards, students will reach what Smith and Tindell (1997) call a "memory block" or what Runco and Chand (1995) called "functional fixedness" (pp. 247, 355).

CATEGORIZING CREATIVITY IN NEW JERSEY

The Common Core State Standards (CCSS) and New Jersey Core Curriculum Content Standards (NJCCS) were analyzed utilizing Webb's protocol and the DOK levels derived from the Webb Alignment Tool (Webb et al., 2005). The DOK was used as an analytical tool to code and compare the cognitive complexity of the standards between the CCSS and the NJCCCS in Grades 9–12 in ELA and Math. All standards and substandards from the NJCCCS and CCSS were included in the analysis. During the analysis of the standards a code was specified for every standard and substandard within the Grades 9–12 ELA and Math CCSS and NJCCCS.

Each standard was rated on a 1–4 continuum based on its corresponding DOK level. Utilizing the step model as a guide, a coding agenda was created, using Mayring's (2000) template and the DOK definitions, examples, and coding rules as described in the Webb Alignment Tool (WAT) training manual. Two analysts using Webb's coding protocol coded each standard based on its Depth of Knowledge complexity (Sato, Lagunoff, & Worth, 2011; Yuan & Le, 2012). Inter-rater reliability was addressed by involving a qualified and trained second coder in order to increase the validity within the standards categorization process.

REDUCED OPPORTUNITIES THROUGH COMMON CORE

Overall, the previous NJCCCS curriculum standards for mathematics and English language arts provided more opportunities for creative and strategic thinking. The CCSS require students to demonstrate mastery of more procedural and declarative information.

English Language Arts

The Grades 9–12 ELA CCSS rated lower in cognitive complexity, with a combined DOK Level 1 and 2 of 72%, as compared with the combined 62% standards rated at DOK Level 1 and 2 coded within the Grades 9–12 ELA NJCCCS. The Grades 9–12 ELA NJCCCS provide students with the potential of reaching higher levels of cognitive complexity and creativity, with a combined 38% of standards rated at a DOK Level 3 and 4 as compared to 28% of the Grades 9–12 ELA CCSS rated at a DOK Level 3 and 4. Although the majority of both sets of standards clustered around levels 1 and 2, overall the NJ ELA standards provided more standards and potentially more opportunities for higher-level creative thinking.

Mathematics

Within Grades 9–12, 62% of the 2009 NJ math standards were rated DOK Levels 1 and 2. Levels 1 and 2 standards involve basic recall of facts and processes and use of simple, one-step problem-solving skills. Approximately 38% of the NJ math standards were rated at levels of complex and creative thinking, DOK Levels 3 and 4. Specifically, 10% of the NJCCCS in mathematics were rated at the DOK Level 4.

Overall, the Grades 9–12 Math CCSS were rated lower in cognitive complexity and creativity. We were astounded to see 90% of the 9–12 CCSS math standards were categorized as either Level 1 or Level 2. None, 0%, of the CCSS mathematics standards were determined to foster Level 4 thinking, leaving the remaining 10% categorized as Level 3.

As a whole, the 2009 New Jersey math and English language arts curriculum standards for grades 9–12 included more opportunities to develop course curricula providing potential opportunities for teachers to develop creative and complex thinking for students than did the grades 9–12 CCSS.

IMPLICATIONS

We submit that state education bureaucrats and officials at accreditation agencies have a professional responsibility to ensure their mandates and monitoring structures do not impede access to and attainment of a quality public education for students in the system. In our opinion, they also have an obligation to know and be transparent about the strengths and limitations of the interventions they foist upon K–12 public school children and teacher education programs.

Teacher Preparation Programs

Some could argue whether the development of creativity and strategic thinking is important to support in the public education system of states. There might be some states in which education bureaucrats and policymakers see the state's responsibility as providing only a basic education based on procedural and declarative knowledge. There might be some states in which policymakers do not see it as the role of teacher education programs to focus on creative and strategic thinking as part of initial preparation. Perhaps some policymakers see that as the role of graduate schools of education.

In states in which education officials and policymakers accept the view that creative and strategic thinking are important parts of a public education, the results from the existing literature and our pilot study provide models for others to conduct reviews comparing their state's previous and current curriculum standards in mathematics and language arts to determine which sets of standards better help to operationalize creative and strategic thinking. We believe it necessary for state education bureaucrats and policymakers to explore the extent to which the claims made by the vendors of the CCSS match the reality that policy seeks to actualize.

Because teacher education program administrators in many states have joined initiatives aimed at indoctrinating preservice teachers to deliver the CCSS to their future students with fidelity, it is vital to know what fidelity of implementation would bring in terms of creative and strategic thinking. Then perhaps teacher education administrators could make more informed decisions as to whether they want to strive for more fidelity within their programs. Without such studies, state education policy is flying blind.

Teacher Preparation Accreditation Agencies

Officials at accreditation agencies should also conduct studies similar to our pilot in order to provide multiple sources of data to better determine whether it is appropriate to require fidelity of implementation to the Common Core and evidence of competency with teaching to the Core. Essentially, accreditation entities that promote adherence to the Core in teacher preparation programs should apply Dewey's (1917) conception of critical reflection to their work. Accreditation officials should also take a clear stance on what the goal of teacher preparation programs should be in terms of the type of thinking teachers should be able to foster with their students. Once that stance is clear, then perhaps accreditation officials can critically reflect on whether their mandates and teacher preparation program criteria match their reported goals for teacher preparation programs.

Program administrators in states that require teacher preparation programs be nationally accredited generally try to align their program goals and programs to the accreditation requirements. This poses yet another potential problem. If those accreditation requirements call for evidence that candidates have been prepared to deliver the CCSS with fidelity, then the program faculty have the right to know what it is they are aligning to in terms of the types of thinking and learning opportunities their candidates will eventually provide to children. At least then program administrators and faculty could dialogue about the empirically discovered strengths and weaknesses of the CCSS in relation to their accreditation agency's requirements and their own program mission. Without information derived from empirical study, the entire system becomes informed by opinion, myths, and mistaken claims about the efficacy of the CCSS to provide opportunities for creative and strategic thinking.

CONCLUSION

The employees at the NGA and CCSSO (2010) contend that the CCSS emphasize the strategic thinking, problem-solving, and creativity skills some in the business community stated that public school students lack. However, the results of our pilot study and other studies suggest otherwise. The results suggest that the type of thinking required by the Common Core is primarily geared toward utilitarian, economic uses, more suitable for the desires of the for-profit, private sector. The type of thinking required by the Common Core seems to be in contrast to Dewey's (1917) ideas of free inquiry and critical reflection and Greene's (1995) concept of social imagination and the "ability to invent visions of what should be and what might be in our deficit society" (p.5). The thinking required by the Common Core seems to lack a humanistic focus and be void of a concern for socially conscious problem solving. The Common Core content appears to be fixed on economically utilitarian uses.

Are teacher education program administrators and faculty potentially repeating an unsuccessful method of education associated with the likes of the Gary Plan and the Lancastrian models by training preservice teachers to implement, with fidelity, a set of curriculum standards that in some states might decrease the opportunities for creative and strategic thinking in students? If teacher preparation administrators and faculty design program curricula aimed at teaching preservice candidates to deliver the CCSS with fidelity, then they must recognize the creativity gap that might exist in some states within the CCSS.

Although our preference would be creativity and strategic thinking aimed at socially conscious problem solving, we would welcome the intermediate step of those who lead teacher education programs identifying the areas of learning where the CCSS might be an advancement over previous state standards, and the areas in which programs and accreditation agencies might need to work for and advocate for improvements in the Core.

REFERENCES

Achieve, Inc. (2004a). Our history. Retrieved from www.achieve.org/history-achieve

Achieve, Inc. (2004b). Ready or not: Creating a high school diploma that counts. In series *The American diploma project.* Washington, DC: Achieve, Inc. Retrieved from www.achieve.org/files/ReadyorNot.pdf

Achieve, Inc. (2008). *Out of many one: Toward rigorous Common Core Standards from the ground up*. Washington, DC: Achieve, Inc. Retrieved from www.achieve.org/OutofManyOne

Achieve, Inc. (2015). The common core shifts at a glance. Retrieved from achievethecore.org/page/277/the-common-core-shifts-at-a-glance

Adobe. (2012). State of create study: StrategyOne. Retrieved from www.adobe.com/aboutadobe/pressroom/pdfs/Adobe_State_of_Create_Infographic.pdf

Albert, R. S., & Runco, M. A. (1998). A history of research on creativity. In R. J. Sternberg (Ed.), *Handbook of creativity* (pp. 16–34). Cambridge, UK: Cambridge University Press.

American Society for Training and Development (ASTD). (2010). *Bridging the skills gap*. Retrieved from www.td.org/magazines/td-magazine/bridging-the-skills-gap-new-factors-compound-the-growing-skills-shortage

Association of Public and Land-Grant Universities. (n.d.-a). About SMTI. Retrieved from www.aplu.org/projects-and-initiatives/stem-education/science-and-mathematics-teaching-imperative/about-us/index.html

Association of Public and Land-Grant Universities. (n.d.-b). Common Core State Standards and teacher preparation: The role of higher education. Retrieved from www.aplu.org/projects-and-initiatives/stem-education/SMTI_Library/APLU-SMTI-Paper-2/file?id=3482

Barrett, C. (2010, April 6). The case for common educational standards. *Wall Street Journal.* Retrieved from www.wsj.com/articles/SB1000142405270230401740457516568 2594015398

Beach, R. W. (2011). Issues in analyzing alignment of language arts Common Core Standards with state standards. *Educational Researcher, 40*, 179–182.

Belkin, D. (2015, January 16). Test finds college graduates lack skills for white collar jobs. *The Wall Street Journal.* Retrieved from www.wsj.com/articles/test-finds-many-students-ill-prepared-to-enter-work-force-1421432744

Bronson, P. & Merryman, A. (2010, Jul. 10). The creativity crisis. *Newsweek*. Retrieved from www.newsweek.com/creativity-crisis-74665

Cisco Systems Inc., Intel Corporation, Microsoft Corporation, & University of Melbourne. (2010). Assessment and teaching of 21st century skills (ATC21S). Retrieved from www.cisco.com/c/dam/en_us/about/citizenship/socio-economic/docs/ATC21S_Exec_Summary.pdf

Cobb, P., & Jackson, K. (2011). Assessing the quality of the Common Core State Standards for Mathematics. *Educational Researcher, 40,* 183–185.

Cody, A. (2013, November 16). Common Core Standards: 10 colossal errors [Blog post]. *Education Week Teacher*. Retrieved from blogs.edweek.org/teachers/living-in-dialogue/2013/11/common_core_standards_ten_colo.html

Conference Board of Mathematical Sciences. (2012). *The mathematical education of teachers II*. Providence, RI: American Mathematical Society. Retrieved from www.cbmsweb.org/archive/MET2/met2.pdf

Council on Competitiveness, The. (USCOC). (2018). Clarion call. Launch of the national commission on innovation and competitiveness frontiers. Retrieved from www.compete.org/storage/reports/2018%20clarion%20call%20final.pdf

Council on Competitiveness, The. (USCOC). (2007). Competitiveness index: Where America stands. Retrieved from www.compete.org/reports/all/357-competitiveness-index-where-america-stands

Craft, A. (2005). *Creativity in schools: Tensions and dilemmas.* New York, NY: Routledge.

Dewey, J. (1917). The need for a recovery of philosophy. In Dewey (Ed.), *Creative intelligence: Essays in the pragmatic attitude* (pp. 3–69). New York, NY: Holt.

Dewey, J. (1929). *The sources of science in education.* New York, NY: Liveright.

Drucker, P. (1969). *The age of discontinuity: Guidelines to our changing Society.* New York, NY: Harper and Row.

Duncan, A. (2013, December 3). *The threat of educational stagnation and complacency*. U.S Department of Education. Retrieved from www.ed.gov/news/speeches/threat-educational-stagnation-and-complacency

ETS. (2015). *America's skill challenge: Millennials and the future.* Retrieved from www.ets.org/millennials

Florida State University. (2013). *CPALMS*: Content complexity rating. Retrieved from www.cpalms.org/Standards/dok.aspx#

Gardiner, G. S. (1972). Complexity training and prejudice reduction. *Journal of Applied Social Psychology*, 2, 326–342. doi: 10.1111/j.1559-1816.1972.tb01284.x

George, B. (2012, March 2). Developing global leaders is America's competitive advantage. *Harvard Business Review.* Retrieved from hbr.org/2012/03/developing-global-leaders-is-a

Greene, M. (1995). *Releasing the imagination: Essay on education, the arts, and social change.* San Francisco, CA: Jossey-Bass.

Hess, K., Jones, B., Carlock, D., & Walkup, J. (2009). *Cognitive rigor: Blending the strengths of Bloom's Taxonomy and Webb's Depth of Knowledge to enhance classroom-level processes.* Dover, NH: National Center for Improvement of Educational Assessment.

IBM Study. (2012). *Global chief executive officer study*. Retrieved from http://www- 935.ibm.com/services/us/en/c-suite/ceostudy2012/

Jackson, S. A. (2003). *Envisioning a 21st century science and engineering workforce for the United States: Tasks for university, industry, and government*. Washington, DC: National Academies Press.

Karp, S. (2013). The problems with the Common Core. *Rethinking Schools*, *28*(2), 10–17.

Kyllonen, P. C. (2012, May). *Measurement of 21st century skills within the Common Core State Standards*. Paper presented at the K–12 Center at ETS Invitational Research Symposium on Technology Enhanced Assessments. Retrieved from www.ets.org/Media/Research/pdf/session5-kyllonen-paper-tea2012.pdf

Mathis, W. J. (2010). *The "Common Core" standards initiative: An effective reform tool?* Boulder and Tempe: Education and the Public Interest Center & Education Policy Research Unit. Retrieved from nepc.colorado.edu/sites/default/files/PB-NatStans-Mathis.pdf

Mayring, P. (2000). Qualitative content analysis. *Forum: Qualitative Social Research, 1*(2). National Commission on Excellence in Education. (1983). *A Nation at risk.* Washington, DC: U.S. Department of Education.

National Council on Teacher Quality. (2014). *2014 teacher prep review*. Retrieved from www.nctq.org/dmsView/Teacher_Prep_Review_2014_Report

National Education Association. (2012). *Preparing 21st century students for a global society: An educator's guide to "the four Cs."* Washington, DC. Retrieved from www.nea.org/assets/docs/A-Guide-to-Four-Cs.pdf

National Governors Association Center for Best Practices & Council of Chief State School Officers. (2010). *Common Core State Standards*. Washington, DC: NGA and CCSSO.

National Governors Association and Council of Chief State School Officers. 2010. *Myths v. facts about the common core standards.* Washington, DC: NGA and CCSSO. Retrieved from www.corestandards.org/assets/CoreFacts.pdf

New Jersey Department of Education. (2014). Common Core State Standards: Preparing students for college and careers. Retrieved from www.state.nj.us/education/sca/

Padget, S. (2013). *Creativity and critical thinking.* Milton Park, UK: Routledge.

Poliokas, K. (2014). Preparing teachers for the common core: Aligning preparation program curricula. American Institutes of Research. Retrieved from www.gtlcenter.org/sites/default/files/Teacher_Preparation_Common_Core.pdf

Porter, A., McMaken, J., Hwang, J., & Yang, R. (2011). Common Core Standards: The new U.S. intended curriculum. *Educational Researcher, 40*(3), 103–116. doi: 10.3102/0013189X11405038

Runco, M. A., & Jaeger, G.J. (2012). The standard definition of creativity. *The Creativity Research Journal, 24*(1), 92–96.

Runco, M. A. (2007). *Creativity: Theories and themes: Research, development and practice.* San Diego, CA: Elsevier Academic Press.

Runco, M. A., & Chand, I. (1995). Cognition and creativity. *Educational Psychology Review*, 7(3), 243–267.

Sato, E., Lagunoff, R., & Worth, P. (2011). SMARTER balanced assessment consortium Common Core State Standards analysis: Eligible content for the summative assessment. (Final Report). Retrieved from files.eric.ed.gov/fulltext/ED536959.pdf

Sawchuck, S. (2014, November 10). In light of Common Core, d. schools look to transform math teacher prep. *Education Week*. Retrieved from www.edweek.org/ew/articles/2014/11/12/12cc-teacherprep.h34.html

Sforza, D., Tienken, C. H., & Kim, E. (2016). A comparison of higher-order thinking between the Common Core State Standards and the 2009 New Jersey Content Standards in High School. *AASA Journal of Scholarship and Practice, 12*(4), 4–30.

Simon, S., & Shah, N. (2013, Sep. 18). The common core money war. *Politico*. Retrieved from www.politico.com/story/2013/09/education-common-core-standards-schools-096964

Smith, S. M., & Tindell, D. R. (1997). Memory blocks in word fragment completion caused by involuntary retrieval of orthographically similar primes. *Journal of*

Experimental Psychology: Learning, Memory and Cognition, 23, 355–370.

Spencer, H. (1883). What knowledge is of most worth? (Originally published in 1859). In *Education: Intellectual moral, and physical* (pp. 1–96). New York, NY: Appleton.

Sternberg, R. (1998). *The Handbook of Creativity.* Cambridge, UK: Cambridge University Press.

Tanner, D., & Tanner, L. (2007). *Curriculum development: Theory into practice*. Upper Saddle River, NJ: Pearson.

Tienken, C. H. (2011). Common core state standards: An example of data-less decision making. *AASA Journal of Scholarship and Practice*, 7(4), 3–18.

Tienken, C. H. (2017). *Defying standardization: Creating curriculum for an uncertain future.* Lanham, MD: Rowman and Littlefield.

Tienken, C. H., & Mullen, C. A. (2014). The curious case of international student assessment: Rankings and realities in the innovation economy. In S. Harris & J. Mixon (Eds.), *Building cultural community through global educational leadership* (pp. 146–164). Ypsilanti, MI: NCPEA Press.

Tienken, C. H., & Orlich, D.C. (2013). *The school reform landscape: Fraud, myth, and lies*. New York, NY: Rowman & Littlefield.

Tienken, C. H., & Zhao, Y. (2013). How common standards and standardized testing widen the opportunity gap. In P. Carter and K. Welner (Eds.), *Closing the opportunity gap: What America must do to give every student a chance* (pp. 111–122). New York, NY: Oxford University Press.

Turnipseed, S. (2012). *Partnership for 21st Century Skills*. Retrieved from www.p21.org/news-events/p21blog/1067

Tyack, D. B. (1974). *The one best system*. Cambridge, MA: Harvard University Press.

U.S. Department of Commerce. (2012). *The competitiveness and innovative capacity report.* Retrieved from www.commerce.gov/sites/default/files/migrated/reports/thecompetitivenessandinnovativecapacityoftheunitedstates.pdf

Vander Ark, T. (2013, May 21). Common Core: A platform for equity and innovation. *HuffPost.* www.huffingtonpost.com/tom-vander-ark/common-core-equity-innova_b_3309994.html

Vander Hart, S. (2014). Common Core: The silent revolution in education policy. In Lombard (Ed.) *Common ground on common core* (pp. 3–18). Madison, WI: Resounding Books.

Ward, T. B., Smith, S. M., & Finke, R. A. (2010). Creative cognition. In R. J. Sternberg (Ed.), *Handbook of Creativity* (pp. 189–212). New York, NY: Cambridge University Press.

Webb, N. L., Alt, M., Ely, R., & Versperman, B. (2005). Web alignment tool training manual. Wisconsin Center for Education Research. Retrieved from wat.wceruw.org/index.aspx

World Competitiveness Center. (2013). *World competitiveness ranking*. Lausanne, Switzerland: Institute for Management Development.

Yuan, K., & Le, V. N. (2012). *Estimating the percentage of students who were tested on cognitively demanding items through the state achievement tests.* Santa Monica, CA: RAND Corporation.

Zhao, Y. (2012). Doublethink: The creativity-testing conflict [Blog post]. Retrieved from zhaolearning.com/2012/08/16/doublethink-the-creativity-testing-conflict

Zheng, Y. (2015). Students as professionals: Prepare learners for the global workforce. *The Asia Society*. Retrieved from asiasociety.org/education/students-professionals

Chapter 3

Toward the End of Teacher Education?

edTPA as the Next Guardian Sentinel of Teacher Certification

Westry Whitaker and Jim Burns

Discourses of education reform have had a long and often troubling history in the United States. Various power factions and educational movements such as life-adjustment education, social efficiency, social meliorism, and others have battled for predominance over American education (Bestor, 1952; Hofstadter, 1962; Kliebard, 2004). Underlying that struggle is an endemic anti-intellectualism and a concomitant conceptualization of education as instrumental schooling predicated on a means–ends calculus, which illustrates the social engineering function of schooling that American schools and society remain "reluctant to abandon" (Pinar, 2006, p. 109). The anti-intellectualism inherent in the history of American schools and society, a product of the Protestant ethic reworked and delivered to capitalism (Chow, 2002; Pinar, 2006, 2012; Weber, 1930/2001), has privileged instrumental intelligence over the development of intellect:

> In our education, for example, it has never been doubted that the selection and development of intelligence is a goal of central importance; but the extent to which education should foster intellect has been a matter of the most heated controversy, and the opponents of intellect in most spheres of public education have exercised preponderant power. (Hofstadter, 1962, p. 25)

Hofstadter's differentiation between intelligence and intellect suggests that the historic preference for education that privileges intelligence over intellect demonstrates the cultural enthrallment to the production of "practical" intelligence that "works within the framework of limited but clearly stated goals" rather than the development of intellect, the "critical, creative, and contemplative side of the mind" (Hofstadter, 1962, p. 25). The increasingly strident demands of corporatized education policy reveals education as an essential disciplinary institution that functions in a general economy of power to habituate bodies as part of a carceral society (Foucault, 1977/1995). Education, reduced to instrumental schooling, produces governable bodies for insertion into prevailing modes of production rather than cultivating the country's intellectual, social, and cultural capacity.

Education reform discourses in the wake of national security "crises" such as the 1957 launch of Sputnik by the Soviet Union and the economic crisis narrative contained in *A Nation at Risk* (published in 1983) have tended to frame social, political, and economic crises in terms of school failure and, more specifically, the failure of teachers and teacher education programs. Consistent with past crisis narratives of educational failure, contemporary education accountability discourses have increasingly overinflated the role of the teacher in assuring student success, itself defined by measurable predetermined performance objectives (see Tyler, 1949). The purposeful and politically expedient disciplinary gaze focused on teachers has subjected teachers and teacher education programs to a "politics of scapegoating" in which teachers are held solely accountable in a reductive reconfiguration of education as the measurement of quantifiable gains in student learning (Pinar, 2006, p. 110). The infiltration of neoliberal market fundamentalism into K–12 and higher education (Giroux, 2012) through the burgeoning and profitable education accountability industry reduces political processes like education, as Dewey (1931/1985) warned, to "the shadow cast on society by big business" (p. 163). The near-religious devotion to market fundamentalism and its radical privatization agenda seeks nothing less than the marketization of every aspect of public life, the elimination of public sector unions via "right to work" legislation, and the *de facto* privatization of K–12 and higher education through charter school expansion, school choice legislation, crippling budget pressures, and increasingly punitive accountability policies (Lafer, 2017). Post-Katrina New Orleans illustrates this: the tactic of disaster capitalism (Klein, 2007), effected through crisis manipulation and management, quickly rendered New Orleans a 100 percent charter district as part of the city's broader gentrification plan (Buras, 2011; Lafer, 2017).

According to contemporary education crisis logic, failing schools, bad teachers, greedy unions, ineffective teacher education programs, a lack of competition and accountability, and the purported inefficiency and inferiority of the public sector threaten our economic and national security (Berliner & Glass, 2014; Giroux, 2012; Hatch, 2015; Kumashiro, 2008, 2012; Pinar, 2012). That pretext has produced four frames that predicate current punitive anti-public education "reform" discourses (Kumashiro, 2008, p. 28):

- Mandate standards for students, teachers, schools, and teacher education programs;
- Hold students, teachers, schools, and teacher education programs accountable through performance-based standardized assessments;

- Institute systemic rewards and sanctions based on assessment results; and
- Create choice initiatives that empower parents to move their children to purportedly better-performing schools.

The education reform frames identified by Kumashiro (2008) reflect a policy commitment to the standardization of teaching itself by exercising power over teachers through the disciplinary tactic of exercise-examination, which continuously subjects preservice teachers and teacher education programs to the compulsory extraction of a regime of truth through "rituals of verification" (Shore & Wright, 2000, p. 84). This chapter focuses on the regime of truth based on the assessment of preservice teacher readiness—the Educational Teacher Performance Assessment (edTPA). Consistent with the crisis narrative built on the construct of self-serving "bad" teachers who emerge from "ineffective" teacher education programs, education reformers maintain that only "outsiders who are not tied to the education establishment" can and should design and implement educational accountability systems (Hatch, 2015, p. 74). Current corporate "school deform" (Pinar, 2012, p. 12) discourses have traced their lineage to early 20th-century social efficiency educators such as David Snedden and Ross Finney, who promoted the application of industrial priorities of efficiency and standardization. Their goal was to produce a "coolly efficient, smoothly running society" that would efficiently deliver mass education designed to prepare students for the workforce, prevent social upheaval, and meet the demands of business (Kliebard, 2004, p. 24).

The language of contemporary corporate education reform, produced to support the current trivialities of power (Nietzsche, 1874/1997) and discourses of humiliation (Giroux, 2012) deployed against teachers, public schools, and teacher education programs, "has the power to mask certain realities or to de-historicize certain concepts to the extent that only certain types of initiatives count as 'reform' and only certain actors are viewed as reformers" (Kumashiro, 2012, p. 10). Free-market capitalist—neoliberal—critics of public education have exploited K–12 students, teachers, and schools, as well as university professors and teacher education programs, as easy targets because they "are the faces of education" to whom everyone can relate: "Americans don't think in terms of a *system* of education; they focus on teachers in classrooms. The educational reform public relations machine understands this phenomenon and makes teachers the primary target as attacks are orchestrated" (Hatch, 2015, pp. 11–12, emphasis in original). Despite a lack of public support for the corporate education agenda and the empirical disproval of flawed causal claims related to teacher and student accountability, both major political parties, at the behest of powerful corporate interests, embrace and promote punitive corporate education reform discourses at the national, state, and local levels (Lafer, 2017). The punitive, broad-based anti-public corporate agenda positions education as the singular target of school deform zealots who blame schools for failing to solve complex, intersected social issues:

> Indeed, there must be consequences for school failure, as politicians pretend there are in business. Indeed, schools should *become* businesses: test scores are the same as profits; test scores, not erudition or understanding, are the bottom line.... Never mind that the consequences of academic study are rarely short term, and cannot be traced through quantified cause-effect chains. And recall that it is *only* schools that have been subjected to such simplistic and sadistic scrutiny. (Pinar, 2012, pp. 220–221, emphasis in original)

In the context of the sadistic scrutiny deployed against public schools, teachers, and teacher education programs, some of the most punitive recent accountability initiatives have emanated from the Obama Administration, as evidenced by former President Obama's 2009 admonition that "It's time to start rewarding good teachers, stop making excuses for bad ones" (Kumashiro, 2012, p. 11). Donald Trump's appointment of Betsy DeVos, a billionaire committed to using schools to "advance God's kingdom" (Rizga, 2017), as U.S. Secretary of Education, has emboldened state-level initiatives such as those in Florida to arm teachers, narrow the scope of science education, further reduce charter school regulation, and facilitate the flow of public education funds to private and religious schools through so-called "opportunity scholarships," a thinly-veiled choice/privatization tactic.

Having established the general sociopolitical context related to contemporary education reform discourses, we endeavor in this chapter to trace the production of edTPA as a tactic of punitive disciplinary power. First, we discuss the conditions of possibility through which edTPA emerged. Second, we analyze edTPA through a Foucauldian lens as a disciplinary system of governmentality that effects subtle, quotidian disciplinary power-knowledges to order, classify, hierarchize, and fix individuals in a social grid and to produce self-auditing teachers and teacher educators. Third, we offer a brief synopsis of Foucault's analysis of counter-conduct and *parrhēsia*, or free-spokenness, through which we might subvert punitive disciplinary technologies like edTPA and reclaim the teaching profession. Our analysis focuses on edTPA as a disciplinary technology that casts a punitive gaze on teachers and teacher education programs and positions them as both the objects and instruments of power, which we consider a threat to the K–12 teaching profession and to teacher education programs in the guise of alternative pathways to certification (Madeloni, 2013). Yet it is crucial to remain mindful that edTPA is merely one aspect of a vast, complex assemblage of power comprised of politically unaccountable foundations and think tanks funded by neoliberal philanthrocapitalists, xenophobic neoconservative reactionaries, a fascistic form of authoritarian populist Christian fundamentalism (Apple, 2001; Hedges, 2006) politicians, policymakers, and even some in the educational establishment. We can neither fully understand nor appreciate the threats posed by edTPA to the future of teacher education and, by extension, the K–12 teaching profession, without historically contextualizing edTPA in a more expansive economy of power.

WHAT IS THE EDTPA?

On October 22, 2009, in a speech hosted by Teachers College at Columbia University, then-Secretary of Education Arne Duncan called for a standardized, performance-based and summative testing system that would bring "revolutionary change, not evolutionary tinkering" to the nation's schools, colleges, and departments of education (U.S. Department of Education, 2009, para. 3). Referring to these programs as "cash cows" of mediocrity (U.S. Department of Education cited in Dover & Schultz, 2016, p. 96), Duncan theorized that this revolution would bring about major reform in teacher preparation. It would, he indicated, allow public education to, again, become Horace Mann's "great equalizer" while simultaneously accomplishing Barack Obama's ambitious goal of allowing the United States to reclaim its position as "the nation with the highest proportion of college graduates in the world" (cited in U.S. Department of Education, 2009, para. 4–5). Paternalistically reminding the many teacher educators in attendance of the importance of retaining "great" talent and recruiting "effective" science and math teachers and teachers of color (in particular Hispanic and Black males), Duncan's planned reform would allow colleges of education to "recruit, reward, train, learn from and honor a new generation of talented teachers" (U.S. Department of Education, 2009, para. 11). His plan for accomplishing this goal: a national, free-market Teacher Performance Assessment (TPA) requiring a performance-based and standardized exit exam designed to measure candidate readiness and the quality of a credential program.

With support from the American Association of Colleges for Teacher Education (AACTE), the Stanford Center for Assessment, Learning, and Equity (SCALE) responded to Duncan's vision for "revolution" by creating a new TPA modeled after the Performance Assessment of California Teachers (PACT). Implemented and distributed nationally by Pearson Education, the new TPA (now known as the Education Teacher Performance Assessment, or edTPA) website (edtpa.aacte.org) hosted by SCALE and the AACTE describes the edTPA as the "first nationally accessible preservice teacher assessment and support program" (AACTE, n.d.-b). Its goals, again as found on the website, include: improvement of student outcomes, improvement of the information base guiding improvement of teacher preparation programs, the strengthening of the information base for accreditation and evaluation of program effectiveness, its combined utilization with other measures as requirement for licensure, and the guiding of professional development for teachers across the career continuum (AACTE, n.d.-b). The expectation for candidates is multifaceted. All new teachers graduating from edTPA-participating colleges of education must demonstrate proficiency in content, pedagogy, classroom management, and, importantly, the ability to utilize data collection and analysis to inform instructional decisions (Darling-Hammond, 2010). Candidates are expected, in other words, to demonstrate this proficiency via an online proposal representing the standardization of planning, the implementation of teaching and management strategies, and the ability to connect those strategies to theoretical foundations and data collection. Perhaps most insidiously, the edTPA has been designed to provide extensive data allowing participating departments of teacher preparation to be measured by their ability to prepare candidates to successfully complete this time-consuming and intricately woven assessment process. edTPA's enunciated goals clearly classify the examination as a technology of coercive accountability through which preservice teachers are evaluated based on student learning outcomes, which are traced back to the teacher education program, and data are collected to refine the punitive nature of the examination itself.

Simply put, SCALE, AACTE, and Pearson designed the edTPA to assess a specific series of tasks—planning, teaching, and assessment. AACTE purports that the edTPA, like the bar exam for a law degree, confirms to the world a new teacher's graduation and classroom readiness. Requirements for successful completion include demonstrated content area proficiency and student learning as related to planning, instruction, and assessment. Specifically, in order to demonstrate this proficiency, candidates must:

- upload a 20-minute video of their teaching;
- submit an extensive 3- to 5-day lesson plan describing the instructional setting and demonstrating the ability to use previously gathered data to inform current instruction, implement practical and relevant teaching strategies and assessments, link those plans or decisions to educational theory, and provide evidence of specific feedback; and
- provide extensive written, narrative analysis (totaling 25–30 pages) focused on the representation of each contextualized pedagogical, instructional, and/or planning decision.

Each complete proposal is submitted in the form of learning segments by the candidate to a Pearson website where external evaluators review the proposal package. Each evaluator has, according to SCALE, completed rigorous training, referred to as "calibration," designed by SCALE and implemented by Pearson. These evaluators, contracted Pearson employees, use 15 rubrics (five for each task) designed to assess the impact of student learning. Rubrics are aligned to the expectations of each task and scored on a 1–5 scale with 3 being considered "target." Scores for each task are totaled and measured according to an overall aggregate determined by individual states participating. This academic year (2017–2018), Pearson requires states to choose a passing score between

37 and 42 for middle and secondary schools and between 44 and 50 for early childhood assessments. Evaluators are paid $75 per portfolio completed. They have no direct knowledge or understanding of the candidate, his or her school, classroom, students, or community, and evaluators are encouraged to spend approximately 2–3 hours on each submission. Three to 4 weeks after submission, candidates receive their scores in the form of a simple number. There is no discussion; there is no feedback. The organic and meaningful relationship developed between teaching candidate and professor—one built upon a foundation of observation, supervision, context, community, trust, and understanding—has been reduced to a generic "good teacher" recipe (articulated as a set of quantifiable rubrics) and a false attempt at quantifiable empiricism.

While passing scores are not required for graduation from a credential program, school, or college, a passing score is required in order to receive a teaching credential in an edTPA implementation state or school. Candidates are required to pay $300 for a single administration. In the event that a candidate does not pass the assessment, the candidate desiring certification is required to arrange a retake. Each retake costs an additional $150. All costs required for completion do not include the inevitable requirements for personal technology and/or extensive access to computers, video collection devices, cameras, and document-scanning technology that will be necessary to upload classroom artifacts. Additionally, teaching candidates are expected to complete the edTPA proposal process while they are enrolled in their university's teacher certification program. Each preservice teacher must, in other words, balance the requirements of edTPA with the expectations of their undergraduate degree including full-time teaching internships, coursework, and for some, full- or part-time jobs. Currently, there are 757 Educator Preparation Programs in 41 states and the District of Columbia participating, either with policy in place or, as is the case with Texas, Ohio, and Connecticut, taking steps toward implementation of edTPA (AACTE, n.d.-a). Montana, New Hampshire, Maine, Massachusetts, North Dakota, Kansas, Missouri, Nevada, and New Mexico are states that have openly opposed edTPA implementation (AACTE, n.d.-a).

edTPA's purported benefits include the suppositions within Arne Duncan's cliché-ridden discussion, the goals as outlined on AACTE and SCALE's edTPA website, and the claim by some teachers and professors of education that the test is designed "for the profession, by the profession" (Ayers as cited in Ravitch, 2015, para. 3). The detail- and task-oriented approach to the submission, some claim, prepares a candidate for appropriate rigor and data utilization during the candidate's planning process. The controversy surrounding edTPA implementation is, however, as diverse and multifaceted as the assessment's many requirements. With its pass/fail design, edTPA takes on a disciplinary approach to credentialing that forces upon teacher candidates a very specific definition of what it means to be a *good* teacher.

Because of the high-stakes nature of the requirement for a state credential, because credential programs are measured by their ability to pass students on the assessment, and because teacher education faculty members are *not* allowed to provide feedback or evaluation of a candidate's progress prior to submission, schools of education that choose to implement edTPA must carve out significant space in their curriculum for projects, assignments, or lesson plan formats that imitate or simulate the edTPA process. These programs and their faculty members are essentially forced into a process of teaching to the edTPA in a manner that increases the likelihood of a candidate receiving a passing score. This *teaching to the test* reduces candidate risk taking, subdues creativity, restricts independence (in favor of a nearly religious obsession with rubrics), and dulls the curriculum. The eventual forfeit of context-specific teaching in favor of a prescribed model of accepted and standardized practice allows for the occupation of important curricular space that formerly nurtured crucial professional discussions centered upon diversity, social justice, marginalized groups, progressive teaching theories, cultural relevance, critical pedagogies, and engaging teaching strategies (Chiu, 2014; Dover & Schultz, 2016).

As such, Au (2013) reported the sanitized nature of student work limited by candidate fears of losing points for not subscribing to the conformity of traditional expectations prescribed by the narrowly focused edTPA. Similarly and perhaps most importantly, Dover and Schultz (2016) share the decision-making process of one of their own students considering a "risky" unit on Kendrick Lamar's hip-hop album *good kid, m.A.A.d. city* in his edTPA:

> As I get ready to film my lesson segment for edTPA this week, I want to take chances. I want to take that which I've built from scratch, what I've put my own creative energy into, and give it a go. After all, this is work that I believe in, and the only thing that will convince me that I shouldn't believe in it, is if I've tried and seen it fail. But there lies my hold up. I don't like failing. I'm in a place weighing the risks and rewards. I believe risks to be worth taking in the classroom. However, my mind tells me to play it safe because this is the BIG assessment for the semester. On the other end, I don't know if the folks at Pearson will really get a feel for the teacher I actually am and I want to be, unless I teach the way I believe I should. (Dover & Schultz, 2016, p. 103)

The struggle of this teaching candidate is an indicator of the problematic nature of edTPA. As representative of the docilization of teachers and the standardization of the teaching profession, this latest version of TPA is a major force in, if not the new guardian sentinel[1] of, the overall war on public education.

Keeping in mind that Pearson's "calibrated" evaluators are paid $75 per submission scored, encouraged to spend no more than 2–3 hours scoring each submission, and completely removed from the community, the classroom, and the situational setting of each lesson they score (using only a 20-minute video to provide the visual context of the teaching), we are reminded that the scorers neglect if not ignore the importance of student/teacher rapport, communication, classroom climate, academic context, community and cultural relevance, and student engagement over time in their assessment of "quality." Instead, scorers and all those who entrust the teaching profession to edTPA are assuming that a 20-minute video accompanied by 3–5 days of lesson plans will provide all necessary information regarding the success, ability, and "readiness" of the candidate. Additionally, because Pearson requires all edTPA scorers to meet a set of requirements, including current or past experience in higher education (edTPA Scorer Qualifications, n.d.), we must consider that these "calibrated" evaluators likely[2] reflect the overwhelmingly White teaching population in the United States (National Center for Education Statistics, 2017). We should, therefore, assume a certain cultural hegemony in scoring that neglects culturally relevant or progressive approaches in favor of more conventional pedagogies (Dover & Schultz, 2016).

In contrast to edTPA's evaluation process, local faculty members of teacher education programs, schools, and colleges are optimally placed to evaluate and mentor candidates over time and within all relevant contexts including community, student, and individual candidate factors. External evaluators are optimally placed to make judgment calls based on snapshots in time and space solely within the confines of the rubrics to which their judgments have been calibrated. In the case of the latter occupying more relevance in the process of molding new teachers, it seems that disciplinary technologies like edTPA define *good teaching* as a prescribed, traditional, and formulaic approach that is centered upon assessment, planning, and distanced constructs. *Relevant teaching* is, however, more of an art embodied through a dynamic, relationship-driven, community-, character-, and actor-dependent balance where planning and assessment can only occupy a part. Thus, edTPA clearly represents a punitive technology of power and knowledge creation about teachers and teacher educators through which to exercise disciplinary control and produce docile bodies that comply with institutional norms produced through the data collected by the examination itself.

"THE EXAMINATION": EDTPA, COERCIVE ACCOUNTABILITY, AND DOCILE BODIES

> The success of disciplinary power derives no doubt from the use of simple instruments; hierarchical observation, normalizing judgement and their combination in a procedure that is specific to it, the examination. (Foucault, 1977/1995, p. 170)

> Thus discipline produces subjected and practiced bodies, "docile" bodies. Discipline increases the forces of the body (in economic terms of utility) and diminishes these same forces (in political terms of obedience). In short, it dissociates power from the body; on the one hand, it turns it into an "aptitude," a "capacity," which it seeks to increase; on the other hand, it reverses the course of the energy,

> the power that might result from it, and turns it into a relation of strict subjection. (Foucault, 1977/1995, p. 138)

Tactics of coercive accountability such as edTPA effectuate disciplinary power through the bodies of pre- and inservice teachers and teacher education professors. The corporate audit technologies associated with coercive accountability that have infiltrated the public sector since the 1970s have solidified neoliberal capitalism as a hegemonic discourse (Harvey, 2005). The institutionalization of public sector coercive accountability is fundamentally connected with neoliberal economic "reforms" driven by International Monetary Fund (IMF) structural adjustment policies predicated on draconian austerity policies that subject public institutions to market logics that have been sold to the public as necessary to promote public sector economy, efficiency, and effectiveness (Shore & Wright, 1999, 2000). Neoliberal policies have largely reconfigured public K–12 and higher education throughout the Global North as a private benefit rather than a public good. Those logics are being exported to the Global South through neoliberal globalization. At the state level in the United States, education legislation and policies reflect a commitment to the *de facto* privatization of public education in an "evidence-free zone of public policy" (Lafer, 2017, p. 139) through disinvestment, punitive accountability, and the upward redistribution of public education funding into private hands. In that broader legislative context and policyscape, audit culture, the "discourses and practices that have accelerated the standardization and quantification of educational experience" (Taubman, 2009, p. 13), has introduced new terminology to education, embedded "new ways of thinking and acting," and formed "the epistemological foundation for the rise of new institutions and the discourses that sustain them and legitimize their activities":

> Thus, in the case of education, "audit" is now associated with a revealing new cluster of terms, including "performance" and "quality assurance" (or "quality enhancement" and "control"), "discipline" and "accreditation," "accountability" and "transparency," "efficiency" or "effectiveness" and "value for money," "ownership" and "responsibility," "benchmarks" and "good practice," "peer-review" and "external verification," "stakeholder" and "empowerment." (Shore & Wright, 1999, p. 559)

The assumptions underlying the lexicon of educational audit culture and coercive accountability have been adopted at all levels of government in the United States by both the political right and, absent a viable progressive alternative, the center-right now occupied by the Democratic Party. Those assumptions have created a policy environment amenable to the increasingly intrusive and expansive data collection, measurement, and assessment demands established by the Bush Administration's No Child Left Behind Act (NCLB) and the Obama Administration's Race to the Top initiative. Successive presidential administrations have consistently advocated for legislation and implemented policy predicated on behaviorist performance standards and standardized assessment, which underlie the panoply of punitive educational accountability technologies such as edTPA, accreditation, and value-added measurement (VAM) of teacher and teacher education program effectiveness (Amrein-Beardsley, 2014; Berliner, 2014; Berliner & Glass, 2014; Hatch, 2015; Kumashiro, 2008, 2012; Pinar, 2012; Taubman, 2009).

As a disciplinary regime, audit culture functions to conceal the workings of power by reframing the political issues inherent in education in the "ostensibly detached language of science, reason, normality, and common sense," which "conceals the ways institutional mechanisms operate to introduce new forms of power" (Shore and Wright, 1999, p. 560; see also Foucault, 1970/1994). The disaggregation of the practice of teaching into discrete, quantifiable, auditable tasks, reduced to and represented as quantifiable data, presents standardized assessment-based accountability and its purportedly scientific truth claims as adhering to de-politicized, objective, legal–rational practices (Foucault, 1970/1994). Assessments like edTPA produce a regime of truth (Foucault, 2008) through the introduction of "instruments for new forms of governance and power" that seek to create a new subjectivity: "self-managing individuals who render themselves auditable" (Shore & Wright, 2000, p. 57). Part of the allure of technologies of coercive accountability like edTPA is the purported empowerment of "individuals and institutions to ensure quality and improve performance . . . by allowing people to be judged by the targets that they set for themselves" (Shore & Wright, 2000, p. 62). The disingenuous marketing tactic that edTPA was designed for and by the profession obfuscates the fact that the targets toward which teachers and teacher educators work are actually framed by an assessment created, administered, and scored by external authorities. Professionals such as teachers and teacher educators therefore operate in institutions where preestablished audit metrics encourage their embodiment of "playpen creativity" and "playpen critical thinking" where they become habituated to perform creative work, but only within the confines of a pre-established institutional ideology (Schmidt, 2000, p. 40). Despite lofty promises of individual empowerment expressed in the corporate lexicon of entrepreneurship, innovation, quality, and efficiency, audit systems have created a pervasive "culture of compliance" in which teachers and teacher educators actually subject themselves to "new self-disciplines which together are re-shaping our sense of professionalism" (Shore & Wright, 1999, p. 568).

The historic emergence of technologies of management and inquiry, and the sequestration of bodies in modern disciplinary institutions, including schools and universities, demonstrates the capability of normalizing disciplinary power to fix "individuals to the production apparatus . . . by forming habits through a play of coercion and punishment, apprenticeship and chastisement" (Foucault, 2015, p. 239). edTPA therefore functions as one of many technologies through which ostensibly scientific, rational, objective disciplinary knowledges and truth claims are produced about the nature of being teachers and teacher educators. Techniques like edTPA also illustrate the insidious nature of power, which renders many teachers, teacher educators, and others in the education order complicit in perpetuating a carceral state (Foucault, 1977/1995). Technologies such as edTPA—the normalizing, ritualized examination—which have become common sense in K–12 and higher education policy discourses, have created and transformed an "economy of visibility into the exercise of power" and reconfigured individuals as the "effect and object of power, as effect and object of knowledge" (Foucault, 1977/1995, pp. 187, 193). edTPA subjects individuals to a field of comparison based on rules to be followed; quantitatively measures, differentiates, and hierarchizes them; and establishes measures of conformity through which to define the norm (Foucault, 1977/1995). The quotidian bureaucratic disciplinary processes embedded in technologies like edTPA constitute a "specific subject . . . whose merits are analytically identified, who is subjected in continuous networks of obedience, and who is subjectified through the compulsory extraction of truth" (Foucault, 2007, pp. 184–185).

The subjectivation of teachers and teacher educators through technologies of coercive accountability like edTPA, which create tension and anxiety through constant surveillance, habituates the objects of power, such as teachers and teacher educators, to "scrutinize their own behavior and eventually adopt the norm of conduct desired by the disciplinary institutions" (Shore & Wright, 2000, p. 77). The impacts of edTPA therefore cannot be understood without being contextualized in long-term, broad-based neoliberal attacks on public institutions like education, public sector unions, antagonism against public employees, the defunding and outsourcing of public services, alternative teacher certification programs, the vast expansion of charter schools, and school choice initiatives (Giroux, 2012; Kumashiro, 2012; Lafer, 2017). The most damaging legislation and policies associated with public K–12 and higher education have occurred at the state level (Lafer, 2017), but the significance of that historic trend has tragically been overlooked as educational advocacy tends to focus on the federal level. Further, the coercive accountability movement, in which edTPA plays a significant role, has spawned a "new audit industry" comprised of a "plethora of new parasitical professions" (Shore & Wright, 2000, p. 80) that form the audit chain's culture of compliance and benefit financially from the punitive audit explosion. The audit industry has thus created and relies on "specialized personnel" whose sole "indispensable" purpose is their constant surveillance over a system of production (Foucault, 1977/1995, p. 174).

Whatever distaste academics profess about coercive accountability and the competitive pecking order created between teachers, students, schools, and teacher education programs, audit culture has become widely accepted and perpetuated by the education establishment. While not romanticizing the past, neoliberal coercive accountability, effectuated as a tactic of disciplinary power-knowledge, seeks to replace systems of academic study and professional collegiality based on autonomy and trust with punitive power-knowledges based on subtle tactics of the sanction effected by the hyper-visibility and normalizing judgments inherent in panoptic surveillance (Foucault, 1977/1995, 2015). As one's subjectivity as an autonomous agent shifts through technologies of disciplinary power such as edTPA toward a self-auditing subjectivity, power as habit becomes invisible and natural, and one can lose the capacity to critique audit systems that appear objective and become complicit in perpetuating them, whether professing to like them or not (Shore & Wright, 2000; Taubman, 2009).

Political technologies of the body such as the ritualized public examination are tactics of governmentality that focus on "conducting the conduct of others" to produce a complex docility in which disciplinary power develops individual bodies as both useful and governable (Foucault, 2011 p. 4). Thus, edTPA functions as a method of inquiry—a "political anatomy" tied to a "mechanics of power" (Foucault, 1977/1995, p. 138)—that produces knowledges to habituate individuals to institutional behavioral norms and habituates bodies for insertion into prevailing systems of production, including schooling. Docility "joins the analyzable body to the manipulable body," a body "that may be subjected, used, transformed and improved" (Foucault, 1977/1995, p. 136). The examination produces docile bodies by effecting increasingly detailed disciplinary power, which, effected as knowledges of the body itself, function at a micro level through infinitesimal coercions that elicit control over bodily mechanisms including the efficiency of movement, gestures, and attitudes (Foucault, 1977/1995).

The modality of the disciplinary docility–utility relationship reflects constant coercion and supervision over the processes inherent in activities that have been disassembled into their most basic elements (Foucault, 1977/1995) and, in the case of technologies like edTPA, reduced to ostensibly commensurable quantifiable data. The docile body is therefore both a body whose movements, dispositions, and habits are developed, optimized, and mobilized through disciplinary tactics for institutionally defined productive purposes and a body that has been subjectivated and rendered politically obedient (Foucault, 1977/1995; Ziarek, 2001).

In the following section, we rethink edTPA as a technique of audit-based coercive accountability through two salient aspects of Foucault's (1977/195) analysis of disciplinary power: edTPA's function as an instrument of inquiry through which to produce a regime of truth about teaching and teacher education, and the panoptic surveillance facilitated by edTPA that fixes a punitive gaze over teachers and teacher education programs. Finally, considering the threats to professional teacher education programs, school choice initiatives, and recent legislation in Arizona (SB 1042) that allows individuals in certain disciplines to bypass formal certification (Silber, 2017), we offer some possibilities through which we might embody a truth quite different than that produced through disciplinary regimes like edTPA.

PANOPTICISM AND THE MEANS OF CORRECT TRAINING

> The examination combines the techniques of an observing hierarchy and those of a normalizing judgment. It is a normalizing gaze, a surveillance that makes it possible to qualify, to classify and to punish. It establishes over individuals a visibility through which one differentiates them and judges them. That is why, in all the mechanisms of discipline, the examination is highly ritualized. In it are combined the ceremony of power and the form of the experiment, the deployment of force and the establishment of truth. (Foucault, 1977/1995, p. 184)

> Hence the major effect of the Panopticon: to induce in the inmate a state of conscious and permanent visibility that assures the automatic functioning of power. So to arrange things that the surveillance is permanent in its effects, even if it is discontinuous in its action; that the perfection of power should tend to render its actual exercise unnecessary. (Foucault, 1977/1995, p. 201)

The normalizing, ritualized, public examination is a technique of discipline that produces individuals by positioning each person as both the object and instrument of the exercise of normalizing disciplinary power (Foucault, 1977/1995). The examination facilitates a two-pronged procedural field through which to effect discipline: hierarchical observation and normalizing judgment. Through an "analytical-practical grid," discipline "analyzes and breaks down . . . individuals, places, time, movements, actions, and operations . . . such that they can be seen, on the one hand, and modified on the other" (Foucault, 2007, p. 56). Disciplinary power classifies the components inherent in specific processes or tasks such as teaching and learning according to specific objectives, seeks to optimize those processes, "fixes the processes of progressive training and permanent control, and finally, on the basis of this, it establishes the division between those considered unsuitable or incapable and the others":

> Disciplinary normalization consists first of all in positing a model, an optimal model that is constructed in terms of a certain result, and the operation of disciplinary normalization consists in trying to get people, movements, and actions to conform to this model, the normal being precisely that which can conform to this norm, and the abnormal that which is incapable of conforming to the norm . . . . [T]here is an originally prescriptive character of the norm and the determination and the identification of the normal and the abnormal become possible in relation to this posited norm. (Foucault, 2007, p. 57)

Thus, edTPA is a multifarious tool of inquiry that produces the norm of teaching practice, prescribes the optimal model of teaching based on predetermined outcomes that aspiring teachers must be habituated to embody, and establishes a regime of truth about being a teacher that must be extracted from preservice teachers in the form of the exam itself. The examination forms a pedagogy of constant exercise and examination in a disciplinary system that coerces through technologies of observation, which subtly coerce the individuals through whom disciplinary power flows by rendering them clearly visible. Importantly, power effected through technologies of compulsory visibility transcends being physically seen because normalizing power-knowledge technologies like edTPA scrutinize individuals as represented by data, which comprises an archive that creates individuals and situates them on a field of intelligibility that hierarchically classifies them in minute detail. Pedagogical surveillance effected through a continuous dynamic of exercise and examination institutionalizes a regime of truth that links knowledge formation with the exercise of power in four ways (Foucault, 1977/1995).

First, the examination is a "ceremony of objectification" that transforms "the economy of visibility into the exercise of power" through compulsory visibility that maintains disciplined individuals in their subjection (Foucault, 1977/1995, p. 187). The subjection of individuals to a network of examinations, measurement, reporting, and gathering of evidence to demonstrate their effectiveness as defined on normalizing rubrics associated with edTPA perpetuates an "age of infinite examination and of compulsory objectification" (Foucault, 1977/1995, p. 189). That process renders teachers and teacher educators the hypervisible objects and instruments of disciplinary power. Second, the examination "introduces individuality into the field of documentation," which subjects teachers and teacher educators to an asymmetrical relationship of submission-obedience to an external authority predicated on the maintenance of a "meticulous archive" of documentary materials that "capture and fix them" in a "field of surveillance" (Foucault, 1977/1995, p. 189). The "apparatus of writing" (Foucault, 1977/1995, p. 190), of which edTPA is a significant part, also constitutes teachers and teacher educators as analyzable objects "under the gaze of a permanent corpus of knowledge" and contributes to a "comparative system" that describes groups, calculates gaps between individuals, and distributes them in a given population (Foucault, 1977/1995, p. 190). Third, edTPA "makes each individual a 'case'" that can be "described, judged, measured, compared with others in his very individuality" (Foucault, 1977/1995, p. 191), which yields knowledges of training, correction, classification, normalization, and exclusion. Fourth, the examination combines "hierarchical surveillance and normalizing judgment" to assure the "disciplinary functions of distribution and classification" through which individuals are fixed and aggregated within institutions to optimize their aptitudes and use of time (Foucault, 1977/1995, p. 192).

The panoptic surveillance embedded in the ritualized public examination and in disciplinary power more broadly is both a modern technology of power-knowledge, realized in Bentham's panoptic design for the prison, and the archaic "oldest dream of the oldest sovereign" (Foucault, 2007, p. 66). Panopticism has institutionalized a "system of permanent registration" (Foucault,

1977/1995, p. 196), creating the individual who is seen, but does not see, and who is positioned as the "object of information, never a subject in communication" (p. 200). Perhaps most insidious in surveillance technologies like edTPA is the panoptic effect of inducing in the object of the punitive, normalizing gaze consciousness of their visibility, and so inscribing in individual teachers and teacher educators the docility, or self-auditing subjectivity, that renders each the author of their own subjection. Panoptic institutions function as laboratories whose technologies of inquiry facilitate experimentation on individuals and produce disciplinary knowledges through which to analyze the "transformations that may be obtained from them" (Foucault, 1977/1995, p. 204). Disciplinary technologies like edTPA are indispensable both to effecting power through teachers and teacher educators and to facilitating the supervision of the mechanisms of the disciplinary institutions themselves (Foucault, 1977/1995). The examination is neither objective nor benign. Rather, it is a political technology of power-knowledge that: produces racialized, gendered, sexualized, culturally and linguistically exclusionary norms of observable behavior; differentiates bodies according to their performative capabilities, aptitudes, and behaviors; arranges them hierarchically on a normalizing scale that ostensibly reflects their ability to replicate the performative objectives inherent in the norm; and affirms the normal and excludes the abject other.

Viewed from the perspective of normalizing institutional power, the ramifications of edTPA for teaching and teacher education are profound, which is striking considering that this examination effectuates punitive disciplinary power through the banal, technocratic, "insidious, quotidian, habitual form of the norm" (Foucault, 2015, p. 240). It is also stunning to consider the extent to which so many in the education establishment have simply acceded to the logic associated not only with edTPA, but with the totality of an increasingly punitive accountability agenda associated with standards, standardized testing, VAM, accreditation, and the megalomaniacal (Pinar, 2006) and melancholic (Taubman, 2009) social engineering fantasies deeply embedded in the history of American education. Too many of us, teachers and teacher educators alike, have, paradoxically, become enthralled to the promises and power claims (presented in terms of objectivity and scientific rationality) of disciplinary technologies like edTPA and its attendant punitive accountability discourses as articles of faith and hope. That faith and hope have been grievously misplaced.

COUNTERING THE DEMISE OF TEACHER EDUCATION

The corporate "school deform" (Pinar, 2012) agenda, including disciplinary techniques like edTPA, threatens the K–12 teaching profession and teacher education. The agenda—charter school expansion; school choice, voucher, and alternate certification legislation; punitive accountability measures such as edTPA, VAM, and accreditation—and the agenda's financial backers—the

American Legislative Exchange Council (ALEC), Chamber of Commerce, State Policy Network, Americans for Prosperity, and the Gates, Broad, and Walton Foundations among others—has been well documented (see Hatch, 2015; Lafer, 2017; Ravitch, 2013). Substantive analysis of the corporate education agenda should be contextualized as part of a coordinated assault on the public sector and very concept of the public good (Lafer, 2017). Tactics like edTPA are part of the long-term neoliberal project, which targets public-sector unions through "right to work" legislation that contributes to the increasingly precarious nature of work (the "gig" economy), has reconfigured K–12 and university teaching as contingent labor, and expanded the power of corporate wealth to subvert democracy at the national and state levels. The edTPA marketing campaign that more standardization will "reprofessionalize" the teaching profession is insulting to teachers and teacher educators and succumbs to the logic described by Schmidt (2000) in which teachers perform creative work within the disciplinary "playpen" created by a set of rubrics. Hatch (2015) responds that teachers must reclaim the teaching profession by speaking truth to power and weaving counternarratives to the corporate agenda. While we agree with Hatch, speaking truth may not be enough. To conclude, we discuss two conceptual lenses through which we may work toward regaining our voices, agency, and profession: a different view of power and the embodiment of truth.

Rethinking Power

To understand the subtleties of disciplinary power, we must historically contextualize our institutional practices and study how modern institutions function to effect power in systems of governmentality (Foucault, 2007). Analyzing edTPA in the context of a general economy of power reveals it to be a disciplinary tactic utterly consistent with the neoliberal project. We should also question how effectively we can investigate institutional power-knowledges on their own terms. For example, our inquiry could focus on how, when, and why the institutionally defined objects of knowledge and research methods we currently take for granted emerged to form disciplinary regimes of truth. Why did the examination emerge as a technology of inquiry and a tactic of disciplinary power, and whose interests does it serve? Understanding the genealogies of disciplinary power-knowledges could reveal fissures through which those tactics can be discredited and subverted.

We also suggest rethinking common schemas of power analyses. Foucault (2015), for example, rejected four common schemas of power analysis: power as appropriation; the location of power solely in the state; power as a form of reproduction; and the effectuation of power as ideology. First, rethinking analysis of power as appropriation suggests that power is not possessed by some at the expense of others and is not monolithic. Rather, power is exercised "over the whole surface of the social field, according to a whole system of relays, connections, [and] points of support" (Foucault,

2015, p. 228). Power is thus always contestable. Second, power is not located solely or primarily in state apparatuses, but runs "through the whole of the social body" (Foucault, 2015, p. 230). State power functions in collaboration with the numerous institutions and technologies that co-constitute a general economy of power.

Third, power does not emerge from specific modes of production to reproduce them. Rather, disciplinary power is "one of the constitutive elements of the mode of production and functions at its heart" (Foucault, 2015, p. 231). Educational institutions sequester bodies and help co-constitute production and consumption patterns and habituate those within the institution to production by organizing individuals' activities and time. Fourth, Foucault (2015) rejects dichotomous power analyses that claim power functions either "in the silent fashion of violence, or in the discursive and wordy fashion of ideology" (p. 233). Institutions exercise power through the application of various knowledges that assure discipline, not simply by transmitting ideology. The institutional production of new disciplinary knowledges through sophisticated techniques of surveillance and data collection enables the exercise of power, which, in turn, forms new disciplinary knowledges. In discussions of edTPA, and educational accountability discourses generally, teachers and teacher educators should remain mindful of our own political agency to critique and subvert disciplinary knowledges like edTPA, which are presented as politically neutral and scientifically objective but in reality are neither.

The Courage of Truth

While not romanticizing the past, we teachers and teacher educators currently find ourselves in a system that has reduced education to disciplinary schooling, credentialism, and the acquisition of marketable skills in pursuit of a return on investment. Yet paradoxes, contradictions, and cracks in the absurd logics and claims of systems of governmentality are inherent in the systems themselves. Foucault's later research, for example, reworked his previous analysis of confession "as a forcible extraction" of truth toward a notion of confession as "an act of speech in which the subject 'publishes himself,' gives himself in words, engages in an extended act of self-verbalization . . . as a way of making the self appear for another" (Butler, 2005, p. 112). The reversal of the act of confession as a form of counter-conduct against disciplinary power demonstrated that spaces exist within institutions in which to rework disciplinary tactics and nullify, subvert, and reconfigure power. Confession as a form of *parrhēsia*, or free-spokenness, illustrates counter-conduct in which speakers embody their subjective agency by narrating their truths in public dialogue with others. Confession as a public accounting of oneself is "a kind of doing, a form of action, one that is already a moral practice and a way of life" (Butler, 2005, p. 126). That public accounting of oneself is the embodiment of the truth one speaks not just in how one speaks, but in how one lives.

The conditions under which true *parrhēsia* occurs includes speaking truth plainly, binding onself to the truth one speaks, and assuming the risks involved in embodying truth in one's speech and in one's actions. *Parrhēsia* demonstrates an ethic of care for the self in order to care for others, and a commitment to a life dedicated to building solidarity with all humankind. As teachers and teacher educators, the embodiment of our truth regarding disciplinary technologies like edTPA might subvert the reduction of the act of teaching, itself the commitment to an ethic of care, to a banal "to-do list" of predetermined outcomes defined by a rubric and performed under edTPA's disciplinary gaze (Taubman, 2000). The conceptualization of teaching as a standardized practice measured by predefined behaviors represented on rubrics subsumes curriculum and teaching under a ritual of verification that places teachers and education professors inside a critical thinking playpen, rather than professionalizing teaching. We teachers and education professors could embody the courage of truth by refusing to remain complicit in perpetuating a quotidian system of production effectuated through instruments like edTPA. Institutionalized power is eminently contestable, and examples of counter-conduct against disciplinary techniques like edTPA, and against punitive accountability discourses more broadly, abound in figures like Barbara Madeloni (Madeloni & Gorlewski, 2013), who questioned and refused an institutionalized object of power-knowledge—edTPA—at great cost.

The most insidious aspect of technologies like edTPA is that they establish regimes of truth based on spurious, or at best partial, claims of objectivity. The embodiment of the courage of truth requires teacher educators to scrutinize those truth-power claims, expose the political agenda behind those claims, and like Madeloni, refuse to remain complicit in perpetuating them. To those who seek to professionalize our profession through standardizing inherently creative, intellectual, and political work, we must, as Madeloni did, refuse, speak out, organize, and embody something else, which will look different in different contexts.

We are the guardians of our own profession. Our professional accountability should be assured through relationships of collegial trust based on critical educational scholarship that appreciates and affirms the nature of our work as an ethic of care for ourselves, each other, our children, and the world rather than on algorithmic thinking that seeks to measure teaching and learning through production line causal chains. As Taubman (2009) asserts, we have given up too much and, in effect, submitted to an abusive relationship predicated on submission to a system of coercive accountability through which we futilely attempt to prove our worth to our examiners on the terms they set for us. As professional educators, a crucial aspect of our courage of truth lies in the creation of a new public pedagogical model of dialogical encounter through which "social relationships become less combative, manipulative, and self-serving and, instead, more educational" (Pinar, 2006, p. 8). Our profession—teaching and teacher education—is in peril, and it is past time to reclaim our voices and our political agency by embodying our truth, subverting punitive disciplinary power, and caring for each other.

NOTES

1. We borrow the concept of the "guardian sentinel" from Gabriel & Lester's (2013) analysis of the emergence of valued-added measures of accountability in Tennessee.

2. Pearson has not made public any data regarding the demographic of its evaluators.

REFERENCES

American Association of Colleges for Teacher Education. (n.d.-a). Participation map. Retrieved from edtpa.aacte.org/state-policy

American Association of Colleges for Teacher Education. (n.d.-b). About edTPA: Overview. Retrieved from edtpa.aacte.org/about-edtpa

Amrein-Beardsley, A. (2014). *Rethinking value-added models in education: Critical perspectives on tests and assessment-based accountability.* New York, NY: Routledge.

Apple, M. W. (2001). *Educating the "right" way: Markets, standards, God, and inequality.* New York, NY: RoutledgeFalmer.

Au, W. (2013). What's a nice test like you doing in a place like this? The edTPA and corporate education "reform." *Rethinking Schools, 27*(4). Retrieved from www.rethinkingschools.org/archive/27_04/27_04_au.shtml

Berliner, D. C. (2014). Exogenous variables and value-added assessments: A fatal flaw. *Teachers College Record, 116*(1), 1–31. Retrieved from www.tcrecord.org/content.asp?contentid=17293

Berliner, D. C., & Glass, G. V. (2014). *50 myths & lies that threaten America's public schools: The real crisis in education.* New York, NY: Teachers College Press.

Bestor, Jr., A. (1952). "Life adjustment" education: A critique. *Bulletin of the American Association of University Professors (1915–1955), 38*(3), 413–441.

Buras, K. (2011). Race, charter schools, and conscious capitalism: On the spatial politics of whiteness as property (and the unconscionable assault on Black New Orleans). *Harvard Educational Review, 81*(2), 296–330.

Butler, J. (2005). *Giving an account of oneself.* New York, NY: Fordham University Press.

Chiu, S. (2014). edTPA: An assessment that reduces the quality of teacher education. *Teachers College, Columbia University Working Papers in TESOL & Applied Linguistics, 14*(1), 28–30. Retrieved from journals.cdrs.columbia.edu/wp-content/uploads/sites/12/2015/04/3.3-Chiu-2014.pdf

Chow, R. (2002). *The Protestant ethnic & the spirit of capitalism.* New York, NY: Columbia University Press.

Darling-Hammond, L. (2010, October 19). Evaluating teacher effectiveness: How teacher performance assessments can measure and improve teaching. Center for American Progress. Retrieved from www.americanprogress.org/issues/education-k-12/reports/2010/10/19/8502/evaluating-teacher-effectiveness/

Dewey, J. (1985). The need for a new party. In J. Boydston (Ed.), *John Dewey: The later works, 1925–1953 Volume 6: 1931–1932*. Carbondale, IL: Southern Illinois University Press, pp. 156–181. (Original work published 1931)

Dover, A., & Schultz, B. (2016). Troubling the edTPA: Illusions of objectivity and rigor. *The Educational Forum, 80*, 95–106.

edTPA (n.d.). Scorer Qualifications. Retrieved from scoreedtpa.pearson.com/become-an-edtpa-scorer/edtpa-scorer-qualifications.html

Foucault, M. (1994). *The order of things: An archaeology of the human sciences*. New York, NY: Vintage Books. (Original work published 1970)

Foucault, M. (1995). *Discipline & punish: The birth of the prison* (A. Sheridan, Trans.). New York, NY: Vintage Books. (Original work published 1977)

Foucault, M. (2007). *Security, territory, population: Lectures at the Collège de France 1977–1978* (G. Burchell, Trans., M. Senellart, Ed.). New York, NY: Picador.

Foucault, M. (2008). *The birth of biopolitics: Lectures at the Collège de France 1978–1979* (G. Burchell, Trans., M. Senellart, Ed.). New York, NY: Picador.

Foucault, M. (2011). *The courage of truth: Lectures at the Collège de France 1983–1984*. (G. Burchell, Trans., F. Gros, Ed.). New York, NY: Picador.

Foucault, M. (2015). *The punitive society: Lectures at the Collège de France 1972–1973*. (G. Burchell, Trans., B. E. Harcourt, Ed.). New York, NY: Palgrave Macmillan.

Gabriel, R., & Lester, J. N. (2013). Sentinels guarding the grail: Value-added measurement and the quest for education reform. *Education Policy Analysis Archives, 21*(9). Retrieved from files.eric.ed.gov/fulltext/EJ1015334.pdf

Giroux, H. A. (2012). *Education and the crisis of public values: Challenging the assault on teachers, students, & public education*. New York, NY: Peter Lang.

Harvey, D. (2005). *A brief history of neoliberalism*. New York, NY: Oxford University Press.

Hatch, J. A. (2015). *Reclaiming the teaching profession: Transforming dialogue on public education*. Lanham, MD: Rowman & Littlefield.

Hedges, C. (2006). *American fascists: The Christian right and the war on America*. New York, NY: The Free Press.

Hofstadter, R. (1962). *Anti-intellectualism in American life*. New York, NY: Vintage Books.

Klein, N. (2007). *The shock doctrine: The rise of disaster capitalism*. New York, NY: Picador.

Kliebard, H. (2004). *The struggle for the American curriculum: 1893–1958* (3rd ed.). New York, NY: Routledge.

Kumashiro, K. K. (2008). *The seduction of common sense: How the right has framed the debate on America's schools*. New York, NY: Teachers College Press.

Kumashiro, K. K. (2012). *Bad teacher! How blaming teachers distorts the bigger picture*. New York, NY: Teachers College Press.

Lafer, G. (2017). *The one percent solution: How corporations are remaking America one state at a time*. Ithaca, NY: Cornell University Press.

Madeloni, B. (2013, February 5). Pearson comes to teacher education, and we are supposed to be cool with that? *National Education Policy Center*. Retrieved from nepc.colorado.edu/blog/pearson-comes-teacher-education-and-we-are-supposed-be-cool

Madeloni, B., & Gorlewski, J. (2013). Wrong answer to the wrong question: Why we need critical teacher education, not standardization. *Rethinking Schools, 27*(4). Retrieved from www.rethinkingschools.org/articles/wrong-answer-to-the-wrong-question-why-we-need-critical-teacher-education-not-standardization

National Center for Education Statistics. (2017). *The condition of education 2017.* Retrieved from nces.ed.gov/programs/coe/indicator_cge.asp

Nietzsche, F. (1997). On the uses and abuses of history for life. In D. Breazeale (Ed.), *Untimely meditations* (R. J. Hollingdale, Trans.) (pp. 59–123). Cambridge, UK: Cambridge University Press. (Original work published 1874)

Pinar, W. (2006). *The synoptic text today and other essays: Curriculum development after the reconceptualization.* New York, NY: Peter Lang.

Pinar, W. (2012). *What is curriculum theory?* (2nd ed.). New York, NY: Routledge.

Ravitch, D. (2013). *Reign of error: The hoax of the privatization movement and the danger to America's public schools.* New York, NY: Alfred A. Knopf.

Ravitch, D. (2015, November 13). Rick Ayers: EdTPA is ruining teacher professionalism. [Web log post]. Retrieved from dianeravitch.net/2015/11/13/rick-ayers-edtpa-is-ruining-teacher-professionalism/

Rizga, K. (2017). Betsy DeVos wants to use America's schools to build "God's kingdom." *Mother Jones.* Retrieved from www.motherjones.com/politics/2017/01/betsy-devos-christian-schools-vouchers-charter-education-secretary/

Schmidt, J. (2000). *Disciplined minds: A critical look at salaried professionals and the soul-battering system that shapes their lives.* Lanham, MD: Rowman & Littlefield.

Shore, C., & Wright, S. (1999). Audit culture and anthropology: Neo-liberalism in British higher education. *The Journal of the Royal Anthropological Institute, 5*(4), 557–575.

Shore, C., & Wright, S. (2000). Coercive accountability: The rise of audit culture in higher education. In M. Strathern (Ed.), *Audit cultures: Anthropological studies in accountability, ethics, and the academy* (pp. 57–89). New York, NY: Routledge.

Silber, C. (2017, May 2). Ducey signs bill expanding teacher certifications. *The Associated Press.* Retrieved from www.usnews.com/news/best-states/arizona/articles/2017-05-02/ducey-signs-bill-expanding-teacher-certifications

Taubman, P. M. (2000). Teaching without hope: What is really at stake in the standards movement, high stakes testing, and the drive for "practical reforms." *Journal of Curriculum Theorizing, (16)*3, 19–33.

Taubman, P. M. (2009). *Teaching by numbers: Deconstructing the discourse of standards and accountability in education.* New York, NY: Routledge.

Tyler, R. (1949). *Basic principles of curriculum and instruction.* Chicago, IL: University of Chicago Press.

U.S. Department of Education. (2009). Teacher preparation: Reforming the uncertain profession—remarks of Secretary Arne Duncan at Teachers College, Columbia University. Retrieved from www2.ed.gov/news/speeches/2009/10/10222009.html

Weber, M. (2001). *The Protestant ethic and the spirit of capitalism.* New York, NY: Routledge Classics. (Original work published 1930)

Ziarek, E. (2001). *An ethics of dissensus: Postmodernism, feminism, and the politics of radical democracy.* Stanford, CA: Stanford University Press.

Part II

IMPACTS ON TEACHER PREPARATION AND THE TEACHING PROFESSION

CHAPTER 4

Impacting Education Through Privatized Graduate Schools

Strategic Fields, Charter Networks, and the Relay Graduate School of Education

Jamie C. Atkinson and Brian W. Dotts

> The control of a large force is the same principle as the control of a few men: it is merely a question of dividing up their numbers . . . [and] the spot where we intend to fight must not be made known; for then the enemy will have to prepare against a possible attack at several different points.
>
> —Sun Tzu, *The Art of War*

It distresses us that opening a chapter on teacher education with words composed about warfare is relevant. However, there is a battle going on over the control of public education. For decades, ideological groups have been working successfully to privatize public charter schools in the United States. These groups include conservative philanthropies, neoliberal organizations, and charter management companies; their ideological goals are often shared by state legislatures. Their work continues to undermine traditional public schooling by transferring public management of and responsibility for schooling to private companies subsidized by public tax dollars. A recent addition to the privatization movement has moved beyond a focus on public charter schools and is manifested in the development of a new alternative teacher preparation program known as the Relay Graduate School of Education. Privately funded and operated by a network of organizations of the kind mentioned above, Relay was established in 2011 as an unconventional certification program for future teachers. In this chapter we analyze the Relay Graduate School of Education, its establishment and organization, and its required courses and certification requirements, and we compare Relay to traditional schools of education. Our findings illustrate how Relay may serve as a pinnacle achievement in the privatization movement in education, particularly since it enables the entire movement to stand alone as a self-perpetuating and self-fulfilling network supplanting public responsibility for schooling from kindergarten through graduate education.

We now have a dual system of schooling and teacher training in the United States. With the Relay Graduate School at its apex, the privatization of schooling has resulted in thousands of public charter schools throughout the U.S. operated by charter management organizations; the increased use of Teach For America (TFA) graduates to fill teaching positions in those schools; and now the establishment of the Relay Graduate School of Education to fast-track teacher certification, creating a pool of teachers to work with TFA and fill the teacher shortages in privately managed public charter schools. We believe teachers who complete programs such as Relay's are not encouraged to critique our current state of education, but rather are normalized to standards, accountability, and neoliberal visions of marketized educational systems—education as a market, or economic, segment that can be compared against productivity measurements and global competition.

PRIVATIZATION DEFINED

The privatization of education and schooling can take many forms, and its goals are pursued by a complex network of private interests. For our purposes, we define the privatization of education as the process of outsourcing traditional public school functions and responsibilities to private companies. Sometimes referred to as "marketization" due to a "pro-business climate" (Bartlett, Frederick, Gulbrandsen, & Murillo, 2002, p. 6.), privatization in the K–12 arena tends to take place in public charter schools whose deregulation facilitates the outsourcing of school functions and school-business partnerships. Privatization occurs when a state or school system contracts with a private charter management organization (CMO) to operate and manage a public charter school in exchange for an "administrative fee" (Miron, Urschel, Yat Aguilar, & Dailey, 2012, p. 10). The Relay Graduate School is a newly created, stand-alone organization funded by a cadre of private conservative philanthropies who share interest in privatizing the alternative teacher certification process. While they identify themselves as nonprofit for tax purposes, organizations like Relay can earn profits as long as they are reinvested in the organization via salaries, consulting fees, and organizational expansion (Kuan, 2001). As we discuss below, Relay is not only funded by private conservative philanthropies, it is organized by a network of individuals who have been involved in the K–12 privatization movement.

ALTERNATIVE CERTIFICATION PROGRAMS

The number of states accepting alternative pathways to teacher certification has grown from just eight in 1983 to all 50 today (Humphrey & Wechsler,

2007; Klemme, 2008; Woods, 2016). Alternative pathways include state-based systems operating within universities and government-sanctioned accredited private alternative certification programs. According to a 2012 survey conducted by the National Center of Education Statistics (NCES), the number of teachers in public schools who had received their certification from alternative pathways had grown to 14.6% (NCES, 2012). Breaking those statistics down further, we find that within charter schools 22.6% of teachers received their training by way of alternative certification programs. This number has surely grown since 2012 based on the rampant growth of programs such as the Relay Graduate School of Education, TFA, The New Teacher Project, and smaller programs such as Urban Teachers and Bank Street. Many states, including New York, have put forth legislation requiring schools to utilize "motivators similar to those of K–12 charter schools" and trading "increased accountability for student performance . . . for less regulation and oversight of teacher training" (Stitzlein & West, 2014, p. 2). The growth of alternative certification programs is due to factors including, but not limited to, teacher shortages and the need to quicken certification processes to fulfill this increased demand (Woods, 2016). The demand for teachers has opened up opportunities for groups interested in the privatization of schooling to pursue their interests in stand-alone alternative certification options.

An analysis of privatized teacher education graduate schools and programs must take into account the complex ideological mechanisms which have shifted the purposes and aims of education, and acknowledge the rapid rise of the charter school movement and the associated connections embedded within strategic action fields. Strategic action fields (SAFs) are "meso-level social orders" focused on a connective ideological agenda, or philosophy; those meso-level orders then act as "the basic structural building block of modern organizational life in the economy, civil society, and the state" (Fligstein & McAdam, 2012, p. 3). Ideological operatives utilize the social mechanisms within SAFs to encourage continued privatization of education and the growth of charter schooling. The contemporary atmosphere of education reform has created fertile ground for the charter school movement and alternative teacher preparation programs. According to Fabricant and Fine (2012), "[T]he contemporary charter movement has deployed and consolidated financial, cultural, media, and political sources to [market] charters to Americans as a wedge institution" (p. 3). A wedge institution utilizes broad social, political, and academic mechanisms to limit the influence of dominant institutions, in this case government or state education, by providing alternatives that divide and conquer, just like wedge movements within military operations. Those same mechanisms are utilized to market privatized graduate schools of education to educators and state educational policymakers as an efficient and pragmatic approach to usher in a new generation of educators free from the usual requirements within traditional programs of study.

The rapid growth of alternative teacher certification pathways has mirrored the growth in the K–12 privatization movement and added a new layer to the already complex and diffuse discourse. Efforts to privatize education have moved beyond K–12 schooling and now include teacher preparation and licensure. New public management theories and new institutionalisms embedded within the neoliberal (defined below) ideological framework "envision a society in which third-party organizations (both for profit and not-for-profit) play a much more central and government-endorsed role" (Burch & Smith, 2015, p. 193) in providing, evaluating, and executing traditional government services.

Our examination must first attend to the ideological formations which have created the choice movement and the ushering in of competition and other market-based reforms leading to charter schools. We then examine one alternative program that has been growing nationwide—the Relay Graduate School of Education—comparing Relay's teacher education programs to traditional teacher certification programs focusing on the formation of teacher knowledge and the pedagogical skill sets teachers are expected to use in their pre–K through 12 classrooms. Finally, we discuss the potential implications of the Relay Graduate School framework.

IDEOLOGY AND EDUCATION POLICY

Neoliberal and *neoconservative* ideas and motives can be found across a spectrum of politics ranging from the centrism of "Third Way" Democrats to the extremism of far-right Republicans. Generally speaking, neoliberals favor privatization—subjecting public institutions and public services to the actions of the market. They advocate consumer choice, competition, deregulation, efficiency, and accountability as the appropriate remedies to improve education and schooling. Basically synonymous with libertarian ideology, neoliberals' "theoretical archetype [is] not democracy or government, but the market," and their idea of a "functionalistic society [places] government as secondary to the market" (Dotts, 2019, p. 457). We wish to add that despite neoliberals' market rhetoric, the privatization of public schooling often takes place outside market competition. In other words, charter management organizations rarely compete for government contracts, and their fees and profits are subsidized by taxpayer revenue. In other venues, the school privatization movement might be better referred to as a mechanism for obtaining corporate welfare.

Neoconservatives, on the other hand, we define as American traditionalists, conservative intellectuals who tend to view American culture and institutions ethnocentrically, and evangelicals who largely support the privatization of public education in order to facilitate the transfer of public school students to private religious schools (through, for example, voucher programs and tax credit scholarships). It was evangelical Christians, originally led by Reverend Jerry Falwell, who claimed America's public schools as "Godless institutions" after the U.S. Supreme Court's 1962 ruling in *Engel v. Vitale*, which prohibited teacher-led prayers in public schools (Dotts, 2019, pp. 457–459). While neoliberals prioritize the freedom of the market, neoconservatives focus on traditional, conservative, Christian morality. Despite their potential ideological contradictions (freedom is often antithetical to morality), the groups find common ground in their support for school privatization.

It should also be noted that while neoliberals and neoconservatives are largely embedded on the Right, these education policy and teacher certification ideas, especially in their neoliberal guise, are often supported by conservative Democrats. Neoliberalism especially continues to dominate the discourse and remains the most significant ideological formation challenging government-centered schooling. "For neoliberals, the capitalist economy (i.e., the "free market"), is the archetype and framework for which all other institutions should be modeled upon, including and more specifically, education" (Atkinson, 2017, p. 3). As Michael Apple asserts (1995),

> we live in a period in which our educational system has become increasing politicized [and marketized] . . . The Spencerian question, what knowledge is of most worth, has now been replaced with an even more pointed question, whose knowledge is of most worth, and the fact that this latter question has become so powerful highlights the profoundly political nature of educational policy and practice. (p. 2)

The macro-issue of educational reform has instigated meso-level strategies and initiatives focused on teacher education and teacher certification processes. Political and "public opinion, as well as state and federal policies, have increasingly endorsed the charter school movement in the United States," and teacher certification and preparedness have been substantively tied to school choice, standardization, and the charter movement (Stitzlein & West, 2014, p. 1). Neoliberals see education as a "private consumable service that can be shopped for measuring cost against quality and [thus] can be improved the way business people attempt to improve businesses" (Saltman, 2014, p. xxii). Thus, alternative certification programs serve as another choice mechanism within the field of privatized educational services. Additionally, Wendy Brown (2006) has discussed the hybridization of neoliberalism and neoconservatism, which has led to a "new form of governmentality [situating] citizens in an undemocratic form of society" (p. 693). The blending of those two ideologies positions citizens as "economic units—*homo economicus*—normalized and evaluated against business models and market measurements of worth and performance and subjectified as commodities" (Brown, 2006, pp. 691, 693). Thus,

> what has emerged—our contemporary construct of the state and society—is a fundamental realignment in social, political, and economic systems. We have reached an unprecedented time in our history marked by sociopolitical transformation, de-democratization, and the marketization of schooling that has now set the stage

> for a complete commodification of schooling, including the teaching profession [to include teacher preparation and certification processes]. (Atkinson, 2017, p. 3)

Both ideological positions, neoliberal and neoconservative, favor school choice and teacher preparation centered on the charter school concept because it separates teacher preparation from typical state (government-controlled) accreditation processes. The prevailing discourse of education has produced new subject positions and social relations, and the meaning, force, and effect of this new discourse is framed by "an overbearing, economic, and political context of international competitiveness" (Ball, 2007, p. 2). In short, the traditional notion of civic virtue—knowing and acting in the public realm to improve the self and the public good—is being replaced by a narrower capitalistic righteousness and an ethos characterized by an unexamined political allegiance to the dominant culture. To understand the significance of how ideology connects with our focus, the Relay Graduate School of Education, we must recognize the underlying mechanisms at work to reconfigure education policy.

SAFS, TEACHSTRONG, AND THE RELAY GRADUATE SCHOOL

Interlocking networks of neoliberal groups (e.g., charter advocacy organizations), nongovernmental and/or quasi-governmental actors, philanthropies, etc., are working to change the way educational policies are developed and instituted (Au & Ferrare, 2015; Ball, 2007, 2012; Lubienski, Brewer & La Londe, 2016; Sondel, Kretchmar & Ferrare, 2015). Those interlocking networks are situated within strategic action fields (Fligstein & McAdam, 2012) and driven by neoliberal and neoconservative ideological actors who work to influence educational policy, teacher certification requirements, and standards of curriculum and instruction at both the macro- and meso-levels. Strategic action fields, or field theory, is a useful tool to explain the networks and ideological formations driving the push for alternative teacher certification programs, such as the Relay Graduate School, and the larger charter school movement. Fligstein and McAdam's theory includes several elements we find useful in discussing the processes ideologically motivated actors utilize to influence education policy, teacher education, and other education reform initiatives.

At the core of this issue is the existence of strategic action fields. A strategic action field is a "constructed meso-level social order in which actors . . . are attuned to and interact with one another on the basis of shared . . . understandings" including a desired course of social and/or political action (Fligstein & McAdam, 2012, p. 9). These meso-level sociopolitical orders operate primarily on the state level through a network of ideologically similar actors exerting pressure on state legislatures to modify and codify education reform initiatives. Strategic action field theory recognizes both "social power" and "mutually attuned actors" as the underlying mechanism providing "both the structure and logic of any given field" and the field's "taken for granted everyday reality" (Bourdieu, 1977; Fligstein & McAdam, 2012, p. 10; Jepperson, 1991). While the number of "mutually attuned actors" and the complexity of the field are both too great to discuss in their entirety, we will discuss some specific entities.

Two large, and substantially connected, advocacy conglomerates are the State Policy Network (SPN) and the American Legislative Exchange Council (ALEC). These two organizations (or networks of affiliate groups) have considerable sway over state legislative agendas. Much of the funding for these organizations originates in dark money contributions from a web of like-minded large philanthropic organizations, often operating through a macro-philanthropic group known as the Donors Trust that includes such notables as the Koch brothers, Bill and Melinda Gates, and the Walton family. It is this web of philanthropic organizations and their legislative operatives (SPN & ALEC) that pushes state educational policy agendas leading to the acceptance of alternative teacher certification entities like the Relay Graduate School.

As Tompkins-Stange (2016) notes, the "philanthropic involvement in policy arenas is not new; indeed, foundations have exercised influence in public policy since their origins in the early 20th century. . . . [However], the past two decades represent a water-shed change in the visibility and the centrality of philanthropy" (p. 2) in influencing state legislative agendas, especially as it relates to matters of education and teacher certification. As Hess & Henig (2015) discuss, large philanthropic organizations, which includes organizations such as the Koch Family Foundations and Walton Family Foundation, along with the charter networks and an extensive list of think tanks, have trended toward ideologically attuned "convergent grant-making" that influences national and state policymakers and education reformers through extensive strategic fields (p. 32). How this all happens is rather interesting in that groups—at times disparate groups—seem to coalesce into these fields advocating for similar ideological agendas. One example, as discussed in a November 2015 *Washington Post* article (Layton, 2015), illustrates how the Center for American Progress, a self-ascribed non-partisan (though slightly left of center on some social issues) policy think tank, gathered a strategic like-minded group aimed at "modernizing and elevating" the teaching profession. The Center for American Progress, a third-way, centrist neoliberal group, promotes charter schools and alternative pathways for teacher certification (Layton, 2015). Furthermore, this coalition and agenda seems to include "the American Association of Colleges for Teacher Education and the National Council on Teacher Quality, which has questioned the quality of many of the 1,400 teacher preparation programs run by colleges" (Layton, 2015).

The Center for American Progress became the hub of a strategic field, making use of social skills and policy connections and operating within a broader field focusing on the development and growth of charter networks and alternative teacher preparation programs, and leveraging state education policy connections through the ALEC and the SPN (Layton, 2015). They are an "incumbent" actor within this field—an actor who can "wield disproportionate influence within a field and whose interests and views tend to be heavily reflected" in the current momentum of education policy (Fligstein & McAdam, 2012, p. 13). Organizations such as the Center for American Progress attempt to create and sustain these networks by securing the cooperation of others. This group of actors now operates under the umbrella of an advocacy coalition, a strategic ideological field, called TeachStrong, which now consists of over 60 organizations who have ties to a larger web—the "Russian Doll" model of embedded fields (Fligstein & McAdam, 2012; Layton, 2015). The members of this coalition work through connected state fields, via the SPN, representing the meso-level structure of these coalitions, to influence state-level educational policy decisions resulting in the growth of charters and creating openings for alternative routes to teacher preparation and certification.

The Relay Graduate School of Education, used here as an example of an alternative teacher pathway, is part of the larger strategic action field devoted to charters and educational reform. What follows is a summary of networked groups of state and national nonprofits, think tanks and policy centers, professional advocacy groups, alternative teacher preparation programs, and other education development groups: non-governmental actors working within a strategic action field centered on the TeachStrong initiative of the Center for American Progress who either directly advocate or indirectly support charters and alternative teacher preparation such as Relay's. Some may surprise you.

Alternative Teacher Education/Certification, and Professional Development: The Relay Graduate School of Education, TFA, Bank Street College of Education, and Urban Teachers.

National Nonprofits, Think Tanks, Political Action, and Policy Groups: Alliance for Excellent Education, America Achieves, Battelle for Kids, Center for American Progress, Center on the Future of American Education—Georgetown University, Chiefs for Change, Clayton Christensen Institute for Disruptive Innovation, Democrats for Education Reform, Digital Promise, Education Post, Education Reform Now, Education Counsel, Educators Rising, Hope Street Group, Generation Scholars Network, Golden Apple, Institute for the Study of Knowledge Management in Education, Knowledge Alliance, Leading Educators, Massachusetts Business Alliance for Education, National Center for Teaching Residencies, National Center on Time and Learning, National Commission on Teaching America's Future, National Council on Teacher Quality, National Institute for Excellence in Teaching, National Women's Law Center, National Writing Project, New America Foundation—Education Policy Program, New Leaders, New Teacher Center, Pritchard Committee for Academic Excellence, Profound Gentlemen, Public Education Business Coalition, Public Impact, Southern Education Foundation (formerly the George Peabody Education Fund), Stand for Children,

Students for Education Reform, The Teacher Salary Project, Teaching Matters, Teach NY, Third Way, The New Teacher Project, The Viva Project, and the Woodrow Wilson National Fellowship Foundation.

Professional Advocacy Groups: American Association of Colleges for Teacher Education , American Federation of Teachers, Association for Supervision and Curriculum Development , Council of Chief State School Officers, Deans for Impact, Educators 4 Excellence, Kappa Delta Pi, Learning Forward, National Academy of Advanced Teacher Education, National Association for the Education of Young Children, National Board for Professional Teaching Standards, National Center for Learning Disabilities, National Education Association, National Indian Education Association, National Network of State Teachers of the Year, Teach Plus, and TESOL International Association.

One challenge for any researcher and supporter of public education is in the fact that many of these organizations offer up initiatives that help public schools. It is imperative to dissect the various initiatives and determine possible hidden motivations of the various actors within the strategic field, or network. Another challenge for education policy researchers is that many of the organizations listed above are themselves part of a larger group of actors—the hubs of other ideologically related fields. Mapping the networks can be a maddening endeavor, though nonetheless important. Many of the organizations have strong ties to large philanthropic organizations wishing to influence national and state education policy centered primarily on neoliberal and libertarian ideals of the free market, choice, and competition (Brewer, Hartlep, & Scott, 2018).

This TeachStrong network of associated groups promoted nine goals that became campaign principles that were adopted by both political parties during the 2016 election cycle (Center for American Progress, 2015). The nine goals included:

- Identifying and recruiting more teacher candidates with great potential to succeed, with a deliberate emphasis on diversifying the teacher workforce;
- Reimagining teacher preparation to make it more rooted in classroom practice and a professional knowledge base, with universal high standards for all candidates;
- Raising the bar for licensure so it is a meaningful measure of readiness to teach;
- Increasing compensation in order to attract and reward teachers as professionals;
- Providing support for new teachers through induction or residency programs;
- Ensuring tenure is a meaningful signal of professional accomplishment;

- Providing significantly more time, tools, and support for teachers to succeed, including through planning, collaboration, and development;
- Designing professional learning to better address student and teacher needs and to foster feedback and improvement; and
- Creating career pathways that give teachers opportunities to lead and grow professionally.

What stands out in the above list are principles that indicate a reimagining of teacher preparation to make it primarily rooted, in classroom practice with universal high standards; raising the bar for licensure; and designing professional learning to better address student and teacher needs. While those principles seem admirable and would be hard to argue against if one advocates for a strong educational system, the language utilized is deceptive in the fact that it diminishes the essential sociological, philosophical, historical, and other foundational work required in typical programs. The reality of teacher licensure is that while traditional university programs face increasing pressure to raise standards (e.g., edTPA, reduction of social foundations of education courses, more emphasis on practice versus theory, and more credit hours required in programs of study), other programs such as the Relay Graduate School of Education and TFA avoid many of the traditional requirements of colleges and universities and often are taught by less-qualified instructors, require fewer courses, and refrain from using widely accepted scholarly research (Ravitch, 2012; Stitzlein & West, 2014; Strauss, 2012; Zeichner, 2013).

This situation creates an alternative system, tailored for charters, and streamlined to generate more teachers for certain high-needs schools (urban, majority minority areas, and impoverished locations) and areas of teaching (early childhood, math and science, and special education). It also challenges and dilutes traditional teaching pathways, creating a new breed of teacher, raised under the legacy of standards, accountability, and efficiency, and politically averse to pushing back against neoliberal and neoconservative ideological norms. Those teachers then may passively promote the narrative that education is primarily a vehicle for global competition, relying heavily, if not exclusively, on standardized test scores. The Relay Graduate School of Education is an excellent example of the insurgency of these alternative programs of study.

THE RELAY GRADUATE SCHOOL OF EDUCATION

The Relay Graduate School of Education (formerly known as Teacher U) was established in 2011 by private charter networks including Achievement First, KIPP, and Uncommon Schools, and hosted by Hunter College in New York City after obtaining approval from the New York Board of Regents. Achievement First is a network of 34 charter schools operating in five cities in Connecticut, Rhode Island, and New York under a 501(c)3 tax designation. However, in 2004, it formed a 501(c)4 organization in Connecticut with several partners to advocate for education reform and charter schools as alternatives to district-operated public schools. This advocacy group, named Connecticut Coalition for Achievement Now (ConnCAN) and with ties to 50CAN, a nonprofit educational advocacy group that promotes the school choice agenda, is free to lobby for Achievement First because of its IRS designation. In addition, its funding originates from multiple philanthropic organizations that have a vested interest in charter schools and have ties to large corporations and hedge fund managers. ConnCAN advocates for increasing the number of charter schools and the number of students in those schools, and for flexible funding options and flexible pathways to teacher certification. ConnCAN/50CAN act through state affiliates of the SPN by lobbying for alternative teacher certification models, which is just one example of how SPN state affiliates attempt to influence state education policymakers (Vogel, 2016).

KIPP, by and large, provided the most significant impetus in establishing the Relay Graduate School of Education with the idea of charter teachers passing on their experience to the next generation of charter teachers while potentially circumventing traditional teacher preparation programs. KIPP (officially known as the Knowledge Is Power Program) has close ties to TFA, as well as an extensive philanthropic and advocacy base. For example, Wendy Kopp, founder of TFA, is married to Richard Barth, who is the CEO of KIPP, and KIPP's founders were two TFA alums, Mike Feinberg and Dave Levin. KIPP also has its own foundation, which received $15 million as seed money from the founders of GAP, Inc., in 1994. This foundation, along with advocates in ALEC and the SPN, works to increase the influence of charter schools in all 50 states. It is within this action field of 501(c)(3) and 501(c)(4) organizations, philanthropies, and charter school networks, many of which are mentioned above, that mutually attuned actors have created social and political coalitions—those "complex webs"—driving educational policy reform toward a massive charter system. Within that system, alternative teacher preparation programs fulfill a non-governmental role in providing teachers who are indoctrinated into the charter networks and the philosophy of charter-based systems.

Relay is now a private, stand-alone institution, without affiliation with other universities, granting only a Master of Arts in Teaching (MAT), primarily for early childhood education. Relay's teacher preparation model emphasizes standardization, clinical experiences, mentorships, and numerous teaching modules, mostly conducted online or in blended formats. The overall curriculum is identified by some as performatively "prescriptive," while Relay's website describes its teaching model as a focus on "honing the teaching craft," while serving "in high needs schools," making significant use of Doug Lemov's book, *Teach Like a Champion* (Mungal, 2016, p. 16). According to its website (relay.edu/about-us/institution), Relay's MAT degrees in Early Childhood Education, Middle School Generalist, and Middle School Generalist, have been accredited by the National Council for Accreditation of Teacher Education (NCATE) and the Middle States Commission on Higher Education (MSCHE).

So How Does Relay Compare to Traditional Programs?

For the purposes of comparison, we reviewed 10 state public institutions in order to understand their academic requirements for teacher education majors. While we have details regarding each institution's requirements, they are broadly similar and will be provided here in average numbers for the sake of space. The public institutions we reviewed were the University of Colorado, University of Connecticut, University of Delaware, University of Illinois, Louisiana State University, Pennsylvania State University, Rutgers University, State University of New York New Paltz, University of Texas Austin, and the University of Tennessee. We focused on the course and student teaching requirements for elementary-grade (early childhood) majors since the Relay Graduate School of Education awards master's degrees primarily in this area. Finally, for each of these public institutions, we have reviewed their specific requirements for students who choose alternative graduate certification routes.

We chose the public universities listed because they are major institutions in states where the Relay Graduate School has established a presence through its growing satellite campuses. We compared these 10 public institutions in order to obtain a thorough understanding of the undergraduate requirements that must be undertaken for students majoring in elementary-age certification. Students at the Relay Graduate School may or may not have acquired similar bachelor's degrees. Equally, if not more, importantly, we examined the alternative certification requirements at each public institution for students majoring in elementary education since these routes offer equivalents to a master's degree and certification/teaching licensure. It is graduate education that Relay claims to offer its students as part of their elementary education certification.

Public University Requirements

At the 10 public institutions reviewed, elementary education majors were required to complete between 120 and 147 credit hours before being awarded a Bachelor of Science degree. Most institutions required a 120-hour minimum, and Rutgers University required completion of 147 credit hours. No institution required less than 120 credit hours to earn the degree. As expected, each institution required students to complete a majority of their coursework in a variety of academic disciplines including the social and natural sciences and the humanities. As teacher education majors, students are required to complete anywhere from 10 to 20 professional education courses including a variety of practicums, field experiences, and student teaching experiences. The University of Illinois, for example, requires numerous professional education courses that focus on educational psychology, language varieties, cultural learning differences, child development, teaching children mathematics and algebraic equations, social studies, science, literature, and reading, art education, and cultural identities, diversity, and social justice. A 12-credit-hour student teaching experience finalizes the requirement for UI's Bachelor of Science degree.

The other nine institutions are very similar to the University of Illinois, but they vary in the specialized courses they offer. For instance, other universities required a variety of courses including, but not limited to, music education, exceptionalities (special needs and/or gifted education), analysis of research in the field, learning assessment, study of bilingual education, teaching methods and strategies for diverse children, educational linguistics, teacher leadership and organization, differentiated learning and assessment, and adolescent health and movement. Other courses included the visual and performing arts, law and ethics in education, curriculum, critical reflection on teacher decisionmaking, information sciences, inclusive classrooms, health and physical education, development of symbolic representations, educational technology, urban education, classroom management and organization, and training in the prevention of bullying, harassment, and intimidation. All institutions offer one or more required courses in educational foundations that usually include such courses as critical and contemporary issues in education, history of education, philosophy of education, education policy, and sociocultural perspectives on issues of diversity and multiculturalism.

During their 4-year undergraduate education, students are required to complete 12 to 15 credit hours of practical student teaching across a 12-week period (roughly a semester), with other practicums, field work, or experiences requiring dozens of hours in schools, school-related organizations, or community centers, with the highest number of outside hours totaling 130 hours of practical experiences, not including student teaching. These undergraduate degrees, therefore, require students to complete a majority of courses spread across academic disciplines at each respective university along with teacher education course requirements and electives that cover a wide array of specialized and focus course offerings dependent on interest and areas of expertise, and to accrue a good deal of practical observations and experiences during or following coursework. For alternative graduate certification programs across nine of the 10 public institutions (one institution's requirements were not available online), requirements generally include the completion of 32–48 hours of graduate coursework and a student teaching experience. At these public universities, courses are generally taught by academics holding PhDs in a variety of education-related areas and EdDs.

Relay Graduate School of Education Master of Arts in Teaching

Students entering the Relay Graduate School must hold a bachelor's degree from an accredited institution of higher education with a cumulative grade point average of 2.5 or higher on a 4.0 scale. If a student's GPA is lower than a 3.0, they must provide a letter of recommendation. The only Relay campus that requires completion of the Graduate Record Examination (GRE) is the

New York City campus. The MAT requires a 2-year commitment that includes coursework and practical training combined with what Relay refers to as a Teaching Residency in an AmeriCorps school program. This Residency includes the following requirements, according to Relay's website:

- Five days of summer training before the school year starts
- Weekly 3- to 4-hour sessions of intensive, deliberate practice
- Approximately 5 hours of weeknight sessions a month of Relay Graduate School of Education core pedagogy instruction (2–4 times)
- One 5-hour Saturday session per month for Relay Graduate School of Education content pedagogy coursework
- Online instruction (8–10 hours per month)
- Aligned Relay assessments that require Residents to demonstrate mastery of key teaching skills
- Regular observations of Residents by the Relay Graduate School of Education Dean and faculty

The National Council for Accreditation of Teacher Education (NCATE) utilizes the designation of Initial Teacher Preparation (ITP) to distinguish programs meeting the minimum requirements for certification. Relay states that its Middle Grades certification programs are accredited by the Middle States Commission on Higher Education (MSCHE). While Relay continues to tout its programs to a wide audience, the NCATE has only accredited Relay's following programs leading to the MAT degree (note: Relay also offers a certification-only option—non-degree—to its students):

Childhood Education

- Program has ties to the Association of Childhood Education International (ACEI), a Specialized Professional Association (SPA)
- Grade: (K–6)
- Degree: Master's
- Level: ITP

Middle School Generalist (NY)

- Program has ties to the Association for Middle Level Education (AMLE) formerly known as the National Middle School Association (NSMA)
- Grades: 5—9
- Degree: Master's
- Level: ITP

Middle School Science (NY)

- Program has ties to the National Science Teachers Association (NSTA)
- Grades: 7–12

- Degree: Master's
- Level: ITP

Relay's course offerings were difficult to find online, so much so that it seemed well-guarded. Their courses are taught primarily through online delivery, utilizing Coursera and Canvas as the two primary Learning Management Systems. We were able to distinguish six known online courses that Relay Graduate School created and that are presented through Coursera and Canvas. The course descriptions below are drawn directly from Relay's website and from the two platforms Relay utilizes for the courses. Many of the courses are packaged/re-packaged courses with recorded lessons, while some are taught face-to-face or in blended settings. The following courses are just a few examples:

Teaching Character and Creating Positive Classrooms

- Positive psychology meets K–12 pedagogy. This course explores key ideas of positive psychology and shows how great teachers apply those lessons to maximize student engagement and accomplishment. Through lectures, discussions, interviews, and footage of great educators in action, you'll learn how to integrate character-based objectives into your own teaching.
- 10–15 hours of videos and online assessments
- Taught entirely online through Coursera by Dave Levin

Get Organized: How to Be a Together Teacher

- This course is designed for classroom teachers who juggle time-sensitive tasks and often-exhausting teaching schedules. With an eye toward long-term sustainability, The Together Teacher examines the purpose for planning ahead, provides tools for tracking time commitments, deadlines and tasks, and helps teachers develop a personal organization system that interacts with their day-by-day practices. All teachers, from the pen & paper list maker to the tech-savvy digital maven, will benefit from the no-nonsense approach to "togetherness" that's presented in this course. We don't care what format you use; we care that you know when you have free time during the day, and that you have a plan for using it.
- 8 hours of videos, readings, and projects
- Taught entirely online through Coursera by Maia Heyck-Merlin

(HE) Teacher Certification Exam Preparation

- Are you an inspiring teacher or novice teacher? This course will help to prepare you to pass your content knowledge exam for teacher certification or licensure.
- Expected Commitment is 7–10 hours

(K–12) BL-101: Beginning to Blend

- Have you ever wanted to have more one-on-one time with students, to engage students in their own learning, or to give students choice around path and pace? If you answered yes to one or more of these questions, this course is for you.
- Self-paced
- Expected Commitment is 6 hours

(K–12) BL-102: Rolling Out Blended

- When rolling out blended/personalized learning in your classroom or school, there are three key pieces: space, routines, and culture. This course will give you concrete strategies to start rolling out these key components and blending your practice.
- Self-paced
- Expected Commitment is 6 hours

(K–12) BL-103: Teaching Each Student

- In a blended/personalized classroom, data can be overwhelming. This course will give you the tools you need to focus your data analysis, so you can provide a more personalized experience for each student.
- Self-paced
- Expected Commitment is 6 hours

(K–12) BL-201: Extending your Blending

- You're currently blending your curriculum and have seen how personalization helps push student growth, agency, engagement, and much more. Now it's your turn to start sharing your best practices, become a blended leader, and extend your reach.
- Self-paced
- Expected Commitment is 6 hours

Relay's instructors and staff are listed in Table 4.1. Note the network of charters, charter management organizations (CMOs), and the Relay Graduate School of Education.

In addition to the few courses we could locate, we were also curious about the materials utilized in Relay's courses. There appear to be only a few books used in any of the courses offered by Relay, which include the following: (1) *Driven by Data* by Paul Bambrick-Santoyo, published by Jossey-Bass, 2010; (2) *Teach Like a Champion—49 Techniques that Put Students on the Path to College* by Doug Lemov, published by Jossey-Bass, 2015; (3) *Teaching as Leadership* by Steven Farr (who serves on TFA's national staff), published by Jossey-Bass, 2010; and (4) *The Skillful Teacher* by John Saphier, Mary Ann Haley-Speca, and

Table 4.1. Relay's Instructors and Staff

Instructors and Staff	Responsibilities and Connections	Education
Dave Levin	Co-founder of the Relay Graduate School Co-founder of Knowledge Is Power Program (KIPP) and associated programs: the Character Labs and Zearn Math, Inc. Became a teacher through TFA Achievement First Uncommon Schools (Both of these are charter management organizations that helped establish Relay and both utilize and supply Relay's graduates in their respective schools.)	Bachelor's degree from Yale University
Maia Heyck-Merlin	Became a teacher through TFA Worked at TFA in several capacities including managing their summer training camps Chief Talent Officer and Chief Operating Officer for Achievement First, a charter school management organization operating 20 schools in Brooklyn and Connecticut	Bachelor's degree in Child Development from Tufts University
Lindsay DeHartchuck	(HE—Teacher Certification Exam Prep) at Relay LJD Education Consultant	Master's degree in Early Childhood Special Education from The George Washington University
Juliana Finegan	Partner, The Learning Accelerator TFA Teaches for Relay Graduate School Designed elements of Relay's science curriculum and blended learning curriculum Partner with The Learning Accelerator project focusing on Blended Learning models Courses: BL-101, -102, -103, & -201	Master's degree in Secondary Science Education from Loyola Marymount University

Robert Gower, self-published by Saphier's own publishing company, Research for Better Teaching, Inc., in 2007. The text *Teaching as Leadership* is particularly noteworthy because it is utilized in other charter-based alternative teacher certification programs, such as TFA's teacher certification program. As Steudeman (2015) notes, this text "fails to recognize the controversies surrounding learning standards and testing" (p. 50; see also Au & Ferrare, 2015). Steudeman further adds that training acquired in alternative certification programs is often solipsistic, failing to recognize alternative perspectives and competing theories regarding education and pedagogy.

CONCLUSION

What does the evidence in this chapter tell us about the current state of teacher education, the future of teacher education, and the subsequent impacts on classroom pedagogy? First, in a tactic that Sun Tzu would appreciate, strategic action fields made up of charter networks and their allied teacher education programs such as the Relay Graduate School of Education act as a wedge dividing the education community into, not only the former divisions of private and public, but also those institutions that are charter and traditional. As alternative teacher education formulas are instituted, traditional programs that may not provide flexibility and minimized time and course requirements, such as university colleges of education, face increased pressure to change their formatting and requirements to recruit and retain teacher candidates. Additionally, traditional programs, which often include courses in social foundations of education to develop teachers in a holistic manner, are relegated to electives or eliminated entirely in order to minimize course hours required and focus on practice instead of theory.

In this new environment, standardization, conformity, universalism, and efficiency are valued over individualism, creativity, independent, and critical thinking. Charter networks, funded by philanthropic organizations and businesses, proselytized by neoliberal and neoconservative ideologues, and lobbied for by the SPN and the ALEC, are increasing their footprint in various states. Many states have adopted charter-based school turnaround programs which are often separated from the Department of Education in the state with a CEO acting as a state school turnaround officer. Once a state deems a district in need, programs are often instituted, including staff development, which then link to programs such as Relay's and many more mentioned in the list of organizations earlier in this chapter. The question for us, then, is how independent and critical and prepared are the educators coming through, or influenced by, these programs? We believe teachers who complete programs such as Relay's are not encouraged to critique our current state of education, but rather, are normalized to standards, accountability, and neoliberal visions of marketized educational systems—education as a market, or economic, segment and compared against productivity measurements and global competition. Does this uncritical mentality, this era of *homo economicus*, translate into the K–16 classrooms a perpetuating cycle of market-oriented educators who normalize standard curricula and accountability based on standardized testing? Further research should be conducted to determine the attitudes and positionalities of teachers who graduate and gain teacher certification through programs such as the Relay Graduate School of Education and how those positionalities affect their classroom practices.

REFERENCES

Apple, M. (1995). Is social transformation always progressive? Rightist reconstructions of schooling today. In M. E. James (Ed.), *Social reconstruction through education: The philosophy, history, and curricula of a radical ideal* (pp. 1–26). Norwood, NJ: Ablex Publishing.

Atkinson, J. C. (2017). Countering the neos: Dewey and a democratic ethos in teacher education. *Democracy & Education, 25*(2), Article 2.

Au, W., & Ferrare, J. J. (2015). Introduction: Neoliberalism, social networks, and the new governance of education. In W. Au & J. J. Ferrare (Eds), *Mapping corporate education reform: Power and policy networks in the neoliberal state* (pp. 1–22). New York, NY: Taylor & Francis.

Au, W., & Ferrare, J. J, (2015). *Mapping corporate education reform: Power and policy networks in the neoliberal state.* New York, NY: Taylor & Francis.

Ball, S. (2007). *Education plc: Understanding private sector participation in public sector education.* New York, NY: Routledge.

Ball, S. (2012). *Global Education Inc: New policy networks and the neo-liberal imaginary.* New York, NY: Routledge.

Bartlett, L, Frederick, M., Gulbrandsen, T. & Murillo, E. (2002). The Marketization of Education: Public Schools for Private Ends. *Anthropology & Education Quarterly, 33*(1), 5–29.

Bourdieu, P. (1977). *Outline of a theory of practice.* Cambridge, UK: Cambridge University Press.

Brewer, T. J., Hartlep, N. D., & Scott, I. (2018). Forbes 30 under 30 in education: Manufacturing "edu-preneur" networks to reinforce privatization/marketization. *Education Policy Analysis Archives, 26*(76), 1–39

Brown, W. (2006). American nightmare: Neoliberalism, neoconservatism, and de-democratization. *Political Theory, 34*(6), 690–714.

Burch, P., & Smith, J. M. A. (2015). Enterprise education policy and embedded layers of corporate influence. In W. Au & J. J. Ferrare (Eds.), *Mapping corporate education reform: Power and policy networks in the neoliberal state* (pp. 190–206). New York, NY: Routledge.

Center for American Progress. (2015, November 10). *40 education organizations unite to launch TeachStrong, a campaign to modernize and elevate the teaching profession.* Retrieved from www.americanprogress.org/press/release/2015/11/10/125052/release-40-education-organizations-unite-to-launch-teachstrong-a-campaign-to-modernize-and-elevate-the-teaching-profession/

Dotts, B. W. (2019). *Educational foundations: Philosophical and historical perspectives.* New York, NY: Cambridge University Press.

Fabricant, M., & Fine, M. (2012). *Charter schools and the corporate makeover of public education: What's at stake?* New York, NY: Teachers College Press.

Fligstein, N., & McAdam, D. (2012). *A theory of fields.* New York, NY: Oxford University Press.

Hess, F. M., & Henig, J. R. (Eds.). (2015). *The new education philanthropy: Politics, policy, and reform.* Cambridge, MA: Harvard Education Press.

Humphrey, D. C., & Wechsler, M. (2007). Insights into alternative certification: Initial findings from a national study. *Teachers College Record, 109*(3), 483–530.

Jepperson, R. (1991). Institutions, institutional effects, and institutionalism. In W. Powell and P. DiMaggio (Eds.), *The new institutionalism in organizational analysis* (pp. 143–163). Chicago, IL: University of Chicago Press.

Klemme, D. (2008). New directions in teacher preparation programs. *Journal of Family and Consumer Sciences Education, 26*(1), pp. 61–67.

Kuan, J. (2001). The phantom profits of the opera: Nonprofit ownership in the arts as a make-buy decision. *Journal of Law, Economics, & Organization, 17*(2), 507–520.

Layton, L. (2015, November 8). How to build a better teacher: Groups push a 9-point plan called TeachStrong. *Washington Post.* Retrieved from www.washingtonpost.com/local/education/how-to-build-a-better-teacher-groups-push-a-9-point-plan-called-teachstrong/2015/11/08/2b28b824-84c8-11e5-8ba6-cec48b74b2a7_story.html?utm_term=.e733629a0ef1

Lubienski, C., Brewer, T. J., & La Londe, P. G. (2016). Orchestrating policy ideas: Philanthropies and think tanks in US education policy advocacy networks. *Australian Education Researcher, 43*(1), 55–73.

Miron, G., Urschel, J. L., Yat Aguilar, M. A., & Dailey, B. (2012). *Profiles of for-profit and nonprofit education management organizations: Thirteenth Annual Report, 2010–2011.* Boulder, CO: National Education Policy Center. Retrieved from nepc.colorado.edu/publication/EMO-profiles-10-11

Mungal, A. S. (2016). TFA, Relay Graduate School, and the charter networks: The making of a parallel education structure. *Education Policy Archives, 24*(17), 1–30.

National Center for Education Statistics (2012). *The condition of education report.* Washington, DC: U.S. Department of Education.

Ravitch, D. (2012). A very bizarre graduate school of education [Web blog post]. Retrieved from www.dianeravitch.net/2012/07/08/a-very-bizarre-graduate-school-of-education

Relay Graduate School of Education. (2019). Teaching residency. Retrieved from www.relay.edu/aspiring-teachers/relay-teaching-residency/apply-teaching-residency

Saltman, K. (2014). *The politics of education: A critical introduction.* Boulder, CO: Paradigm Publishers.

Sondel, B., Kretchmar, K., & Ferrare, J. J. (2015). Mapping the education entrepreneurial network: TFA, charter school reform, and corporate sponsorship. In W. Au & J. J. Ferrare (Eds.), *Mapping corporate education reform: Power and policy networks in the neoliberal state* (pp. 65–85). New York, NY: Taylor & Francis.

Steudeman, M. J. (2015). Ignoring the ghost of Horace Mann: A reflective critique of Teach for America's solipsistic pedagogy. In T. J. Brewer & K. deMarrais (Eds.), *TFA counter-narratives: Alumni speak up and out* (pp. 47–54). New York, NY: Peter Lang.

Stitzlein, S. M., & West, C. K. (2014). New forms of teacher education: Connections to charter schools and their approaches. *Democracy & Education, 22*(2), Article 2.

Strauss, V. (2012, July 5). Is this any way to train teachers? *Washington Post.*Retrieved from www.washingtonpost.com/blogs/answer-sheet/post/is-filling-the-pail-any-way-to-train-teachers/2012/07/04/gJQADViVOW_blog.html

Tompkins-Stange, M. E. (2016). *Policy patrons: Philanthropy, education reform, and the politics of influence.* Cambridge, MA: Harvard Education Press.

Vogel, P. (2016). Here are the corporations and right-wing funders backing the education reform movement: A guide to the funders behind a tangled network of advocacy, research, media, and profiteering that's taking over public education. Retrieved from www.mediamatters.org/research/2016/04/27/here-are-corporations-and-right-wing-funders-backing-education-reform-movement/210054.

Woods, J. R. (2016). Mitigating teacher shortages: Alternative teacher certification. Education Commission of the States. Retrieved from www.ecs.org/wp-content/uploads/Mitigating-Teacher-Shortages-Alternative-Certification.pdf

Zeichner, K. (2013, October 10). Why the "GREAT Teachers and Principals Act" is not great [Blog post]. Retrieved from www.washingtonpost.com/blogs/answer-sheet/wp/2013/10/10/why-the-great-teachers-and-principals-act-is-not-great

CHAPTER 5

Canaries in the Classroom

The Teaching Profession in Trouble

Anthony Cody

For the past decade we have heard that our schools are broken and students are burdened with countless bad teachers who are impossible to fire (Goldstein, 2014; Kumashiro, 2012). This public assault has been accompanied by a wave of policies that have undermined teacher autonomy and professional standing while chipping away at due process and seniority protections. In this chapter, I examine the assault on the teaching profession and the ways in which it is being transformed. I also look at the ways in which teachers are beginning to organize to defend the profession and offer an alternative framework for strengthening their ability to work well with students.

THE WAR ON TEACHERS

Across the nation, enrollment in teacher education preparation programs has steadily declined in recent years (Camera, 2016). Enrollment in teacher preparation programs peaked at 200,000 graduates annually in the 1970s but has shrunk to half of that in 2018 (Whitford, 2018). A MetLife Survey of the American Teacher revealed that job satisfaction among teachers has dropped to its lowest level in 25 years, from 62% in 2008 to 39% in 2012—a total of 23 points (Markow, Macia, & Lee, 2013). A more recent survey of teachers in the state of Georgia provided more detail, noting that "teachers described a profession that was overcrowded with mandated tests, evaluated by unfair or unreliable measures, and constantly being changed without any input from the professionals inside the classroom. All occurring while being compensated poorly when time and experience are taken into account" (Downey, 2016).

When Nancie Atwell won the first Global Prize for Teaching, she was asked during a television interview what her advice was for students who are interested in becoming teachers. Her response should have been shocking as she said,

> Honestly, right now I encourage them to look in the private sector. Because public school teachers are so constrained right now by the Common Core standards, and the tests that are developed to monitor what teachers are doing with them. It's a movement that's turned teachers into technicians, not reflective practitioners. And if you're a creative, smart young person, I don't think this is the time to go into teaching, unless an independent school would suit you. (CNN, 2015)

Can you imagine if the Nobel Prize winner in medicine warned young people not to become doctors? Yet the interviewers expressed some passing sadness and simply moved on. It seems as though nobody is listening to teachers, and the results are playing out in our schools across the country. Teachers have become demoralized and isolated. The teaching profession is in dire straits and few are paying attention as the canaries in the classroom leave in droves. Of course, many dedicated teachers remain but struggle to preserve a sense of equilibrium and moral standing as the pressure mounts to focus on test scores at the expense of students' well-being. Some teachers do their best to put their heads down and hope this will pass, while others—including a great many who are creative and smart—keep their sanity by actively resisting, as teacher walkouts and strikes over the past 2 years attest (Goldstein, 2018a, 2018b; Goldstein & Burns, 2018).

There are several factors that are impacting the working lives of teachers. First of all, the living conditions for our students have significantly worsened, and this has very real impacts on the classroom. Levels of student poverty have risen dramatically over the past decade; the National Center for Education Statistics announced that in 2013 the number of public students living in low income households reached 51%, the highest level of poverty ever recorded (Klein, 2015; Southern Education Foundation, 2015). Decades of research have shown that economic inequality plays a dramatic role in shaping educational opportunities and outcomes for students (Berliner, 2013; Carter & Welner, 2013; Dixon, 2016; Ladson-Billings, 2006, 2013). Teachers' work is affected by the conditions their students must live with since schools are not sealed off from the world. In 1993, 19.5% of teachers indicated that poverty was a serious problem in their schools, while 32.4% did so in 2012 (National Center for Education Statistics, n.d.). While the nation's economy has recovered from the banking crisis of 2008, many states have failed to restore adequate funding to public schools (Leachman & Mai, 2014), which can dramatically impact opportunities for students. Schools facing chronic shortages of supplies must look to teachers to supplement them using their own funds (Ness, 2017). Schools that serve low-income students tend to have lower levels of resources even though the needs there are greater (Semuels, 2016).

In 2010 the *Los Angeles Times* created its own Value Added Model (VAM) to analyze teacher performance and published "effectiveness ratings" for thousands of teachers (Felch, Song, & Smith, 2010)—again, operating on the assumption that teaching and education occur in a vacuum and that low student achievement is the result of bad teachers and not an artifact of systemic inequity. That same Fall, the pseudo-documentary *Waiting for Superman* was released, with a multimillion-dollar publicity budget from the Gates Foundation. The Gates Foundation also sponsored NBC's *Education Nation*, to showcase the film and its stars, and even Oprah devoted two episodes to the effort (Oprah.com, n.d.). The thesis of the film and accompanying TV broadcasts was that public schools were broken and that getting rid of "bad teachers" was impossible. Tenured teachers have "jobs for life" and such protections existed only to protect bad teachers. If we could get rid of all the bad teachers, Bill Gates promised, U.S. rankings on international tests would shoot to the top and our economy would follow. This signaled the rise of a concerted reform focus that had the support of big money philanthropies like the Gates Foundation as well as the federal Department of Education. Federal stimulus dollars went to states willing to include test scores in teacher evaluations, and to adopt "college and career ready standards," such as the Common Core.

Several other trends have contributed to the destabilization of the teaching profession. A narrative has emerged that degrades the importance of teachers' professional knowledge. This has taken several forms, but the common foundation is judging teacher quality on the basis of a capacity to increase test scores. In 2011, Bill and Melinda Gates published an editorial in which they stated,

> It may surprise you—it was certainly surprising to us—but the field of education doesn't know very much at all about effective teaching. We have all known terrific teachers. You watch them at work for 10 minutes and you can tell how thoroughly they've mastered the craft. But nobody has been able to identify what, precisely, makes them so outstanding. This ignorance has serious ramifications. We can't give teachers the right kind of support because there's no way to distinguish the right kind from the wrong kind. We can't evaluate teaching because we are not consistent in what we're looking for. We can't spread best practices because we can't capture them in the first place. (Gates & Gates, 2011)

The Gates Foundation has provided $45 million to the Measures of Effective Teaching project (Bill & Melinda Gates Foundation, n.d.), which has yielded very little in the way of useable research. Despite this, they have pushed hard for the use of VAM systems for purposes of teacher evaluation. Gates has also provided significant funding to the National Council on Teacher Quality, which has published poorly researched rankings of teacher education programs (Cody, 2012). Their ranking system appears to be designed to reward schools that emphasize test preparation and punish those that push back against testing.

There is a widely shared statistic that teachers "come from the bottom third" of college graduates. But as Matthew Di Carlo has pointed out, this statistic is a distortion and is useless as any sort of guide to teacher quality (Di

Carlo, 2011). Nonetheless, this distortion not only helped impel Teach For America (TFA), which supposedly will bring the "best and brightest" to our classrooms (Kopp, 1989, 2001), even if only for a short while, but it continues to provide fodder to its supporters. TFA, in turn, justifies its effectiveness with very thin studies that, as Julian Vasquez Heilig points out, show marginal positive test score effects for their corps members (Vasquez Heilig, 2015) which are not generalizable to the broader TFA population (Vasquez Heilig, 2013a; Veltri, 2013). What is missing from these studies is a look at the effect turnover has on student achievement and on a school's climate overall. When this is examined, researchers find that teacher turnover has major negative impacts on student performance, and the effects were even worse for low-achieving and Black students (Ronfeldt, Loeb, & Wyckoff, 2013).

POLICIES AND PRACTICES DESTROY MORALE

VAMs have been inserted into the evaluation system in many states at the demand of the U.S. Department of Education—as a condition for Race to the Top grants or state waivers to NCLB. Careful research shows these VAM systems to be unreliable, unstable, and to yield particularly poor results for teachers of English Language Learners (ELL) and special education students (Haertel, 2013). The tests aligned with new standards have been made significantly more difficult. The Common Core tests are yielding proficiency rates of around 30% of all students, with scores significantly lower for African American, Latino/a, special education, and ELL populations. Yet, according to reform logic, poor test scores are the result of bad teachers who are protected by teacher unions and due process. If only we could get rid of these slackers, test scores would rise and the achievement gap would close.

Leading reform advocates do not often directly acknowledge their antipathy to veteran teachers, but once in a while it comes out. In 2010, Bill Gates said this about teacher salaries:

> Another feature of school budgets is a bump in pay for master's degrees. But a master's degree has almost no impact on achievement. Nevertheless, my own state of Washington has an average salary bump of nearly $11,000 for a master's degree—and more than half of our teachers get it. That's more than $300 million every year that doesn't help kids. And that's just one state. As a country, we spend $9 billion a year for master's degrees. When we need higher student achievement on lower budgets, we're obliged to review all the money we're spending and ask: does this buy better student achievement? (Bill & Melinda Gates Foundation, 2010)

This thinking has led directly to the attempts to quantify teacher effectiveness, and use this, rather than level of experience and education, to determine pay and due process protections. Paul Vallas, who led the New Orleans

Recovery School District after Hurricane Katrina, did little to hide his true feelings about veteran teachers as he set out to fire all the teachers in the city. He said this in a 2010 interview with the BBC:

> I don't want the majority of my teaching staff to work more than 10 years. The cost of sustaining those individuals becomes so enormous. Between retirement and healthcare and things like that, it means that you are constantly increasing class sizes and cutting programs to sustain the cost of a veteran workforce. (Conway, 2010)

Fully credentialed teachers, many with master's degrees, are now required in many districts and states to complete elaborate portfolios to prove their competence, using copyrighted "frameworks" from Charlotte Danielson or Robert Marzano. Teachers find their teaching subjected to close examination. Many aspects of these teaching rubrics reflect good practices, but teachers report that many of them are being used to set absurd expectations. I posed this question on my Facebook wall on March 28, 2015:

> I have a feeling that the Danielson and Marzano teacher evaluation frameworks—and perhaps ProTeach in Washington state, are being used to send teachers jumping through hoops for no good purpose. Have you experienced these evaluation tools being used to set absurd expectations? Or consume an inordinate amount of time?

The next morning, there were comments from forty teachers, with a general consensus in line with my concern. Some samples:

Donna Y.: My district uses Danielson . . . it has not improved instruction in my building one iota . . . but helps tear down morale, one observation at a time.

Karen A.: The time commitment is way more than previous evaluations and it is very subjective. Your administrator can give you a basic [low score] if they didn't see something in the lesson but that doesn't mean you don't do it. So you have to PROVE you do. You have to collect data and upload artifacts all in an effort to PROVE you are doing your job. The feedback I got was not valuable at all and certainly not worth the time and effort my observation required.

Amanda K.: I had to complete the full evaluation cycle for the Danielson Method for a class I was taking. It took a very long time to go through it with one teacher. My biggest concern is that the conversations that are such a big part of this evaluation method are not authentic. It's meant to be a collaborative method between the evaluator and the teacher. However, it can take a great deal of time to build that level of trust. If that trust is not present, the conversations cannot be authentic and no true growth can result.

Meg N.: Here is the handbook for the Georgia system, which has been horrible. (Georgia Department of Education, 2014). The Georgia system (being hailed as a model) has created massive extra work for both teachers and admin. Basically it is 50% student growth, 40% observation and 10% student surveys. The measurement of student growth is a statistical wonder to behold. A pure lesson in how to compare apples to oranges and destroy professional teachers in the process. The observation portion is where you get into the overkill. Admins must observe every teacher 4 times for 10 minutes each plus two 30 minute observations (one announced, one unannounced). The standards for teachers must be observed and checked off. Some administrators want to see them ALL EVERY time. There is no clear definition of what the admin are observing. For example, what differentiation looks like to one administrator will not be recognized as such by another.

Jon P.: We also use Danielson in Pittsburgh. Time differs dramatically depending on the admin. But by the way the language is written, it is up to the teacher to provide a "preponderance of evidence" for the specific rating. A teacher with 3 basic ratings out of 24 components is in danger of being exited. Fortunately, we are understaffed and it seems like it would be an impossible task to make the system as oppressive as the language would allow.

Kathleen J.: Most of our "Collaborative Team" time is spent trying to prove we are doing our jobs. As with Danielson, it does depend on your administrator, and while I think mine is good, we have to upload charts we are keeping, must have SMART goals of two- to six-week duration, and keep data points towards those goals. I have heard principals complain about how much time using Danielson takes for THEM to use to evaluate teachers; time spent on paperwork as opposed to time spent actually out in the school. Just like the time I spend proving I'm doing my job as opposed to other more productive things I could be doing.

A Wisconsin teacher's husband wrote: I always know when my wife is working with the requirements for these evaluation models. Between it and her lesson planning/IEP work/grading I know she won't have a day off for several weeks, and she will tell me daily, often through tears, that she wants to quit being a teacher, and that other teachers in the building were breaking down in tears from the stress of them on a daily basis. These effectiveness and evaluation models have done more to destroy her will to be a teacher than Scott Walker has. The two combined are devastating.

Paul C.: The truth is that the attempt to use a time consuming evaluation process in order to determine which teachers are not proficient is only taking precious time away from both teachers and administrators. Teachers have less time and energy to work with students as their primary focus is on proving their ability and administration is spending so much time on evaluations that the community building and advocacy for students is suffering. The whole thing is a fool's errand going after a trumped up cause for the supposed failing public schools. Just as voter fraud is not causing harm to our election process, bad teachers are not the reason for a school system that is being overtaxed with continued unfunded mandates and reduced personnel and funding.

In 2016, the Network for Public Education sponsored a survey of teachers and administrators to investigate the impact these evaluations were having on schools. About three thousand educators responded, and the results were unequivocal. The NPE report concluded that,

> Teachers and principals believe that evaluations based on student test scores, especially [VAM], are neither valid nor reliable measures of their work. They believe that VAM scores punish teachers who work with the most vulnerable students. Of the respondents, 83% indicated that the use of test scores in evaluations has had a negative impact on instruction, and 88% said that more time is spent on test prep than ever before. Evaluations based on frameworks and rubrics, such as those created by Danielson and Marzano, have resulted in wasting far too much time. This is damaging the very work evaluation is supposed to improve, as valuable time is diverted to engage in related compliance exercises and paperwork. Of the respondents, 84% reported a significant increase in teacher time spent on evaluations. (Network for Public Education, 2016, p. 2)

Paul C. raised a pertinent question. If a demand for accountability is rooted in authentic concerns over the quality of work, then it can be satisfied by reasonable steps to set standards and raise quality. If, however, accountability demands are a political device used to disempower, deprofessionalize, and scapegoat a profession, then nothing that can be done will satisfy them. Which situation are we in? Bhaskar Sunkara wrote about this ever-growing list of requirements and accountability measures in a 2012 essay entitled "Lean Production." The essence of this model is to increase the demands on teachers, with ever-rising expectations for performance and paperwork. Sunkara wrote:

> The goal of lean education isn't teaching or learning; it's creating lean workplaces where teachers are stretched to their limits so that students can receive the minimum support necessary to produce satisfactory test scores. It is critical for teachers to see this clearly because lean production is indeed "continuous": in other words, it's insatiable. The harder teachers work to satisfy the demands of lean managers,

> the harder we will be pushed, until we break down. There is no end to this process. (Sunkara, 2012)

The recent wave of teacher strikes has begun to shift national media coverage of the teaching profession. *Time Magazine*, which in 2014 featured a cover story that asserted "It's nearly impossible to fire a bad teacher" (Strauss, 2014), changed their tune in 2018, with a series of much more sympathetic covers showing teachers with captions such as "I have 20 years of experience, but I can't pay to fix my car, see a doctor for headaches, or save for my child's future. I am a teacher in America" (Stone, 2018).

TEACHERS DEFEND THEIR PROFESSION

The resistance evident in the 2018 and 2019 teacher strikes has been building for several years. A small but growing number of educators have declared themselves *Teachers of Professional Conscience,* and are refusing to administer standardized tests to their students (Teachers of Professional Conscience, n.d.). Julianna Kreuger Dauble wrote this in the statement she read to her school board in Renton, Washington:

> Students cannot realize their full potential at school when we have cut counselors, nurses, art, music, extracurricular activities, behavior support, classroom aides, science materials, field trips, and most of all cut sacred TIME for teachers to plan innovative instruction. With No Child Left Behind teachers have been assigned more duties for student data collection, we must fulfill new evaluation rubric requirements, we are handed still more tests that are not aligned with curriculum or students' developmental needs and are riddled with errors, we have additional certification requirements that take time away from classroom work, we are expected to perform new leadership duties, we must navigate new technology without training or working equipment, we have to teach to pacing guides that are often impossible to follow, we somehow complete report cards thoughtfully even though they do not match new standards and the new tests, and we still must learn what the new standards even mean without any time to do so thoughtfully; and all this with a lack of high-quality aligned curricular materials while our students come to school needier than ever. This is not just a workload issue. This is literally driving teachers out of the profession. This reality is unconscionable and I cannot remain silent. I ask others to stand up with me for children and our future. (Dauble, 2015)

Some teachers are organizing within their unions to provide protection for their colleagues who wish to share information with parents and students about opting out of tests. Michelle Gunderson has offered a Teachers Pledge on the Ethical Use of Data, which provides a solid foundation teachers can use to limit some of the damage that the obsession with test scores can do (Dauble, 2015). Gunderson has also written about what she describes as the "triumvirate of upheaval," Common Core, PARCC tests, and "Framework evaluations" (Gunderson, 2015). She believes it is time to resist these evaluations, and has begun this process in Chicago, noting,

> I realize that it is very hard for teachers to publicly speak about evaluation. Teachers have been vilified as lazy public sector workers who refuse to do their jobs, and talking about the harshness of our current evaluations plays into some of the rhetoric that as workers teachers do not want to be accountable. But for the sake of our students, our profession, and the future of public schooling, teachers need to be speaking out about their personal experiences with punitive evaluations. (Gunderson, 2015)

She goes on to say,

> In the fight against the upheaval we are experiencing in our schools, this might be the most personal and difficult stance to take. Sharing your evaluation is like baring your soul. The Chicago Teachers Union has arranged for members to share their evaluations with the union so they can analyze trends and abuses. I have shared mine. I realize that my union's organizational skills and strengths are different than other locals, but I can envision groups of teachers doing the same whether at their school site or through union caucus work. (Gunderson, 2015)

When I first read Linda Darling-Hammond's book, *The Right to Learn* (1997), I was inspired by her suggestion that the National Board process could help the teaching profession gain respect, like other professions. The many "framework" evaluations being used now bear a passing resemblance to the National Board process. They describe what good teaching should look like, and include rubrics that observers use. Like National Board portfolios, they provide teachers with the chance to provide evidence of their work. But the experiences of teachers do not suggest these evaluations are enhancing the profession. In the current policy context, where the imperatives center on ridding our schools of "bad teachers" and raising test scores, these evaluations do more harm than good. They invoke fear that corrodes the trust needed for real collaboration, reflection, and growth.

HONOR TEACHERS BY EMPOWERING THEM

The fundamental premises and assumptions that have brought us here must be turned on their heads if we are to rescue and elevate the teaching profession. Contrary to what Bill and Melinda Gates wrote in 2011, we know a great deal about what makes an effective teacher. In the broader social context, we must directly confront the ways that poverty affects students, and ensure genuine opportunities await them once they have graduated.

We know from Daniel Pink's (2011) description of research into human motivation that for complex work such as teaching, people are motivated by three key factors: autonomy, mastery, and purpose. To these three, I would add trust. Trust allows for autonomy. Trust allows us to give and receive feedback from our colleagues, allowing us to actively collaborate. This then builds our mastery as teachers, and allows us to fulfill our true purpose.

Conversely, learning and growth are shut down when we cannot safely trust those around us. When we lack autonomy, we are not actually responsible for our actions. Mastery is impossible if we are following someone else's script. When our true purpose is removed, and instead we must pursue test scores, we become subject to coercion and control that does not benefit students or the teaching profession.

As inequality has grown, schools serving the have-nots have become stigmatized and pathologized. Our elites cannot bear that our increasingly inequitable economic system submit to the scrutiny that justice demands, so they project blame upon students and their teachers for their failure to transcend the conditions they must endure. Teachers in elite private schools do not face these extraordinary evaluation systems—their students' supposed successes are sufficient proof of the teachers' merit. The teachers in low-income schools, conversely, have students that tend to perform worse than their wealthy peers, and thus students and teachers must be measured, ranked, sorted, and stigmatized for their inferior performance on the tests chosen to reinforce the illusion of merit on the part of the privileged.

Our biggest enemy is not the "bad teacher" who is impossible to fire (truly bad teachers are few, and firing is not impossible, as some may believe). Our biggest enemy within the school setting is the conditions that constrain good teaching and cause good and great teachers to flee (or avoid) the profession. Rather than trying to appease endless demands for teacher accountability, we must reverse the focus of the inspector's lens. Teachers ought to be responsible for teaching, for creating communities of learning within their classrooms and schools. Policymakers must be held accountable for allowing them to do this without onerous systems of coercion and control. And those who have compiled the nation's wealth and political power must be held accountable for the poverty that results from the prioritization of corporate profits above human and environmental concerns.

If accountability demands have as their goal the disempowerment of teachers as a whole, then nothing will satisfy these demands, and teachers are being forced to endure a cruel theater of the absurd. Attempting to prove their competence over and over again to a system that actually will not allow them to succeed is insanity. True reforms aimed at improving our students' lives, in and beyond their schools, should encompass basic economic justice and make meaningful, well-paid work available for all. Reform within our schools should focus on reinforcing traditional teacher preparation programs, giving teachers time to collaborate and the autonomy to select the focus for this collaboration. Teachers need time to learn from one another and to work together to investigate their teaching practice. Rather than trying to rid our schools of experienced teachers, we should strengthen mentoring and educator training programs that leverage their expertise. Rather than investing huge amounts of money in extensive testing systems to monitor achievement, we should be investing in our teachers, and in the conditions that promote stability.

REFERENCES

Berliner, D. C. (2013). Effects of inequality and poverty vs. teachers and schooling on America's youth. *Teachers College Record, 115*, 1–26.

Bill & Melinda Gates Foundation. (2010). Bill Gates: Council of chief state school officers. Retrieved from www.gatesfoundation.org/media-center/speeches/2010/11/bill-gates-council-of-chief-state-school-officers

Bill & Melinda Gates Foundation. (n.d.). Foundation commits $335 million to promote effective teaching and raise student achievement. Retrieved from www.gatesfoundation.org/Media-Center/Press-Releases/2009/11/Foundation-Commits-$335-Million-to-Promote-Effective-Teaching-and-Raise-Student-Achievement

Camera, L. (2016, September 14). The teacher shortage crisis is here. *US News & World Report.* Retrieved from/www.usnews.com/news/articles/2016-09-14/the-teacher-shortage-crisis-is-here

Carter, P. L., & Welner, K. G. (Eds.). (2013). *Closing the opportunity gap: What America must do to give every child and even chance.* Oxford, UK: Oxford University Press.

CNN. (2015). First "Nobel prize of teaching"' winner gets $1 million. *CNN New Day.* Retrieved from www.cnn.com/videos/world/2015/03/17/bts-nancie-atwell-teaching-award-million-dollars.cnn

Cody, A. (2012). Payola policy: NCTQ prepares its hit on schools of education. *Education Week.* [Blog post]. Retrieved from blogs.edweek.org/teachers/living-in-dialogue/2012/05/payola_policy_nctq_prepares_it.html

Conway, Z. (2010, April 8). Education "revolution" in New Orleans. *BBC News.* Retrieved from news.bbc.co.uk/2/hi/8608960.stm

Darling-Hammond, L. (1997). *The right to learn: A blueprint for creating schools that work.* New York, NY: Wiley.

Dauble, J. K. (2015). My statement of professional conscience. Retrieved from www.livingindialogue.com/julianna-kreuger-dauble-statement-professional-conscience/

Di Carlo, M. (2011, December 7). Do teachers really come from the "bottom third" of college graduates? [Blog post]. *Washington Post.* Retrieved from www.washingtonpost.com/blogs/answer-sheet/post/do-teachers-really-come-from-the-bottom-third-of-college-graduates/2011/12/07/gIQAg8HPdO_blog.html?noredirect=on&utm_term=.b99f40ec9cb7

Dixon, J. (2016, November 19). Toxic stress of poverty, violence, pain alter kids' brains. *Detroit Free Press.* Retrieved from www.freep.com/story/news/local/michigan/detroit/2016/11/19/detroit-children-toxic-stress-health/88530796/

Downey, M. (2016). Survey of Georgia teachers reveals "a workforce that feels devalued and constantly under pressure." *Atlanta Journal-Constitution*. Retrieved from www.ajc.com/blog/get-schooled/survey-georgia-teachers-reveals-workforce-that-feels-devalued-and-constantly-under-pressure/gIk7YMIkymZcBl4eLyhqMP/

Felch, J., Song, J., & Smith, D. (2010). Who's teaching L.A.'s kids? *Los Angeles Times*. Retrieved from articles.latimes.com/2010/aug/14/local/la-me-teachers-value-20100815

Gates, B., & Gates, M. (2011). Grading the teachers. *Wall Street Journal.* Retrieved February 13, 2019 from www.wsj.com/articles/SB10001424052970204485304576641123767006518?mg=reno64-wsj&url=http%3A%2F%2Fonline.wsj.com%2Farticle%2FSB10001424052970204485304576641123767006518.html

Georgia Department of Education. (2014). *Teacher keys effectiveness system: Implementation handbook*. Atlanta, GA: Georgia Department of Education. Retrieved from www.gadoe.org/School-Improvement/Teacher-and-Leader-Effectiveness/Documents/FY15%20TKES%20and%20LKES%20Documents/TKES%20Handbook%20-%20FINAL%2010-15-14.pdf

Goldstein, D. (2014). *The teacher wars: A history of America's most embattled profession.* New York, NY: Doubleday.

Goldstein, D. (2018a, April 2). Teachers in Oklahoma and Kentucky walk out: "It really is a wildfire." *New York Times.* Retrieved from www.nytimes.com/2018/04/02/us/teacher-strikes-oklahoma-kentucky.html

Goldstein, D. (2018b, April 3). Teacher walkouts: What to know and what to expect. *New York Times.* Retrieved from www.nytimes.com/2018/04/03/us/teacher-walkouts-strikes.html

Goldstein, D., & Burns, A. (2018, April 12). Teacher walkouts threaten Republican grip on conservative states. *New York Times.* Retrieved from www.nytimes.com/2018/04/12/us/teacher-walkouts-threaten-republican-grip-on-conservative-states.html

Gunderson, M. (2015). The triumvirate of upheaval in our classrooms. Retrieved from www.livingindialogue.com/triumvirate-upheaval/

Haertel, E. H. (2013). *Reliability and validity of inferences about teachers based on student test scores.* Princeton, NJ: ETS.

Klein, R. (2015, January 16). More than half of American public schoolchildren now live in poverty: Study. *Huffington Post.* Retrieved from www.huffingtonpost.com/2015/01/16/southern-education-foundation-children-poverty_n_6489970.html

Kopp, W. (1989). *An argument and plan for the creation of the teacher corps.* (Unpublished bachelor's thesis.) Princeton University, Princeton, NJ.

Kopp, W. (2001). *One day, all children: The unlikely triumph of Teach For America and what I learned along the way.* Cambridge, MA: Public Affairs, Perseus Books Group.

Kumashiro, K. (2012). *Bad teacher! How blaming teachers distorts the bigger picture.* New York, NY: Teachers College Press.

Ladson-Billings, G. (2006). From the achievement gap to the education debt: Understanding achievement in U.S. schools. *Educational Researcher, 35*(7), 3–12.

Ladson-Billings, G. (2013). Lack of achievement or loss of opportunity? In P. L. Carter & K. G. Welner (Eds.), *Closing the opportunity gap: What America must do to give every child and even chance* (pp. 11–22). Oxford, UK: Oxford University Press.

Leachman, M., & Mai, C. (2014). Most states funding schools less than before the recession. *Center on Budget and Policy Priorities.* Retrieved from www.cbpp.org/research/most-states-funding-schools-less-than-before-the-recession

Markow, D., Macia, L., & Lee, H. (2013). *The MetLife survey of the American teacher: Challenges for school leadership*. New York, NY: MetLife. Retrieved from www.metlife.com/content/dam/microsites/about/corporate-profile/MetLife-Teacher-Survey-2012.pdf

National Center for Education Statistics. (n.d.). Percentage of teachers indicating that certain issues are serious problems in their schools, by level and control of school: Selected years,1987–88 through 2011–12. *Digest of Education Statistics.* Retrieved from nces.ed.gov/programs/digest/d13/tables/dt13_210.10.asp

Ness, A. (2017, August 2). Teachers spend hundreds of dollars a year on school supplies. That's a problem. *Education Week.* Retrieved from www.edweek.org/tm/articles/2017/08/02/teachers-spend-hundreds-of-dollars-a-year.html

Network for Public Education. (2016). *Teachers talk back: Educators on the impact of teacher evaluation*. New York: Network for Public Education. Retrieved from mronline.org/wp-content/uploads/2018/07/NPETeacherEvalReport.pdf

Oprah.com. (n.d.). The shocking state of our schools. Retrieved from www.oprah.com/oprahshow/the-shocking-state-of-our-schools

Pink, D. H. (2011). *Drive: The surprising truth about what motivates us.* New York, NY: Riverhead Books.

Ronfeldt, M., Loeb, S., & Wyckoff, J. (2013). How teacher turnover harms student achievement. *American Educational Research Journal, 50*(1), 4–36.

Semuels, A. (2016, August). Good school, rich school; bad school, poor school: The inequality at the heart of America's education system. *The Atlantic.* Retrieved from www.theatlantic.com/business/archive/2016/08/property-taxes-and-unequal-schools/497333/

Southern Education Foundation. (2015). A new majority research bulletin: Low income students now a majority in the nation's public schools. Retrieved from www.southerneducation.org/publications/newmajorityresearchbulletin/

Stone, C. (2018). New *Time* magazine covers show what it's like to be a teacher in America. *Scary Mommy.* Retrieved from www.scarymommy.com/time-magazine-teacher-america-cover/

Strauss, V. (2014, October 25). A *Time* magazine cover enrages teachers—again. *Washington Post.* Retrieved from www.washingtonpost.com/news/answer-sheet/wp/2014/10/25/a-time-magazine-cover-enrages-teachers-again/?utm_term=.df33aa712f5f

Sunkara, B. (2012, September). Lean production: Inside the real war on public education. *Jacobin Magazine.* Retrieved from www.jacobinmag.com/2012/09/lean-production-whats-really-hurting-public-education/

Teachers of Professional Conscience (n.d.). Letters of Professional Conscience—About. Retrieved from teacherslettersofprofessionalconscience.wordpress.com/about/

Vasquez Heilig, J. (2013a). "Does not compute": Teach For America mathematica study is deceptive? Retrieved from cloakinginequity.com/2013/09/23/does-not-compute-teach-for-america-mathematica-study-is-deceptive/

Vasquez Heilig, J. V. (2013b). New mathematica TFA study is irrational exuberance. Retrieved from nepc.colorado.edu/blog/new-mathematica-tfa-study-irrational-exuberance

Vasquez Heilig, J. (2015). Do you have five minutes to understand whether @teachforamerica is effective? Retrieved from cloakinginequity.com/2015/03/10/do-you-have-five-minutes-to-understand-whether-teach-for-america-is-effective/

Veltri, B. T. (2013). Cloaking inequity: Huggy, snuggly, cuddly: Teach For America and mathematica. *National Education Policy Center.* Retrieved from nepc.colorado.edu/blog/huggy-snuggly-cuddly-teach-america-and-mathematica

Whitford, E. (2018, August 13). Report shows drop in students in teacher ed. *Inside Higher Ed.* Retrieved from www.insidehighered.com/quicktakes/2018/08/13/report-shows-drop-students-teacher-ed

Chapter 6

Teacher Preparation in Singapore

Lessons on Neoliberalism

Priya Goel La Londe and Warren Mark Liew

Since the 1980s, education policy elites have expanded systems of managerialism, performance accountability, and incentivism alongside moves to decentralize school governance, privatize public education, and valorize school choice (Kretchmar, Sondel, & Ferrare, 2014). Today, the tenets of individual liberty, free and competitive markets, and deregulation have come to characterize the public policy arenas of healthcare, social services, higher education, and pre-K–12 education. These neoliberal principles congregate in "a theory of political practices that proposes that human well-being can be best advanced by liberating individual entrepreneurial freedoms and skills within an institutional framework characterized by strong private property rights, free market, and free trade" (Harvey, 2005, p. 2). As a politico-economic model of educational governance, neoliberalism has frequently been attacked by critics of contemporary education reform (e.g., Connell, 2013; Zeichner, 2010). Yet its scope and context-specificity cannot be reduced to a generalized indictment of modern-day education systems. As Apple (2017) asserts, "neoliberalism does not stand alone, and it takes on different forms in different contexts. It is also not a unitary movement, since it has contradictory tendencies within it" (p. 148). Amid these debates, it is ever more important to gather conceptual and empirical accounts of how neoliberal logics, in all their heterogeneous and contradictory enactments, are shaping teacher policy and practice around the world.

Teacher policy is an important test site for exploring the multifaceted ways in which neoliberal principles have been applied to contrasting ends and conflicting effects. A central narrative in the move to reform teacher preparation is the apparent crisis of teacher professionalism, where teachers—particularly in low-performing education systems—are regarded as underqualified and ineffective (Berliner & Biddle, 1996). Proponents of teacher education reform suggest this crisis can be remedied through free market competition, incentivism, and curriculum standardization. However, the efficacy of mass, efficient, and performance-focused teacher training continues to be widely debated. While critics link neoliberal forces to the deterioration of teacher professionalism, others point to the positive effects of neoliberal teacher certification on student achievement outcomes (Holloway, Sørensen, & Verger, 2017). The lack of critical consensus suggests the need for more contextualized accounts of the theoretical and empirical benefits of neoliberalism on teacher policymaking around the world.

This chapter examines the ways in which neoliberal principles underscore teacher preparation and professionalization pathways in Singapore. With an education system designated high-performing based on international testing benchmarks, Singapore has garnered a great deal of attention and power on the world stage, and its teacher education policies have been lauded as highly effective. "What works" analyses of Singapore's success have typically identified the elements of policy and practice contributing to Singapore's success in comparative international assessments of student achievement (Darling-Hammond et al., 2017). Less often analyzed, however, is the question of "why what works, works" with respect to the shared contexts and contextual specificities of neoliberal education reform. In this chapter, we invite readers to consider, in the case of Singapore, how the preparation of teachers at the undergraduate and graduate levels, as well as the systematic deployment of teachers across the centralized K–12 education system, might be understood within neoliberal frameworks of theory and practice. Understanding that teachers and teaching interact with foundational policy logics and commitments, we pay attention to the organizational structures, governmental processes, and curricular arrangements of teacher preparation in terms of their local enactments. Our goal is not to provide a comprehensive description of teacher education in Singapore, but rather to offer an interpretive depiction of how one country's efforts at programmatic, policy-driven teacher preparation and professionalization have been actualized, specifically in relation to three paradigmatic expressions of neoliberal ideology: social efficiency, performative meritocracy, and curriculum rationality. By extrapolating theoretical understandings from the concrete specifics of one country's high-performing education system, we hope to enrich current understandings of the ideological logics and implementation logistics of neoliberal teacher preparation across diverse cultural and political contexts.

NEOLIBERAL PARADIGMS IN SINGAPOREAN TEACHER PREPARATION: SOCIAL EFFICIENCY, PERFORMATIVE MERITOCRACY, AND CURRICULUM RATIONALITY

As a policy concept and construct, "teacher quality" is hard to define. Its definitions range in scope and specificity, its measures vary across institutional policies and practices, and its enactments are contingent on culture and context. What counts as teacher quality, why and whether it matters in shaping student outcomes, and how it ought to be measured and assessed are all highly contested issues among policy actors, practitioners, and researchers (Berliner, 2005; Connell, 2009; OECD, 2005). To identify and advocate for "what works" in teacher preparation, policymakers, funders, researchers, practitioners, and the media have turned to international benchmarks of teacher quality. The seminal 2010 partnership between the Obama-led U.S. Department of Education, the Organization for Economic Cooperation and Development (OECD), and the United States National Center on Education and the Economy (NCEE) led to two much-cited publications on high-performing education systems: the 2011 OECD report, *Strong Performers and Successful Reformers in Education: Lessons from PISA for the United States*, and the Harvard University Press book, *Surpassing Shanghai: An Agenda for American Education Built on the World's Leading Systems* (Tucker, 2011). In both publications, Singapore is positioned as an "extraordinary success story" (Tucker & Ruzzi, n.d.), home to a first-class education system backed by images of "beautiful, airy school buildings where student artwork, papers, projects and awards are displayed throughout; libraries and classrooms are well stocked; instructional technology is plentiful; and teachers are well trained and well supported" (Darling-Hammond, 2013, p. 114). The NCEE (2018) attributes Singapore's educational success to the quality of its teachers, assured by rigorous teacher education and training, policies of centralization and merit-based evaluation, and a national ethos of schooling that prizes respect for teachers, hard work, and meritocracy. Missing from the analysis in this report, however, is a deeper theoretical account of how neoliberal tenets underpin this apparent formula for success. In what follows, we attempt such an analysis by describing three paradigmatic expressions of neoliberalism—social efficiency, meritocratic performativity, and instrumental rationality—integral to Singapore's teacher preparation strategy and its supporting policies. In conclusion, we return to a consideration of the limits and potentialities of neoliberal doctrine in teacher education reform, posing questions in search of new answers.

SOCIAL EFFICIENCY

Just as public education is the engine of the nation's economy, so public schools are the generators of human capital for the national and global marketplace. Social efficiency ideology (Kliebard, 1987; Schiro, 2008) views public schooling as a primary lever in the capitalist machinery, calibrated to maximize returns of investment from the (re)production of human capital. Drawing on neo-Marxist theories surrounding the function of schools in the reproduction of capitalist relations, social efficiency frameworks aim to align the processes of schooling with the state's social, economic, and political goals (Bowles & Gintis, 1976). Social efficiency arguments draw support from numerous large-scale studies that point emphatically to the long-term benefits of quality assurance systems, buttressed in state policies and practices regarding teacher selection, education, and certification, on student achievement outcomes (Levin, 2018).

Singapore's economic pragmatism can be reflected in the doctrine of "scientific curriculum management" implicit in social efficiency ideology (Bobbitt, 1924; Tyler, 1949), with practices that systematically align the purposes and processes of curriculum-making with the normative goals of socioeconomic progress. Since gaining self-government in 1959 and independence in 1965, Singapore has consistently pursued a social efficiency agenda under the leadership of former Prime Minister Lee Kuan Yew, whose political party, the People's Action Party (PAP), has dominated the country's parliamentary democracy with policies associated with soft-authoritarian governmentality (Tan, 2012). A geographically small sovereign state with virtually no natural resources, Singapore has achieved astounding economic progress over the past 53 years, becoming the country with the third highest GDP per capita, currently ranked fifth on the United Nations Human Development Index (United Nations Development Programme, 2018). Underpinning the state's developmental policies is an ideology of economic pragmatism (Chua, 1995) grounded in a singular master narrative: that the nation's successes are precariously built, its economic viability dependent entirely on foreign investments and its own human resources, and its political stability dependent on the cohesive citizenship of its multiethnic, multilingual society.

Singapore's educational policies are rooted in the country's aspirations to maintain global economic leadership in pace with globalization, technological change, and intellectual capitalism. Since the late 1980s, the public sectors of telecommunications, transportation, healthcare, postal mail, utilities, and national banks have been privatized in a variety of scopes and ways (Yuen, 1989). In line with Washington Consensus recommendations for open markets and aggressive competition, Singapore has embraced the idea that nation-states can thrive in global competition through privatization and deregulation. The number of private and international schools and tuition centers has increased dramatically over the last 10 years. However, the centralization and nationalization of education policy remains a fundamental feature of the country's public education system. The Ministry of Education (MOE) sets policy, program, and practice goals and guidelines for government-funded education, from kindergarten through higher education, maintaining strict oversight over the design of curriculum and assessment, student enrollment, as well as teacher selection, recruitment, and professional development.

Teacher selection, preparation, and development are at the core of Singapore's policy strategy to train students to take on labor needs in the neoliberal global economy (Ashton & Sung, 1997; Gopinathan, 2007; Liow, 2012). Helming the work of teacher preparation is the National Institute of Education (NIE), the country's sole provider of teacher education and certification. Established in 1991, NIE evolved from its earlier status as the country's only teacher training institute to become an autonomous school within the Nanyang

Technological University (NTU), offering both diploma and degree programs at the undergraduate, master's, and PhD levels. NIE is accountable to both the university and the MOE for the quality of its programs and graduates, its mandate for accountability based on the efficient alignment of teacher education curricula with the curriculum structures of public schooling. For example, the training and allocation of teachers according to content knowledge domains is cohesively structured on the national curriculum's "strong classification rules" (Bernstein, 1990). School subjects are taught separately by different subject teachers according to the learning outcomes specified in each subject-based syllabus. Policies maintain a tight link between candidates' undergraduate majors and teaching subjects. University graduates selected to become teacher trainees[1] undergo an 18-month Postgraduate Diploma in Education (PGDE) program that prepares them to specialize in two curriculum subjects. Graduate teachers are encouraged to major in two subjects during their university studies, and the MOE programmatically assigns graduate teachers to teach the subject areas closest to their undergraduate major and minors. A candidate's first undergraduate degree often determines the subject they are assigned to teach. Thus, graduate teachers with training in humanities, science, and mathematics are typically assigned to secondary school English, math, science, and social studies.

PERFORMATIVE MERITOCRACY

Closely aligned to the government's social efficiency framework for educational governance is the ideology of meritocracy. Official rhetoric echoes popular egalitarian conceptions of meritocracy as a nondiscriminatory system of distributive justice that rewards individuals according to merit, where "merit" is a measurable function of individual talent and hard work. To be sure, the notion of meritocracy has long been problematized, and there exists a wealth of philosophical and empirical literature questioning the effectiveness of meritocratic solutions to the problem of educational equity (e.g., Gutman, 1987; Jencks, 1988). Critics of education policy in Singapore, moreover, have examined the ideological role of meritocracy in legitimizing a highly stratified social order governed by administrative elites who are themselves the products of a merit-based education system (Barr & Skrbis, 2008; Lim, 2013; Tan, 2008). Through the lens of critical theory, "merit" is never an isomorphic set of qualities and achievements to be objectively identified and ratified, but a token of symbolic capital institutionally constructed and transacted in the reproduction of power and privilege (Apple, 1979; Bourdieu & Passeron, 1990; Bowles & Gintis, 1976).

Beyond neo-Marxist accounts of the role that schools play in cultural reproduction, what needs to be further recognized is the extent to which Singapore's meritocratic ideals thrive on a neoliberal culture of competitive individualism based on high-stakes performance outcomes. By *performative meritocracy*, therefore, we refer to a culture of competitive enterprise that produces, and is produced by, institutionalized systems of performance-based accountability. Performance-based accountability uses outcomes, in this case student performance on tests, to measure equity and to determine the quality of teachers, leaders, schools, and education systems. Through competition and high-stakes testing, school leaders are incentivized to focus on outcomes, benchmarks, and penalties, while calling on teachers to recognize improvement in achievement scores as an objective proxy of their quality (Ball, 2003). Concomitantly, education authorities and policymakers use information generated from test scores to justify policy actions that correlate teacher quality with student achievement measures (McDermott, 2011). Rankings and school choice schemes thus hold teachers and school leaders accountable to parents and the public, reinforcing the notion of performative meritocracy in the service of test-based standards of excellence. In Singapore, this accountability system is held in place by three "meritocratic" policy solutions: (1) ability-based tracking of students; (2) ability-based selection and placement of teachers; and (3) performance management of teachers.

Ability-based Tracking of Students

Singapore is well known for its ability-based tracking approach to primary, secondary, and tertiary education, enabled by a centrally administered system of high-stakes standardized testing. Students enroll in primary schools (grades 1 to 6) at the age of 7, then proceed to 4 to 5 years of secondary school education, followed by another 2 to 4 years of high school education (in either junior colleges or polytechnics). Student performance on the Primary School Leaving Examination (PSLE) determines placement in secondary school, where students are sorted into three academic "streams"—Special, Express, or Normal—and taught in classes homogeneously filled by students from the same stream. Students who follow the Special or Express pathway take the Singapore-Cambridge General Certificate of Education Ordinary-Level Examination (GCE O-Levels) after 4 years of secondary education, passing which they can then enroll in junior colleges or polytechnics to complete 2 to 3 years of a high school or diploma program respectively in preparation for university entry. Students with PSLE scores lower than those in the Special and Express streams are placed in the Normal stream, where they are further sorted into either the "Academic" or the "Technical" curriculum, with those in the Normal Academic stream given opportunities to move up to the Express stream on the strength of their year-end examination scores. Normal stream students sit for either the GCE Normal (Academic) or GCE Normal (Technical) examinations at the end of 4 years, and typically go on to attend the Institute of Technical Education for vocational training, or to one of two government-funded private institutions for the arts. In Singapore in 2016, 70,310 (39%) students took the

Normal (academic or technical) track of the 180,000 students enrolled in secondary school (Ministry of Education, 2017a).

Ability-based Selection and Placement of Teachers

An underreported feature of Singapore's success formula is its selective placement of teachers, with the most highly educated teachers concentrated in secondary school core academic subjects. Primary mathematics teachers, for example, are recruited from the top 20% of their cohort (Ingvarson & Rowley, 2017). Based on applicants' school transcripts and interviews, the MOE recruits highly qualified candidates (i.e., preservice teacher candidates) for its teacher preparation programs at NIE. NIE collaborates with the MOE in refereeing the academic qualifications, interview selection processes, and curriculum processes of teacher trainees and practicing teachers. In addition to the qualifications-based criteria outlined above, all applicants undergo screening interviews conducted by Ministry officials, in which they are assessed on their dispositions and attitudes toward teaching.

Just as students are tracked along ability-based educational pathways, so too teachers can ascend their career ladders along three distinct professional tracks: Teacher, Leadership, and Specialist. Selection into, and advancement through, these tracks is crucially based on teachers' performance-based competencies. According to the MOE website:

> Education Officers can choose to move across the different career tracks, as long as they satisfy the standards and criteria of the job / career track they aspire to take on. Like any other profession, career advancement is only limited by your own performance and potential. (MOE, 2017b)

The aim of ability-based career tracking, then, is to provide differentiated opportunities for teachers to develop their individual abilities and career aspirations in line with the resource allocation demands of MOE's hierarchical organizational structure, as shown in Table 6.1.

Performance Management

Upon completion of their teacher education programs, teacher trainees become full-time civil-servant employees of the Ministry of Education, and are given a starting monthly salary ranging from 1,750 SGD to 3,500 SGD per month, where trainees with degree qualifications earn more than trainees without degree qualifications (Ministry of Education [Remuneration & Benefits], n.d.). This salary range remains below average relative to 2017 per capita gross national income of 76,863 SGD (26,248 USD) a year, or 6,405 SGD (4,687 USD) per month (Department of Statistics, 2018). Still, Singapore remains one of the few countries in the world that pays all preservice teachers,

Table 6.1. Classroom Teachers' Career Tracks and Their Hierarchical Levels (MOE, 2017)

Teaching Track	Leadership Track	Senior Specialist Track
Senior Teacher	Subject Head / Level Head	Senior Specialist 1
Lead Teacher	Head of Department	Senior Specialist 2
Master Teacher	Vice Principal	Lead Specialist
Principal Master Teacher	Principal	Principal Specialist
	Cluster Superintendent	Chief Specialist
	Director	
	Divisional Director	
	Director-General of Education	

provides free tuition for the completion of a mandatory teacher education program, and offers social security provisions (in the form of monthly contributions to the Central Provident Fund), annual performance bonuses of up to 30% of monthly salary, retention bonuses, sabbaticals, and 100 hours of professional development (Lee & Tan, 2010; National Center on Education and the Economy, 2018). In return for this sizable economic investment, trainees are "bonded" to MOE as teachers for 3 years (Ministry of Education, Post Graduate Diploma in Education, n.d.). The MOE attributes the low attrition rate of approximately 2% to their teacher remuneration and benefits package (Lee & Tan, 2010).

A centralized performance appraisal system, known as the Enhanced Performance Management System (EMPS), is used to evaluate the quality of teachers and school leaders based on an auditable record of performance measures. Detailed and sophisticated, the EPMS allows for quantitative, standardized comparisons of teachers' observable competencies and measurable contributions based on five "Teaching Competency Clusters" (Table 6.2). Built into this appraisal rubric is a system for pegging teachers' performance grades to annual performance bonuses and promotion prospects. To the extent that these performance metrics stand in as summative proxies for teacher quality, teachers must learn to survive and thrive in their career trajectories by evaluating themselves on these same evaluative frameworks (Liew, 2012, 2013). Through a reflexive logic reminiscent of J. L. Austin's theory of linguistic performativity (Austin, 1962), these performance rubrics do not merely describe or prescribe the qualities of high-performing teachers; they crucially *ascribe* to their referents (i.e., the teachers being assessed) the very competencies that will merit annual salary increments and performance bonuses. Initiated into a neoliberal work order of competitive individualism where "merit" is concretely realized in terms of economic capital, teachers are thus exhorted to make "continual enterprise of [them]selves" (Olssen, 1996, p. 340) through (self)managerialist practices that effectively "govern without governing" (Rose, 1999, p. 298). The apparent efficacy of this performative mechanism for disciplining and motivating teachers might

Table 6.2. The Singapore Ministry of Education's Teaching Competency Model (as cited in Sclafani & Lim, 2008)

TEACHING COMPETENCY CLUSTERS				
1. Nurturing the Whole Child	**2. Cultivating Knowledge**	**3. Winning Hearts and Minds**	**4. Working with Others**	**5. Knowing Self and Others**
• Passion and commitment to nurture the whole child	• Subject mastery • Analytical thinking • Initiative • Teaching creatively	• Understanding the environment • Developing others	• Partnering parents • Working in teams	• Tuning into self • Personal integrity • Understanding others • Respecting others

account for why it has become a central motif in teacher remuneration systems. England and Wales, for example, have moved to an entirely performance-based compensation system for teacher salary (Evans, 2011), and performance pay is in use or has recently concluded in China, India, Israel, Kenya, the United States, and in 28 other OECD nations (Woessmann, 2011). In at least 33 countries, value-added modeling is a central part of teacher evaluation policy discourse and experiments, with student performance and teachers' performance appraisals as primary determinants of teacher performance grading (and sometimes teacher pay) (Amrein-Beardsley, Polasky, & Holloway-Libell, 2016; La Londe, 2017; Smith & Kubacka, 2017; Straubhaar, 2017).

CURRICULUM RATIONALITY

The perennial challenges of teacher preparation frame a diverse set of curriculum objectives, ranging from the technical demands of subject content mastery to the ethical dimensions of teachers' beliefs and professional value orientations. Most teacher education programs feature a collection of courses covering both domains of professional competence, although the ratio of distribution might vary considerably. In general, NIE's teacher preparation programs reflect the features of a knowledge-based, skills-oriented, and practice-based curriculum. Teacher trainees in the Postgraduate Diploma in Education (PGDE) programs (see Table 6.3 for the course structure of the PGDE primary school program) must complete courses comprising 19 Academic Units (AUs) of "Education Studies," 26 AUs of "Curriculum Studies and Subject Knowledge," 3 AUs of "Language Enhancement and Academic Discourse Skills," and 13 AUs for "Practicum" or residency training. As the titles and synopses of these courses suggest, the bulk of the teacher education curriculum is devoted to two primary domains of teacher knowledge: *subject content knowledge* and *pedagogical*

Table 6.3. Curriculum structure of the Postgraduate Diploma in Education (PGDE) (Primary) General Program

Category/Subject	Course Code	Title	No. of AUs
EDUCATION STUDIES			
	QED50A	Educational Psychology: Theories and Applications for Learning and Teaching	2
	QED50B	Pedagogical Practices	4
	QED50C	Teacher-Student Relationship	1
	QED50E	Singapore Kaleidoscope	2
	QED50G	Technologies for Meaningful Learning	2
	QED50H	Professional Practice and Inquiry I	0
	QED50J	Professional Practice and Inquiry II	1
	QED50K	Teaching and Managing Learners at the Primary Level	2
	QED50L	*The Social Context of Teaching and Learning*	1
	QED50M	*Character and Citizenship Education*	1
	QED50N	Assessing Learning and Performance	1
	QED50P	Group Endeavors in Service Learning	1
	QED50Q	Effective Parent Engagement for Teachers	1
Total Academic Units			19
CURRICULUM STUDIES AND SUBJECT KNOWLEDGE (any two as assigned)			
English Language	QCE50D	Teaching English at the Lower Primary Level	5
	QCE50E	Teaching English at the Upper Primary Level	4
	QSE50C	Grammar	2
	QSE50D	Children's Literature	2
Mathematics	QCM50C	Teaching and Learning of Primary Mathematics I	3
	QCM50D	Teaching and Learning of Primary Mathematics II	2
	QCM50E	Teaching and Learning of Primary Mathematics III	2
	QCM50G	Assessment in Primary Mathematics	2
	QSM50C	Number Topics	2
	QSM50D	Geometry Topics	2

Category/Subject	Course Code	Title	No. of AUs
CURRICULUM STUDIES AND SUBJECT KNOWLEDGE (any two as assigned)			
Science	QCS50D	Curriculum and Inquiry in Primary Science	3
	QCS50E	Assessment in Primary Science	2
	QCS50G	Pedagogies for Primary Science	2
	QCS50H	Informal Science Learning Environments for Primary Science	2
	QSS50C	Topics in Physical Science for Primary Science Teaching	2
	QSS50D	Topics in Biological Sciences for Primary Science Teaching	2
Social Studies	QCL50D	Teaching Social Studies in the Primary Classroom I	3
	QCL50E	Teaching Social Studies in the Primary Classroom II	2
	QCL50G	Fieldwork in Primary Social Studies	2
	QCL50H	Managing Diversity in Primary Social Studies	2
	QSL50C	Disciplinary Foundations in Primary Social Studies: Geography	2
	QSL50D	Disciplinary Foundations in Primary Social Studies: History	2
Total Academic Units			26
LANGUAGE ENHANCEMENT AND ACADEMIC DISCOURSE SKILLS (LEADS)			
	QLK50A/B	Practical Pronunciation for Teachers	1
	QLK50D	Communication Skills for Teachers	2
Total Academic Units			3
PRACTICUM			
	QPR50A	Teaching Assistantship	3
	QPR50B	Teaching Practice	10
Total Number of Academic Units			52

Source: NIE (2017), p. 20

content knowledge (Shulman, 1987). Only two courses—titled "Social Context of Teaching and Learning" and "Character and Citizenship Education" under the curriculum section "Education Studies"—are explicitly devoted to the philosophy, history, and sociology of education, and these amount to only two AUs out of a total of 58 AUs. The substantive content of these two courses, moreover, is based on the sociocultural and political contexts of teaching in Singapore, with little attention to comparative analyses of education systems from a larger historical and theoretical perspective. The course synopsis for "Social Context of Teaching and Learning," for instance, states:

> This course aims to promote deeper understanding about the socio-political development of the Singapore education system among pre-service teachers at the National Institute of Education. They will appreciate the functions of the education system in socializing citizens for economic, political and social roles in the context of a multi-ethnic and multicultural society. They will have the opportunity to understand the rationale of major education policies and new government initiatives that impact the work of school leaders, teachers, students and other stakeholders in order to achieve the *Desired Outcomes of Education* laid out by the Ministry of Education. At the same time, they will be made aware of the diverse and multiple roles that are played by teachers in the education system. It is hoped that pre-service teachers will become aware of the challenges that teachers face when engaging in pedagogical developments and initiatives in schools, and be empowered to become innovative, effective and caring teachers. Pre-service teachers are encouraged to link the content learnt in this course to what they have learnt in other courses at NIE, as they discuss major challenges and issues in the Singapore education system. (NIE, 2017, p. 31)

As this synopsis indicates, teachers in Singapore should be primarily concerned with the instrumental aim of "socializing citizens for economic, political and social roles" in the Singapore context, so as "to achieve the *Desired Outcomes of Education* laid out by the Ministry of Education." A normative thrust thus underpins this vision of educators "empowered to become innovative, effective and caring teachers," with little emphasis on the ability to critique, question, or challenge these very goals and their assumptions in relation to the ideologies implicit in the Singapore system's socializing enterprise—including the ideologies that we have identified as part of the neoliberal agendas of social efficiency, performative meritocracy, and curriculum rationality.

Taken together, NIE's teacher education curricula can be seen as responsive to at least two of the three neoliberal pressures identified by Sleeter (2008): (1) an emphasis on preparing teachers as technicians, away from explicit equity-oriented teacher preparation; and (2) the privileging of testable content knowledge as part of teachers' professional knowledge. Given its close alignment with the demands of MOE's public school curricula, this "technicist" emphasis on content-focused, practice-based learning outcomes would seem entirely rational, even if the suspicion of an instrumentalist bias might give some pause. At a time when globalization pressures have spurred curriculum innovation and reform, neoliberal forces have also diverted attention away from the politically transformative aims of education towards a depoliticized vision of human development, where knowledge and skills are transacted as economic goods divested of emotional, cultural, and ideological value. It is not surprising, then, that teacher education curricula built on these instrumental goals would give short shrift to the rich traditions of philosophical scholarship on social justice, equity, and critical pedagogy. One could argue, after all, that teacher education for "conscientization" (Freire, 1970) is ideologically at odds with the utilitarian goals of performative meritocracy, insofar as these utilitarian goals might become, ironically, the principled targets of a critically oriented, problem-posing praxis.

The subordination of critical reflexivity to the exigencies of instrumental rationality is further reflected in the MOE's operational definition of "critical thinking." Prized as a key competency necessary for effective participation in the 21st-century knowledge economy, critical thinking features prominently in the official MOE curricula, but is associated with learning outcomes cautiously detached from the term's liberal-democratic valences. Analyzing official curriculum documents as well as ethnographic classroom data from a public secondary school, Lim (2014) has shown how a logic of instrumental rationality undergirds official articulations of how (far) critical thinking should be taught in schools:

> Far from approximating the dispositions of open-ended, discursive inquiry integral to liberal renderings of the subject[,] critical thinking as it is recontextualized in Singapore's mainstream schools continue to take aim at answering the knowledge economy's call for knowledge workers skilled and disciplined in the technologies of information processing. (p. 699)

The appropriation of critical thinking by an ideology of pragmatism thus redirects "higher order thinking skills" toward problem-solving ends rather than problem-posing means. Accordingly, critical thinking should be focused on developing methods to implement the official curriculum efficiently and effectively, rather than on encouraging teachers to critically examine the curriculum's conflicting means, ends, and paradigms in relation to the context-specificities of culture, power, and ideology (Loh, 2016).

Singapore's schooling system has traditionally relied on a tried-and-tested formula of examination-driven pedagogies to realize its social efficiency goals. In an efficiency-driven curriculum, teacher-technicians ensure delivery of a curriculum script that codifies the aims, contents, and pedagogical approaches for each lesson, including the questions that teachers ask of themselves and of students (Rodriguez & Magill, 2016). Curriculum rationality as such favors predictability over diversity, implementation over experimentation. Several classroom-based studies have found that teachers, particularly in the lower-achieving classrooms of the Normal stream, tend to rely on a prescriptive pedagogy, where learning activities are consistently teacher-directed and highly structured, providing little room for active construction of knowledge and concepts (Albright & Kramer-Dahl, 2009; Curdt-Christiansen & Silver, 2013; Kiss & Mizusawa, 2018; Lim, 2014; Towndrow & Kwek, 2017). Once initiated into a school culture of test-directed instrumental rationality, developing teachers quickly see themselves as agents of neoliberal capital, laboring to prepare students for the demands of high-stakes, standardized national examinations. Freire's (1970) critique of the "banking model of education" comes to mind, with the inclusion of teachers themselves as the passive recipients of professional knowledge deposits. In the remainder of this section, we recount two published case studies of teachers in Singapore that illustrate the workings of this banking model and their potential negative effects on teacher identity.

Loh and Hu (2014) followed the experiences of Natalie, a preservice teacher in Singapore; and Gatti and Catalano (2015) followed the experiences of Rachael, a preservice teacher in the United States. Natalie worked in Singapore's Franjipani Primary School, both as a contract teacher before she joined the graduate teacher education program, and for her teaching practicum. As a new teacher, she was supposed to be assigned only 80% of the full official teaching load, but this reduced workload did not fit the efficiency goals of the schools' resource allocation budget. Instead, Natalie had to teach up to 38 periods per week while assuming the responsibilities of an English Language Coordinator. Meanwhile, she described her lessons as "boring" and absent of "real life artifacts" because worksheets and test-based instruction were the primary modes of learning. Her concerns, ideas, and requests for help were often dismissed by her mentor teacher and Head of Department, who would instead redirect her pedagogical efforts towards the school's "tried and tested" methods. After one year, Natalie "seemed depressed and unhappy": She had given up on critical reflection and had "accepted worksheet efficacy and utility" in favor of a largely "product-oriented approach." Eventually, Natalie found her beliefs challenged and changed, her critical disposition "subdued by the neoliberal school culture that she had attempted to resist" (Loh & Hu, 2016, p. 18).

Rachael's professional identity development was similar. Her professional training began with a teacher preparation program in the United States that was a partnership between a university and a venture capitalist-founded, not-for-profit organization. Gatti and Catalano (2015) examined metaphors in programmatic language (e.g., mission, syllabus objectives) in order to draw links between program philosophy and how teachers constructed their identities and the learning-to-teach process. They examined metaphors that reflected two frames of teaching—teaching as a journey and teaching as a business. The business of learning to teach suggested that teachers are knowledge producers and must be highly skilled in "signature strategies" that yield measurable, replicable results. The program sustained an intense focus on testing, gains, and efficiency through a range of sports metaphors (e.g., "champion teachers," "change the pace," "control the game," and "hit rate"), medical terminology (e.g., "resident student"), and competition via quantification (e.g., "price tag," "minutes count"). Rachael did not fare well with this approach—one that emphasized signature pedagogical methods and scripted lesson-planning—as she wanted to empower her students and viewed teaching as a journey. During her teacher practicum, she experienced three main obstacles: programmatic incompatibility, pedagogical paralysis, and programmatic abandonment. Rachael described herself as a "remote control teacher" who lacked agency and power, particularly in her relationship with her mentor teacher. Just as the role of the mentor teacher was to convey what the teacher education program and the school system valued, so her role was to perform what was expected of her. Disheartened by her inability to disrupt and resist the teacher-as-technician model valorized by the school and her mentors, Rachael eventually left the teacher training program.

Drawing on both Natalie's and Rachael's experiences, Gatti and Catalano point to the ways in which the neoliberal approaches "disrupt the humanizing aims of education, replacing those aims with platitudes of career and college readiness" (p. 156). Neoliberalism, they argue,

> is far from a theoretical abstraction for novice teachers; rather, it is instantiated in discrete practices and policies, whether that is the "worksheet syndrome" that the participant in Loh and Hu's (2014) study describes, or Rachael feeling like she has a "price tag" attached to her. (p. 157)

Rachel and Natalie both experienced what Loh and Hu (2014) describe as "praxis shock," a common but critical juncture in beginning teachers' careers where professional responsibilities, policy mandates, and school politics challenge their beliefs about self and teaching. In the face of performance-based accountability pressures, teachers often surrender to the dominant culture's strictures and sanctions, aligning their practices with the neoliberal ideals of social efficiency, performative meritocracy, and curriculum rationality. Teachers who experience praxis shock are likely to succumb to neoliberal pedagogy because they lack the professional self-confidence to resist neoliberal institutional norms and to face superiors who question their thinking (Loh, 2016).

CONCLUSION: THE PROMISES AND PERILS OF NEOLIBERAL PARADIGMS FOR TEACHER PREPARATION

Premised on social efficiency, performative meritocracy, and curriculum rationality, neoliberal stances hold that teacher preparation policies should aim to recruit, train, evaluate, and retain the best by the most efficient means. Singapore's economic success story, featuring the rise of its education system to the top of international testing benchmarks, appears to bear positive testimony to the government's pragmatic pursuit of neoliberal strategies for teacher selection, recruitment, and remuneration policies. Indeed, as numerous quantitative studies on teacher quality (Carnoy, Beteille, Brodziak, Loyalka, & Luschei, 2009; Ingersoll et al., 2007; Ingvarson & Rowley, 2017; Wang, Coleman, Coley, & Phelps, 2003) suggest, countries that consistently perform well on international tests of student achievement, such as Singapore, Finland, and Chinese Taipei, have strong teacher preparation systems characterized by:

- stringent recruitment, selection, and screening policies;
- institutional systems for reviewing, assessing, and accrediting teacher education providers;
- competitive remuneration packages for high-quality entrants who would otherwise enter other professions;
- strong teacher education curricula for ensuring that graduates meet high standards of performance before gaining certification and full entry to the profession.

There remains, of course, more to be said about the lessons to be learned from the Singapore success story. Over the last 40 years, the globalization of neoliberal politics has significantly correlated with rising income inequalities in many parts of the world, alongside concentrations of wealth and privilege amid the weakening of redistributive mechanisms. Similar trends are evident in Singapore: While the median monthly income for employed Singapore households grew by 4.9% in 2015, the Gini coefficient (the most commonly used statistical measure of income distribution among a nation's residents, with 0 representing perfect equality and 1 representing perfect inequality) fell only slightly from 0.464 in 2014 to 0.463 in 2015 (Liang, 2016). With respect to the distribution of teacher capital, some evidence points to the negative social consequences of social efficiency policies over time. A pattern of stratification exists in the relationship between teacher qualifications, school level placement, and teaching subject. Highly educated teachers are concentrated in core academic subject areas in secondary schools. In 2006, approximately 67% of the nearly 26,000-person primary and secondary teacher force were graduates. Thirty-one percent of graduates were placed in primary schools; 84% of nongraduates were placed in primary schools, and 60% of the 5% of teachers who held a master's degree were placed in secondary schools (Tan, Wong, Gopinathan, Goh, Wong, & Ong, 2007). Since then, however, the disproportionate placement of highly educated teachers in secondary schools has lessened. In 2016, approximately 86% of the 30,453 primary and secondary teacher work force were graduates, and 55% of graduates were placed in secondary school (Ministry of Education, Education Statistics Digest, 2017). In 2016, 358 (2%) of primary school teachers held only a GCE O-Level qualification, while just 83 (0.5%) of secondary school teachers held only a GCE O-Level qualification. Additionally, 1,647 (approximately 11%) of primary school teachers held a master's or PhD, compared to 2,538 (approximately 17%) of secondary school teachers.

These statistics encourage policy actors to approach answers to "what works" in teacher education with informed skepticism. Likewise, teachers and teacher educators should critically reflect on how practices and policies that work in favor of some students may work to the disadvantage of others. Concurring with the critical scholarship on teacher education, we argue that teacher education should go beyond teacher training to focus on the development of critical consciousness, social agency, and equity-oriented praxis (Zongyi, 2006). However, rather than simply re-voicing the outcries of neoliberalism's staunchest critics, our goal in this chapter has been to examine the ways in which neoliberal principles are instantiated in the teacher preparation structures of Singapore's educational economy. By acknowledging the successful efforts of neoliberal policymakers and state authorities, we deepen our rationale for an interrogation of contemporary critiques of neoliberalism. To what extent does the case of Singapore exemplify the purportedly negative consequences of subordinating education's critical–emancipatory goals to the rule of social efficiency, performative meritocracy, and curriculum rationality? How will Singapore's success story of teacher preparation shape future recontextualizations of neoliberalism in teacher policy and broader education policy in the country and around the world? How can neoliberal-minded policy elites and educators collaborate more actively in preparing and empowering teacher professionals to fulfill the emancipatory aims of teaching, especially for students who remain the most underserved in schools? These are questions best served by the continuing efforts of critical scholars of education.

NOTE

1. Non-graduates are selectively recruited into NIE's 4-year BA or BSc program based on their academic performance in the GCE A-Level examinations. A preparatory 2-year Diploma in Education (Dip Ed) program, leading to the BA or BSc program, is offered to those who do not meet the minimum A-level requirements but have completed their Singapore-Cambridge General Certificate of Education Ordinary Level (O-Level) examinations, or hold a polytechnic diploma.

REFERENCES

Albright, J., & Kramer-Dahl, A. (2009). The legacy of instrumentality in policy and pedagogy in the teaching of English: The case of Singapore. *Research Papers in Education, 24*(2), 201–222. doi: 10.1080/02671520902867200

Amrein-Beardsley, A., Polasky, S., & Holloway-Libell, J. (2016). Validating "value added" in the primary grades: One district's attempts to increase fairness and inclusivity in its teacher evaluation system. *Educational Assessment, Evaluation, and Accountability, 28*, 139–159. Retrieved from dx.doi.org/10.1007/s11092-015-9234-5

Apple, M. W. (1979). *Ideology and curriculum*. London, UK: Routledge & Kegan Paul.

Apple, M. W. (2017). What is present and absent in critical analyses of neoliberalism in education. *Peabody Journal of Education, 92*(1), 148–153. doi:10.1080/0161956X.2016.1265344

Ashton, D. N., & Sung, J. (1997). Education, skill formation, and economic development: The Singaporean approach. In A. H. Halsey, H. Lauder, P. Brown, & A. S. Wells (Eds), *Education: Culture, economy, society* (pp. 207–218). Oxford: Oxford University Press.

Austin, J. L. (1962). *How to do things with words.* Clarendon, UK: Oxford University Press.

Ball, S. J. (2003). The teacher's soul and the terrors of performativity. *Journal of Educational Policy, 18*(2), 215–228.

Barr, M. D., & Skrbis, Z. (2008). *Constructing Singapore: Elitism, ethnicity and the nation-building project.* Malaysia: NAIS Press.

Berliner, D. C., & Biddle, B. J. (1996). *The manufactured crisis: Myths, fraud, and the attack on America's public schools.* New York, NY: Perseus.

Berliner, D.C. (2005). The near impossibility of testing for teacher quality. *Journal of Teacher Education, 56*(3), 205–213.

Bernstein, B. (1990). *Class, codes and control: The structuring of pedagogic discourse.* New York, NY: Routledge.

Bobbitt, F. (1924). *How to make a curriculum*. Boston, MA: Houghton Mifflin.

Bourdieu, P., & Passeron, J.C. (1990). *Reproduction in education, society and culture*. London, UK: Sage.

Bowles, S., & Gintis, H (1976). *Schooling in capitalist America.* London, UK: Routledge & Kegan Paul.

Carnoy, M., Beteille, T., Brodziak, I., Loyalka, P., & Luschei, T. (2009). *Teacher education and development study in mathematics (TEDS-M): Do countries paying teachers higher relative salaries have higher student mathematics achievement?* Amsterdam, Netherlands: International Association for the Evaluation of Student Achievement.

Chua, B. H. (1995). *Communitarian ideology and democracy in Singapore.* London, UK: Routledge.

Connell, R. (2009). Good teachers on dangerous ground: Towards a new view of teacher quality and professionalism. *Critical Studies in Education, 50*(3), 213–229.

Connell, R. (2013). The neoliberal cascade and education: An essay on the market agenda and its consequences. *Critical Studies in Education, 54*(2), 99–112.

Curdt-Christiansen, X. L., & Silver, R. (2013). New wine into old skins: The enactment of literacy policy in Singapore. *Language and Education, 27*(3), 246–260.

Darling-Hammond, L. (2013). Diversity, equity, and education in a globalized world. *Kappa Delta Pi Record, 49*(3), 113–115.

Darling-Hammond, L., Burns, D., Campbell, C., Goodwin, A. L., Hammerness, K., Low, E., McIntyre, A., Sato, M., & Zeichner, K. (2017). *Empowered educators: How high-performing systems shape teaching quality around the world.* San Francisco, CA: Jossey-Bass.

Department of Statistics. (2018). *Singapore in Figures 2018*. Singapore: Author. Retrieved from www.singstat.gov.sg/-/media/files/publications/reference/sif2018.pdf

Evans, L. (2011). The "shape" of teacher professionalism in England: Professional standards, performance management, professional development and the changes proposed in the 2010 White Paper. *British Educational Research Journal, 37*(5), 851–870. dx.doi.org/10.1080/01411926.2011.607231

Freire, P. (1970/2005). *Pedagogy of the oppressed* (M. B. Ramos, Trans.). New York, NY: Continuum.

Gatti, L., & Catalano, T. (2015). The business of learning to teach: A critical metaphor analysis of one teacher's journey. *Teaching and Teacher Education, 45,* 149–160.

Gopinathan, S. (2007). Globalisation, the Singapore developmental state and education policy: A thesis revisited. *Globalisation, Societies and Education, 5*(1), 53–70.

Gutman, A. (1987). *Democratic education.* Princeton, NJ: Princeton University Press.

Harvey, D. (2005). *A brief history of neoliberalism*. Oxford, UK: Oxford University Press.

Holloway, J., Sørensen, T. B., & Verger, A. (2017). Global perspectives on high-stakes teacher accountability policies: An introduction. *Education Policy Analysis Archives, 25*(85), 1–18.

Ingersoll, R., Boonyananta, S., Fujita, H., Gang, D., Kim, E. G., Lai, K. C., & Wong, A. F. L. (2007). *A comparative study of teacher preparation and qualifications in six nations.* Philadelphia, PA: Consortium for Policy Research in Education.

Ingvarson, L., & Rowley, G. (2017). Quality assurance in teacher education and outcomes: A study of 17 countries. *Educational Researcher, 46*(4), 177–193.

Jencks, C. (1988). Whom must we treat equally for educational opportunity to be equal? *Ethics, 98*(3), 518–533.

Kiss. T., & Mizusawa, K. (2018). Revisiting the *Pedagogy of Multiliteracies*: Writing instruction in a multicultural context. *Changing English, 25*(1), 59-68. doi: 10.1080/1358684X.2017.1403283

Kliebard, H. M. (1987). *The struggle for the American curriculum, 1893–1958.* New York, NY: Routledge.

Kretchmar, K., Sondel, B., & Ferrare, J. J. (2014). Mapping the terrain: Teach For America, charter school reform, and corporate sponsorship. *Journal of Education Policy, 29*(6), 742–759.

La Londe, P. G. (2017). A failed marriage between standardization and incentivism: Divergent perspectives on performance-based compensation in Shanghai. *Education Policy Analysis and Archives, 25*(88), 1–39. doi: 10.14507/epaa.25.2891

Lee, C. K., & Tan, M. Y. (2010, March). *Rating teachers and rewarding teacher performance: The context of Singapore.* Paper presented at APEC Conference on Replicating Exemplary Practices in Mathematics Education, Thailand, March 7–12.

Levin, H. (2018). Studying privatization in education. In H. Levin (Ed.), *Privatizing education: Can the school marketplace deliver freedom of choice, efficiency, equity, and social cohesion?* (pp. 1–17). New York, NY: Routledge.

Liang, C. Z. (2016, Feb 26). Median monthly income for employed Singapore households grew by 4.9% in 2015. *The Straits Times.* Retrieved from www.straitstimes.com/singapore/median-monthly-income-for-employed-singapore-households-grew-by-49-in-2015

Liew, W. M. (2012). Perform or else: The performative enhancement of teacher professionalism. *Asia Pacific Journal of Education, 32*(3), 285–303.

Liew, W. M. (2013). Effects beyond effectiveness: Teaching as a performative act. *Curriculum Inquiry, 43*(2), 261–288.

Lim, L. (2013). Meritocracy, elitism, and egalitarianism: A preliminary and provisional assessment of Singapore's primary education review. *Asia Pacific Journal of Education, 33*(1), 1–14.

Lim, L. (2014). Critical thinking and the anti-liberal state: The politics of pedagogic recontextualization in Singapore. *Discourse: Studies in the Cultural Politics of Education, 35*(5), 692–704.

Liow, E. D. (2012). The neoliberal-developmental state: Singapore as case study. *Critical Sociology, 38*(2), 241–264.

Loh, J. (2016). From fantasy to depression: A beginning teacher's encounter with performativity. *AsTEN Journal of Teacher Education, 1*(1), 1–12.

Loh, J., & Hu, G.W. (2014). Subdued by the system: Neoliberalism and the beginning teacher. *Teaching and Teacher Education, 41*, 13–21.

McDermott, K. A. (2011). *High-stakes reform: The politics of educational accountability.* Washington, DC: Georgetown University Press.

Ministry of Education, Singapore. (n.d.). Postgraduate diploma in education. Retrieved from www.moe.gov.sg/careers/teach/teacher-training-programmes

Ministry of Education, Singapore. (n.d.). Remuneration and benefits. Retrieved from www.moe.gov.sg/careers/teach/remuneration-benefits

Ministry of Education, Singapore. (2017a). Education Statistics Digest. Retrieved from www.moe.gov.sg/docs/default-source/document/publications/education-statistics-digest/esd_2017.pdf

Ministry of Education, Singapore. (2017b). Teach: Career information. Retrieved from www.moe.gov.sg/careers/teach/career-information

National Center on Education and the Economy. (2018). Singapore: Teacher and principal quality. Retrieved from ncee.org/what-we-do/center-on-international-education-benchmarking/top-performing-countries/singapore-overview-2/singapore-teacher-and-principal-quality/

National Institute of Education, Singapore. (2017). *Postgraduate Diploma in Education (PGDE) programme handbook: December 2017 intake*. Retrieved from www.nie.edu.sg/teacher-education/postgraduate-diploma-in-education-programmes-pgde

Olssen, M. (1996). In defense of the welfare state and of publicly provided education. *Journal of Educational Policy, 11*(3), 337–362.

Organisation for Economic Co-operation and Development. (2005). *Teachers matter: Attracting, developing and retaining effective teachers*. Paris, France.

Organisation for Economic Co-operation and Development. (2011). *Strong performers and successful reformers in education: Lessons from PISA for the United States.* OECD Publishing. Retrieved from dx.doi.org/10.1787/9789264096660-en

Rodriguez, A., & Magill, K. R. (2016). Diversity, neoliberalism and teacher education. *International Journal of Progressive Education, 12*(3), 7–23.

Rose, N. (1999). *Powers of freedom: Reframing political thought*. Cambridge, UK: Cambridge University Press.

Schiro, M. S. (2008). *Curriculum theory: Conflicting visions and enduring concerns* (2nd ed). Los Angeles, CA: Sage.

Sclafani, S., & Lim, E. (2008). *Rethinking human capital in education: Singapore as a model for teacher development.* Washington, DC: Aspen Institute. Retrieved from www.aspeninstitute.org/publications/rethinking-human-capital-education-singapore-model-teacher-development/

Shulman, L. S. (1987). Knowledge and teaching: Foundations of the new reform. *Harvard Educational Review, 57*(1), 1–22.

Sleeter, C. (2008). Equity, democracy, and neoliberal assaults on teacher education. *Teaching and Teacher Education, 24*, 1947–1957.

Smith, W. C., & Kubacka, K. (2017). The emphasis of student test scores in teacher appraisal systems. *Education Policy Analysis Archives, 25*(86). doi:10.14507/epaa.25.2889

Straubhaar, R. (2017). The "power" of value-added thinking: Exploring the implementation of high-stakes teacher accountability policies in Rio De Janeiro. *Education Policy Analysis Archives, 25*(91), doi:10.14507/epaa.25.3034

Tan, K. P. (2008). Meritocracy and elitism in a global city: Ideological shifts in Singapore. *International Political Science Review, 29*(1), 7–27.

Tan, K. P. (2012). The ideology of pragmatism: Neo-liberal globalization and political authoritarianism in Singapore. *Journal of Contemporary Asia, 42*(1), 67–92.

Tan, S. K., Wong, A. F., Gopinathan, S., Goh, K. C., Wong, I. Y. F., & Ong, K. H. (2007). The qualifications of the teaching force: Data from Singapore. In R. M. Ingersoll (Ed.), *A comparative study of teacher preparation and qualifications in six nations* (pp. 71–84). Consortium for Policy Research in Education. Retrieved from eric.ed.gov/?id=ED498318

Towndrow, P., & Kwek, D. B. (2017). The teaching of literature in a Singapore secondary school: Disciplinarity, curriculum coverage and the opportunity costs involved. *Asia Pacific Journal of Education, 37*(3), 389–402. doi: 10.1080/02188791.2017.1302923

Tucker, M. C. (2011). *Surpassing Shanghai: An agenda for American education built on the world's leading systems.* Harvard, MA: Harvard Education Press.

Tucker, M., & Ruzzi, B. B. (n.d.) 9 building blocks for a world-class education system. Washington, DC: National Center on Education and the Economy. Retrieved from ncee.org/what-we-do/center-on-international-education-benchmarking/9-building-blocks/

Tyler, R. (1949). *Principles of scientific management*. New York, NY: Harper.

United Nations Development Programme. (2018). Human Development Reports: Singapore. Retrieved from hdr.undp.org/en/countries/profiles/SGP

Wang, A., Coleman, A., Coley, R., & Phelps, R. (2003). *Preparing teachers around the world.* Princeton, NJ: ETS.

Woessmann, L. (2011). Cross-country evidence on teacher performance pay. *Economics of Education Review, 30*(3), 404–418. doi: 10.1016/j.econedurev.2010.12.008

Yuen, N. (1989). Privatization in Singapore: Divestment with Control. *ASEAN Economic Bulletin, 5*(3), 290–318. Retrieved from www.jstor.org/stable/25770219

Zeichner, K. (2010). Competition, economic rationalization, increased surveillance, and attacks on diversity: Neo-liberalism and the transformation of teacher education in the U.S. *Teaching and Teacher Education, 26*, 1544–1552.

Zongyi, D. (2006). Beyond teacher training: Singaporean teacher preparation in the era of new educational initiatives. *Teaching Education, 15*(2), 159–173.

Chapter 7

Teaching Toward Which Ends?

Residency Candidates Navigating Competing Programmatic Aims

Hilary Conklin, Lauren Gatti, and Kavita Kapadia Matsko

> ... One thing that was very obvious that I saw was that [AUSL and DePaul] did not mix well together, in my opinion. It's not just—there was never a clear sense who is in charge of my educational process. Was it DePaul or was it AUSL? ... it just always seemed like you guys were never on the same page ... [you] had two very different philosophies on how to teach people to be educators and it was kind of funny to see. It was like—it's like seeing those two parents that you know are going to get a divorce, but they're trying to stay together for the kids and it's just not working. It's just that's what it felt like in my residency. (Secondary AUSL social studies resident)

In recent years, policy debates have raged over which forms of teacher preparation lead to the best outcomes for K–12 students, particularly for students of color and students living in poverty. Centrally, these disagreements are over programmatic features such as what learning should be prioritized for effective teaching and what the central aims of preparation should be. At the same time, the field of teacher preparation is experiencing declining enrollments (cf. Sawchuk, 2014). The shrinking pool of prospective teachers is leading many university-based teacher preparation programs to partner with non-university-based pathways to bolster their enrollments and, thus, sustain themselves financially. In these arrangements, novice teachers from both pathways—university-based and non-university-based—take common university coursework but, through differing clinical experiences, may learn different overarching messages about the most important purposes and skills for teaching.

Novice teacher learning is a complex phenomenon that requires attention to many overlapping factors and influences, including the purpose of teachers' learning and the social forces shaping teacher learning (Zeichner & Gore, 1990). Differing pathways might prioritize different central purposes of teacher learning, such as teaching toward democratic orientations (Zeichner,

2003) or learning to follow teaching scripts (Walsh, Glaser, & Wilcox, 2006). These varied features of preparation pathways do not shape teachers' learning in neat, linear ways; rather, learning to teach—in *any* pathway— is a complex, recursive, and often deeply conflictual process (Britzman, 2003; Gatti, 2016). As many university-based teacher preparation programs—especially those in high poverty, urban contexts—increasingly house multiple pathways and partnerships, reconciling and meaningfully integrating differing messages about teaching and learning becomes even more complex.

In this chapter, we illuminate how two individuals preparing to be secondary English teachers in a 1-year pathway sponsored by the Chicago-based urban teacher residency program, Academy for Urban School Leadership (AUSL), and DePaul University's Master in Education program (where one of the authors teaches) experienced and navigated divergent programmatic aims during their residency year and into their first year of teaching. These cases are drawn from a larger, longitudinal study in which we explored how students in DePaul's graduate program and those in the AUSL graduate program learned to teach through their student teaching/residency year and their first year in Chicago Public Schools.

In Spring 2016, we conducted two classroom observations for each resident as they completed their residency placement, and two interviews, one prior to and one following the classroom observations. We also interviewed four program instructors—two at DePaul and two at AUSL—who were close to resident experience, to gain insight into each pathway's programmatic priorities. In school year 2016–2017, we then conducted two rounds of classroom observations with each AUSL teacher in their first year of teaching; we observed 2 consecutive days each in Fall and Spring, followed by an interview.

We focus on two AUSL residents, Abe and Lori. In particular, we shed light on the complicated ways they each negotiated the respective programmatic aims of DePaul (where they completed all of their master's coursework) and those from AUSL (where they were employed, mentored, and coached to teach in the AUSL network of schools). We begin by showing how our participants' DePaul professors and Mentor Resident Coaches (MRCs) from AUSL understood, enacted, and prioritized their respective individual and programmatic aims. Then we offer illustrative examples of how Abe and Lori negotiated the competing aims they experienced in their teacher preparation.

We argue that both AUSL and DePaul strive to prepare teachers to work successfully in underserved communities; however, AUSL places greater priority on classroom management techniques and measurable student learning gains, while DePaul places greater priority on social justice–oriented, democratic aims, and the social theories of learning underpinning teachers' decisionmaking in the context of particular content areas. Over the course of their residency year and subsequent first year of teaching, each AUSL resident thoughtfully processed these overlapping but sometimes competing aims, integrating some with their own personal aims for teaching while actively rejecting others. By analyzing what the programmatic priorities and aims for teaching in underserved communities are in each program and how AUSL residents make sense of them, this chapter illuminates a crucial dimension of teacher preparation that lies at the heart of current policy debates. As these partnerships continue to proliferate, we assert that it should be the burden of the programs—rather than the candidates—to take on the hard work of navigating their shared responsibility for preparing teachers and deliberating the larger aims, or the "teaching toward which ends?"

To preface the discussion that follows, it's important to note that the experiences we discuss below represent one particular moment in time for these programs. In this case, our data come from the inaugural year of partnership between AUSL and DePaul's secondary education program; because of shifts in AUSL's needs in secondary schools, this partnership has not continued. Additionally, our focus in this study—and the majority of the data collection—was about the experience of the teacher residents, their perspectives, and their practices. We worked to gain insight into each program's aims and practices through a selection of interviews and document review; however, we recognize that teacher preparation programs are complex and ever evolving, and acknowledge that the range of curricular emphases featured in each program may extend beyond what we discuss.

ACADEMY FOR URBAN SCHOOL LEADERSHIP

Academy for Urban School Leadership (AUSL) was founded in 2001 by Chicago venture philanthropist Martin Koldyke, Donald Feinstein, and then-CEO of Chicago Public Schools (CPS), Arne Duncan. The program's initial aim was to prepare teachers through a residency model of teacher preparation to teach in the city's underserved and underperforming schools. AUSL's teacher residency program (one of the first residency programs in the country) is based on the medical model of apprenticeship, where novice professionals are paid to learn alongside an experienced mentor and in the real-world context of that profession. In 2006, AUSL expanded their reach in CPS to include school management, creating an independent district-within-a-district. When schools in CPS are labeled failing and slated for turnaround or transformation, they fall under either the aegis of CPS's Office of School Improvement or of AUSL. AUSL currently manages a network of 31 turnaround schools and training academies (schools that have been designated as resident preparation sites), 26 of which are elementary schools and five of which are high schools.

AUSL's residency is focused on attracting and retaining teacher candidates (especially teachers of color and career changers) who are committed to learning to teach in and to staying within AUSL's network of schools. To that end, residents are paid a living stipend for their residency year and are eligible for discounted tuition at one of AUSL's partner universities where they earn their master's degree and their teaching credential. Residents take intensive summer coursework through AUSL leaders as well as with the university partner. Then, during the residency year, AUSL residents are placed in pairs in one of AUSL's training academies. There, they teach Monday through Thursday under the guidance of an AUSL-selected mentor teacher and with additional support from Mentor Resident Coaches (MRCs). Residents attend their university courses at DePaul on weekday evenings and during the day on Fridays, which leads to a master's degree and certification in their area. After successful completion of the residency year—which includes the opportunity to be interviewed and hired for employment in one of AUSL's network schools—residents must remain teaching in CPS for 4 years. If they do not complete this contractual obligation, they are required to repay a prorated portion of their graduate tuition and AUSL stipend.

As a program, AUSL aims to provide "Chicago Public Schools with high-quality teachers prepared to succeed within the demanding conditions of tragically underperforming urban schools" (Academy for Urban School Leadership, 2017). In AUSL's daily work with residents, this overarching mission translates into a clearly structured framework—the "matrix"—that helps residents learn and practice a specific set of defined skills that is intended to enable them to manage classrooms effectively and focus their classrooms on learning. The matrix outlines the scope and sequence of AUSL's monthly instructional cycles, each of which is focused on a different domain from Charlotte Danielson's (2007) framework as well as a particular set of techniques from Doug Lemov's book *Teach Like a Champion* (2010). These techniques are what residents are then assessed on. For example, the matrix requires that all residents practice Lemov's technique of "100%," the idea that classrooms must have a standard of 100% student compliance at all times, during a particular 5-week block (Lemov, 2010).

AUSL's aim to help candidates learn and practice these specific strategies through repetition in the classroom is facilitated by site-based teacher educators, Mentor Resident Coaches (MRCs). MRCs are former teachers and mentors from AUSL's network of schools who are situated within AUSL's training sites and are responsible for supporting, mentoring, observing, and conferencing with between eight and 10 residents (from across disciplines) who are placed in that school. One of the most important things MRCs are responsible for is supporting the resident's practice of the techniques outlined in the matrix. Jim, one of the MRCs, explained:

> So the plan is, for example, one of the strategies might be habits of discussion, right? . . . to have teachers figure out a way so that there's more ratio on students than there are on teachers, right? That's a hugely important thing for teachers to do. And so we really systematically are saying . . . between January 1st and February 15 you're going to work on this habit of discussion by using sentence stems for kids and then I'll coach around that.

The MRCs' emphasis on helping residents practice and hone skills and techniques outlined in AUSL's matrix was linked to the corollary priority of managing the classroom. As Ron, the other MRC, explained,

> . . . we basically hit on management [and] instruction on Domains 2 and 3 in Danielson's framework. I think those are the things that you can see [most] in the classroom. . . . [That's] not to say we don't hit planning and professionalism as well, but you can't teach a class of kids if you can't manage a classroom.

When asked to elaborate on the purposes of classroom management, Ron explained:

> To not have students be kicked out of a room I think is sort of like the end piece, right? [I]f a student's out of the room which means the student isn't learning . . . those kids have 180 days, you have 180 days to get them from A to B. A day outside of your classroom or an hour outside of your classroom is a deficit model. Instead of how do I be proactive instead of reactive to management. And so making sure that residents have something on their tool belt to use so that it's not—it doesn't get to that point, right? And so that's why it's such a focus.

While coaching residents to learn classroom management strategies is one primary aim of the AUSL program, the AUSL network also emphasized helping residents learn common sets of standards and a common curriculum. Jim noted that, in addition to coaching residents on the strategies specified in the matrix, "We use Engage New York as our curriculum in AUSL, so helping people internalize that." Further, he said his instructional priorities included "helping teachers internalize what it looks like to do Common Core aligned work with their students so that they can push their kids' thinking."

Jim and Ron's description of the content and purpose of their MRC work—practicing Lemov techniques from the matrix, working with the AUSL Engage New York curriculum, and managing the classroom—illustrates how the larger programmatic aims become actualized, embodied, and practiced by residents under the direction of the MRCs. AUSL aimed to prepare residents to be ready for their first day of independent teaching and viewed cycles of practice and the assessment of a specific, discrete set of teaching skills and management strategies as the best way to prepare residents for their work in urban schools.

DEPAUL UNIVERSITY

DePaul became AUSL's university partner for secondary teacher preparation in 2015 in part to address what AUSL saw as the need for content-specific preparation for its secondary residents, especially related to pedagogical content knowledge. DePaul is a Vincentian, Catholic university focused on, according to its mission statement, "a sensitivity to and care for the needs of each other and of those served, with a special concern for the deprived members of society" (DePaul Mission Statement, 2018, p. 4). DePaul's College of Education (COE) mission stems from and feeds this larger university mission, aiming to prepare teachers, counselors, and leaders who "are committed to creating equitable, compassionate, intellectually rich, and socially just environments" (DePaul College of Education, 2018). The Vincentian foundations of DePaul underly the central aims of the COE, which is to "cultivate the social conscience, understandings, and practices necessary to address social inequities among and with individuals, communities, and institutions" (DePaul College of Education, 2018).

AUSL residents preparing to be secondary teachers earned their master's degree and certification through DePaul's secondary education program. (See Table 7.1 for course sequencing.) When asked about the overarching purposes and priorities of DePaul's teaching philosophy, Hilary (one of this chapter's authors and the Secondary Education program instructor and director during the 2015–16 year in which Abe and Lori were residents) shared her thinking on how DePaul's mission is implemented in the secondary program. "[I]t's uneven," she said. "I think most of the secondary program faculty share a broad view of aiming to teach all learners, and aiming to teach in sort of broadly constructivist ways. I think beyond that it breaks down a little bit." The secondary program also follows a set of learning outcomes it has developed that, as Hilary explained,

> are all connected to [DePaul's] Vincentian idea . . . [Y]ou have to reach all your students. So we're thinking about diverse learners, . . . they're thinking about their special ed class, they're thinking about English language learners, and that you have to reach all students. I think that is reflected in all of our standards.

Aside from these broad orientations, Hilary described a range of specific aims featured in program coursework that varied depending on the instructor and the course. Some faculty members highlight Charlotte Danielson's framework (Danielson, 2007), for example, while others, like Hilary and another colleague, centralize Fred Newmann's Authentic Intellectual Work framework (cf. Newmann, King, & Carmichael, 2007). Similarly, some coursework emphasizes the role of structural inequalities in education and aims to help students understand how factors like race and culture shape students' experiences in schools.

DePaul's programmatic priorities are further complicated by obligations to meet various state level requirements, such as the state-required Education Teacher Performance Assessment (edTPA) along with addressing the Illinois

Table 7.1. DePaul course sequence for AUSL residents

Summer Quarter 2015	Fall Quarter 2015	Intersession 2015	Winter Quarter 2016	Spring Quarter 2016
AUSL residents take full-time coursework day time and evening	*AUSL residents in high school residency site full time Monday – Thursday with weekday evening and Friday day time classes*			
Curriculum and Instruction in Secondary Education (C)	Teaching (content area) in the High School 1 (I)	Psychology and Education of the Exceptional Child (C)	Teaching (content area) in the High School 2 (I)	Assessment Issues in Secondary Education (C)
Human Development and Learning: Secondary (C)	First content course (I)		Second content course (I)	Register for Student Teaching (C)
Education and Society (C)	Reading and Writing across the Curriculum (C)		Doing Critical Practitioner Research in Education (C)	Student Teaching Reflective Seminar/ EdTPA (C)
Teaching Adolescent English Language Learners across the Curriculum (C)				

Note: (C) indicates course taken only with cohort of AUSL residents on Fridays during the daytime; (I) indicates integrated course taken with AUSL residents and other DePaul Secondary Education Master's students on weekday evenings.

Professional Teaching Standards. Additionally, because DePaul wanted its graduates to be eligible to teach in International Baccalaureate (IB) schools, program faculty must also incorporate standards for IB certification into their coursework.

DePaul's priorities are further differentiated by content areas. Because Lori and Abe were preparing to be secondary English teachers, they were required to take a two-term sequence in Secondary English Methods at DePaul. These courses were taught by Matthew, a faculty member who had been teaching secondary English methods and content area literacy at DePaul for over 15 years. As part of the secondary education faculty, Matthew was responsible for attending to specific requirements related to state licensure, the edTPA, and Illinois Professional Teaching Standards. These requirements, which include an emphasis on instructional planning, delivery, and assessment, surfaced clearly when Matthew was asked to share his priorities for teaching secondary English methods courses. He said,

> For me, the major goal is to help them understand the relationship between assessment activities, and objectives, or standards. So being able to sort of create that connection. If they have a particular objective they're trying to meet, then what type of activities are going to position students to try out and practice meeting that objective in a meaningful way? Then how are you going to assess that objective so that students can demonstrate what they learned? Then beyond that, what are you going to do for students who are struggling?

Matthew extended this thinking, however, by explaining the ways in which he took "procedural type of things" such as instructional planning and used them to think philosophically about the why and how of his work as a secondary English teacher educator. These nuts-and-bolts requirements were couched within larger questions related to the purpose of teacher preparation.

> [W]hat [do] we want for students? . . . what are our obligations to students? We have this content that we want them to learn, or that they're expected to learn. What's our obligation in preparing them? How do we give them the practice? How do we create the relevancy that sort of puts them in a position to succeed?

Matthew worked to make things relevant for his students by modeling the kinds of practices he wanted his novice English teachers to enact, intellectual and pedagogical goals that included "engaging different perspectives" and the ability to "recognize other people's experiences." Most importantly, Matthew's goal for his secondary English students was to understand that "the meaning that's created within the English Language Arts classroom needs to sort of percolate from student experience, from what's going on in student's lives."

Matthew understood classroom management to be related to the quality and purpose of the work they are doing in English Language Arts. When asked to share his definition of classroom management, he explained,

> I think classroom management is a product of student engagement, or lack of engagement. In my own teaching, classrooms have always been kind of messy and chaotic, I'm usually the quietest person in my classrooms. I don't mind the chaos. I don't mind the messiness, but I know that for many people classroom management is an issue. I would define

> classroom management as the classroom environment. What opportunities are you providing for students to express themselves in meaningful ways? Because if you don't provide those type of opportunities, they're going to express themselves in other ways.

Classroom management, therefore, was understood to be a function of student engagement.

Thus, at DePaul, the mission to create "equitable, compassionate, intellectually rich, and socially just environments" and "cultivate the social conscience, understandings, and practices necessary to address social inequities" was lived out in various forms across the program coursework and interwoven with additional frameworks that individual faculty used to instruct their teacher candidates, including the AUSL residents. DePaul faculty members' approach to preparation focused on both conceptual and practical ideas related to teaching and learning designed to prioritize student engagement as a vehicle to classroom management.

FOCAL CASES

Lori

Lori Alvarez, a Cuban American female, grew up in the northern suburbs of Chicago and completed her undergraduate degree in English at a large Midwestern university. She was passionate about English throughout her schooling, and that passion guided her toward her decision to teach. Despite limited early experiences with students, she knew early on in her undergraduate program that she not only wanted to teach, but also had a clear sense of where and why she wanted to teach. She recalled, "I've always said I'm never going to teach in the suburbs, and it's not the suburbs' fault. They're fine, but these kids [on the west side of Chicago] need me way more." This commitment to equity led her to apply to the highly publicized program Teach For America (TFA) during her senior year. Although she was ultimately not accepted into TFA, going through the application process allowed her to learn about and eventually realize her preference for AUSL. A week after her interview with AUSL, she was accepted into the secondary English program. The combination of location (Chicago), the depth and timing of the residency's clinical experience, and the fact that she would be earning a master's degree while teaching sealed her decision to enter the program.

Lori's Residency Year. Lori spent most of her residency year at Caraballo High School, one of the top 20 high schools in the city of Chicago (see Table 7.2). Her residency experience also included two 2-week residencies at Simmons School.

Table 7.2. School Contexts

School	Resident	Student demographics	Percentage low-income students	School Rating	Students enrolled
Caraballo	Lori (primary residency site and first year of teaching)	94% Hispanic; 5% Black	95%	Level 1+ (highest rating): Good standing	1,185
City Academy	Abe (primary residency site)	62% Hispanic; 20% White; 12% Black; 5% Asian	83%	Level 1: Good standing	545
Edwards	Abe (5 weeks during residency)	98% Black	99%	Level 2: Intensive support	262
Simmons	Abe and Lori (2 weeks during residency)	98% Black	94%	Level 2: Intensive support	622
Urban Arts	Abe (first year of teaching)	38% Black; 33% Hispanic; 19% White; 2% Asian	46%	Level 1+ (highest rating): Good standing	613

Lori vividly recalled her first days as a resident. "I was so frightened. I'd never been in a classroom [in a teaching role] my entire life." Her mentor teacher would often step out of the classroom so that Lori and her co-resident could step up and teach. As time went on, her solo teaching experiences became lengthier, morphing into "lead teaching experiences" where AUSL residents assumed full lead-teaching responsibilities in the classroom, often 4 days at a time.

Learning how to manage the classroom was the first thing Lori remembers being prioritized in the AUSL part of her preparation: "making sure students aren't acting out, how to control them . . . this was like all we focused on for like the first 3 months of school." Despite the fact that she was also attending DePaul for her teacher preparation, when she reflected upon her preparation at the end of her first year of teaching on the extent to which DePaul was shaping her development as a teacher, Lori quickly offered "Zero percent." After some consideration, she revised her thinking and commented that learning about the effect of poverty on education in her summer foundations coursework at DePaul had influenced her: "I didn't really . . . see myself as privileged and like digging into that, into why you think the way you think" was valuable. She also acknowledged that although she learned a great deal about planning at DePaul, her most powerful learning came from her experiences planning daily for students through her residency.

With a foot in both worlds, Lori reported feeling confused by what she termed "conflicting information" from each program. For example, she said her English methods instructor:

> . . . takes things a lot slower than we do. He thinks an engaging lesson includes the teacher reading multiple chapters of a book out loud to the class. I think that there is value in reading to your students but I don't think I can do that, I don't think they'll be engaged for that long. Like we just do things as efficiently as possible.

Lori's practice with and exposure to efficiency as a goal came primarily through her mentor teacher. Lori said, "I probably wouldn't have learned half the things that I know now if she didn't push me so much." Lori's perseverance during residency paid off. After successfully subbing for a teacher on maternity leave at Caraballo at the end of her residency, Lori was the only secondary English AUSL resident to get a job there. She would be teaching English to freshmen and juniors.

Lori's First Year of Teaching. The fact that Lori spent a full year in the classroom as a student, combined with being hired at the same school in which she completed her residency, resulted in a smoother transition into her first teaching year than what might be considered typical. "This year is so much easier [than residency]," she reflected. "It's weird because that is not usually what you hear. This does not feel like my first year of teaching, which is amazing." When thinking about the ways in which she felt most prepared to teach, Lori characterized her comfort in just being around the students and her ability to flexibly plan lessons in response to the students' shifting needs as her key strengths. No longer a resident, Lori relished the opportunity to make her own instructional reading materials. However, this love for creating original materials conflicted with AUSL's preference for more scripted curriculum like Engage New York. Lori found it difficult to connect with materials that she had not developed or into which she had little input.

Another reason the Engage New York curriculum proved to be challenging for Lori related directly to her aims in teaching English. In reflecting on the Engage curriculum's inclusion of excerpted classic texts, Lori said,

> I can't imagine (how) you go through your entire high school career without reading an entire book. That is just horrific to me . . . I want [my students] to love to read, like I really just want them to enjoy reading and thinking about the bigger concepts in life, especially now.

Instead of adhering to the prescribed Engage curriculum, Lori opted to organize literature circles around key works for her students, prompting her school-based mentor resident coach to encourage Lori to return to the Engage curriculum. Because of her former status as a resident, Lori felt obligated to comply with such directives, but then reflected more critically: "Sometimes, I forget I'm a real teacher. . . . This is my room and I can't let people tell me what to do, because these are my kids." Over the course of the year, Lori learned to amplify and use her voice, something that she did not exercise often as a resident.

Lori's Navigation of Competing Program Aims: Doing What I Was Told to Do . . . Like most individuals entering a teacher education program, Lori entered hers with very little classroom experience and therefore relied fully on AUSL and DePaul to prepare and shape her for the work of teaching. Aside from her desire to share her love for literature with her students, she was still in the process of forming her own aims for teaching English. In fact, when asked about her aims during her preparation experience, she noted, "I don't even know really if I can speak on what my philosophy is versus what I'm being told to do. . . . All I really know is what I've been told."

Even in the moments when she would internally question the messages she was receiving through AUSL and DePaul, she ended up favoring the views of her mentor and the AUSL program. For instance, Lori struggled to understand the request for her students to "speak louder" because she thought it to be countercultural to their communication style and was worried about being perceived as "mean"; however, she followed through on the feedback she received because she thought it necessary to develop and express authority.

And while she questioned why compliance was so strongly emphasized in her AUSL preparation, she also feared becoming a teacher who could not manage her classroom effectively. She recalled, "I've seen teachers who have no control over their classroom and have no ability to teach because they [the students] walk all over them." The emphasis on behavior management in AUSL strongly influenced Lori and her peers' thinking, particularly in the residency year, and often resulted in dissonance in their coursework at DePaul. For example, when she took her second English methods class, she had been in her residency for almost 6 months. She reflected on some of the methods course experiences that required them to do in-class, practice-teaching demonstrations:

> My peers in the DePaul classroom have not even been in a classroom yet[1]. And like it was hard for us to communicate with them . . . .and I don't blame them at all obviously . . . The teaching demonstrations were so awkward because [my DePaul peers] would say things [providing critiques]—because we'd do a lot of behavior management because that's what we do, and they would be like, that's weird . . . And then they'd do [their demonstrations] and we'd be like "everyone was talking and nobody was listening."

While activities such as the teaching demonstration provoked dialogue in class, a general sense of incongruence between AUSL's and DePaul's priorities prevailed throughout the year. In part, Lori explained, this was because of vastly differing philosophies between the two programs, but it was also because the AUSL program had been newly transferred to DePaul, and there was limited communication between the two entities. She said, "There was so much conflicting information, and no one communicated by any means."

In addition to experiencing vastly differing messages about teaching and learning, the AUSL residents found it hard to take up the content of DePaul's coursework in any meaningful way due to sheer exhaustion. Lori said, "We were dying. Working all day and then coming to class until 9 P.M. and then waking up again at five, working all day. I had Monday and Tuesday night classes the last quarter . . . I was like delusional . . . we (were) struggling very, very hard to survive." The timing and urgency of their residency schedules often meant that the needs of the students in their residency classroom the next morning trumped coursework assignments. There was little time to think about and respond to the things they were learning, much less to develop and articulate clear aims. Lori noted this challenge of not having enough time to reflect on her personal aims during her residency year, saying, "I think I'll probably figure that out more when I have time to be alone in the classroom."

Lori's distance from AUSL requirements in her first year as a teacher of record provided her space to consider and sharpen her own views about teaching, but she continued to be anchored by the AUSL strategies she thought she should be using. She reflected,

> I'm not as strict as I probably should be. . . . I don't mind when students call out answers when they're super excited. Like I will tell them to raise their hands but I'm not going to chastise them for it. I want the classroom environment to be a space where students feel comfortable to say what they think. Actually, when you're a resident, though, you're so much more strict . . . it's black and white because you are still learning. . . . Once you are a teacher, you can put it in a gray area.

Lori's experience in AUSL was intentionally organized to leave little room for alternative perspectives and expectations, particularly around behavior management, but in her own classroom, she felt much more agency to make decisions about how to use "the strategies" and toward what ends.

Abe

When Abe Fuller, a White male, began the AUSL residency, he was considerably more seasoned than many of his resident peers. At age 35, he brought more work and life experiences to his practice than most of the others in his secondary education cohort. He held both a bachelor's degree in English literature and a master of fine arts degree in creative writing, and had prior experiences teaching writing to 18- to 21-year-olds, working for several magazines, and starting and editing his own magazine. Knowing he wanted to teach writing, and after talking with close friends and relatives who had gone through and worked in the elementary AUSL program, he pursued AUSL's secondary program in English education. Although he had heard some stories that concerned him about AUSL's discipline-oriented emphasis, he was persuaded to apply after seeing a high school teacher in an AUSL school run what he viewed as a warm and nurturing classroom. While Abe entered the program with a deep commitment to working in underserved schools, he was primarily motivated by the efficiency of AUSL's year-long path to teaching certification.

Abe's Residency Year. Abe spent his AUSL residency year primarily at City Academy—AUSL's first teacher training site—where he taught English to two classes of freshmen and two classes of sophomores. During his residency year, he also spent time at two schools with significantly different student demographics and higher poverty rates: 5 weeks at Edwards Academy High School, also an AUSL training academy, and 2 weeks at Simmons Academy, one of AUSL's turnaround schools (see Table 7.2).

Abe's residency experiences were significantly shaped by these different school settings as well as the mentors with whom he worked. His primary mentor at City Academy was a 20-year teaching veteran whom Abe described as very hands-off. While she gave Abe considerable autonomy in his teaching—which he appreciated—she did not always model the specific strategies that AUSL trained residents on during their summer professional development experience. His mentor's and City Academy's more "loose" approach to discipline aligned with his approach and personality better than the stricter AUSL tactics, but he was continually evaluated on his use of the AUSL strategies and grew concerned that he was not seeing the required "moves" being modeled. It was in part because of this disconnect that Abe went to Edwards, where he worked with a mentor who modeled the AUSL strategies in more consistent and visible ways.

However, Abe was troubled by what he viewed as Edwards's rigid and punitive approaches to discipline, practices he saw as being closely connected to the African American composition of the student body. He noted that, despite the students being similarly behaved to those at City Academy,

> . . . this student body [at Edwards] is being walked through metal detectors, given demerits when they do things that are bad, and . . . [getting] sent to what's called "refocus," which is this room where they sit with the dean and they don't do any school work and they sit in the room for the rest of the period. . . .

Abe recalls being urged by his Edwards MRC to give students demerits, which ran counter to his own beliefs about the best disciplinary practices for students. As he explained, when a student is misbehaving:

> . . . you have to find a way to fuel that kid or get that kid interested or have them stay after with you and do some extra work. . . . And then there's this [other way of thinking] at urban schools in particular where it's like no, you send them to the dean and the dean deals with it. And I'm so fundamentally opposed to that.

Abe's First Year of Teaching. After interviewing for a position teaching English at Caraballo (Lori's residency site) and being turned down for it, Abe secured a high school English teaching position out of the AUSL network, at a Chicago public high school focused on the arts with a diverse student population (see Table 7.2). According to Abe, Urban Arts enacts restorative justice practices. He was hired there after an interview in which he emphasized his beliefs in the importance of building relationships and using formative assessment. Abe noted that the students at the school are passionate about whatever form of arts they are pursuing.

Abe's Navigation of Competing Program Aims: Picking and Choosing. Like Lori, when Abe reflected on his experience learning to teach, he noted that much of what DePaul espoused seemed to be in direct conflict with what AUSL espoused. When we asked how he reconciled the seeming contradictions between AUSL's and DePaul's perspectives, Abe said, "You get to pick and choose which ones you really believe in and stand by." Across Abe's residency year and his first year of teaching, he shifted in his assessment of the relative value of AUSL's and DePaul's primary aims, taking more from AUSL initially but more from DePaul as he embarked on his own classroom.

Although he had significant critiques of AUSL's approach, by the end of his residency year he seemed to be a strong proponent of many of the behavior management strategies he had learned. Reflecting at the end of his residency year, he noted that implementing many of the AUSL strategies led to his classroom operating more efficiently, such as "starting every class with a timed activity" and "getting everybody back at 100% . . . [That's] key because if you get 100% attention then it's very, very easy to see who's getting off task or who's trying to disrupt the class." Thus, Abe saw the utility of the various *Teach Like a Champion* strategies AUSL had taught him. At the same time, he also felt that AUSL overemphasized these strategies and, in doing so, took away some of the human element of teaching. He explained:

> . . . with some of these [*Teach Like a Champion*] strategies, when you finish this program, if you're good at these strategies they could drop you at any school anywhere and you'll be able to command a classroom . . . However, I think that in trying to train us to manage the classroom so that we have the most time for educational, student-centered learning, I feel that a line has been crossed that we're spending so much time on the behavior management stuff that the students' selves get kind of lost in the shuffle.

In short, Abe felt that teachers in AUSL schools often spent too much time getting students to behave.

As he rounded out his residency year, although he dismissed some of what DePaul offered him as idealistic and disconnected from what is actually required in schools, Abe also found that some of what he learned in DePaul's program about the social contexts that shape schooling helped him make sense of what he was troubled by in AUSL schools. He said:

> [I]t's actually a really cool thing . . . to get these theories and to read *Tuck In Your Shirt*, which is this amazing essay about how terrible uniforms are. And then go into [an AUSL] school that has uniforms where people are telling people to tuck their shirt in.

Some of what he learned at DePaul, then, provided a framework in which to situate his practical experiences, but did so over time and in non-linear ways.

Similarly, Abe noted how some DePaul coursework shaped his thinking. He said, "I had some . . . social justice–minded education classes that were really influential in kind of opening my eyes to certain things that were happening." This coursework appeared to shape his understanding of what he viewed as racist practices in some of the AUSL schools he visited:

> being in a program where I go to [Edwards] and [Simmons] which are 100% African American and there's metal detectors and there's no door ... on the bathroom stalls—and there's the high security presence. And deans, multiple deans, and you can just send the students to, like, a room to sit. And then being here [at City Academy] which is, like, 15% African American and mostly, you know, Hispanic and Polish ... I mean ... it's still low income, right? But they're not African American and they're not being treated like prisoners.

Thus, while Abe found less of immediate practical value from his coursework at DePaul during his residency, the emphasis he learned there on justice-oriented perspectives more broadly shaped his critiques of some of AUSL's practices.

Yet, once Abe entered a new school context in his first year of teaching and was no longer immersed in AUSL's practices or schools, he ultimately abandoned much of his AUSL strategy repertoire and leaned more heavily on the aims and practices emphasized in his DePaul coursework. While at the beginning of his first year of teaching he drew from his AUSL strategies—cold calling, positive narration, clapping to get attention—he began to get resistance from his new group of students and also to feel that he wasn't being authentic to who he was as a teacher. He explained:

> ... I started to do the AUSL stuff and would get so much push back. They'd be like, [Mr. Fuller], we do not do this at this school. This is not who we are.... And it only took like a week to be like you know what, I don't have to do that this year, and I'm not going to.... I'm just going to be myself, which is all I ever wanted to do last year, and see how that works. It's been great.

While Abe still felt that the daily classroom experience with adolescents he had in his residency was invaluable, he no longer prized the Doug Lemov "teacher moves" AUSL had trained him to enact. He noted, "I still put my residency first [in its influence on my practice], ... but I'm not using any of those moves."

In place of the AUSL strategies, in his first year of teaching, he found himself drawing most heavily on DePaul's emphasis on building relationships with students and creating thoughtful, engaging lessons. He contrasted what he viewed as AUSL's "policing" approach to discipline with the "parenting" approach he has adopted with his students at Urban Arts, "treating them more like I'm their parent than like a police officer has opened up a lot more avenues for us to have and build a pretty strong relationship." At the end of his first year of teaching, he noted that he viewed AUSL practices as building walls between him and his students. He said:

> . . . at the beginning of the year I was extremely strategy-focused 'cause I had come out of AUSL and it's just like okay, if you use these strategies the students will come around to you. And I felt like each time I was doing something like okay, clap when I say clap, you know, and each time I would do one of those things I was putting up another little wall . . .

With a year of independent teaching under his belt, Abe reflected on how AUSL had offered valuable immediate practical classroom experience and DePaul initially seemed irrelevant, but now, the planning approaches he learned at DePaul have helped tremendously:

> . . . looking back on this year now . . . I ended up slowly ditching a lot of the strategies and things that I learned from AUSL over the course of the year, whereas the—the curriculum and planning and differentiation and all that kind of stuff that I learned at DePaul ended up being very, very useful to me.

Abe began to see that AUSL was making students "act" like students, but not necessarily fostering genuine engagement. He commented that now, in his first year of teaching, "I just feel like I have students more engaged in learning than just being good and acting like a good student." He credited DePaul with emphasizing the importance of formative assessments—something he incorporates regularly in his teaching—and the principles of well-aligned lesson plans that have clear objectives that are aligned with activities and assessments. Further, the overarching approach to English education that he learned in his DePaul English teaching methods courses became much more salient to Abe. At the end of his first year of teaching, he explained that, while he was initially skeptical of the DePaul English methods approach:

> As I started to . . . really be comfortable with myself in front of the students, I started to find myself doing a lot of those things and seeing them really—really work. And seeing that there is—you don't have to be so strict about time like AUSL is so strict about time. Like if you waste a minute in the classroom you're going to see it on your evaluation, you know? And really there's nothing wrong with the first 5, 10 minutes of class be just everybody settling in and getting ready to learn some stuff.

Thus, through Abe's residency year and across his first year of teaching, he grappled with the competing aims he was learning from AUSL and DePaul, initially gravitating toward some of the practicality of AUSL's methods, but ultimately finding greater philosophical alignment and value in the aims espoused by DePaul.

CROSS-CASE DISCUSSION AND ANALYSIS

Considering Lori and Abe as cases of residents navigating differing programmatic aims, how might their particular residency paths illuminate the broader issue that candidates learning to teach face in this age of partnering programs? Lori's and Abe's cases illustrate there is no single path or learning-to-teach process. Instead, these cases show how a teacher's navigation of competing programmatic aims is a highly contingent process, one that depends on the resident, the various contexts that shape residents' learning, and the strength of particular programmatic influences.

The Resident

Consistent with prior research on teacher learning, Lori's and Abe's cases suggest that residents will grapple with competing programmatic messages in light of the existing experiences and understandings about teaching and learning they already possess. Further, the strength of their existing convictions may influence the extent to which they actively grapple with competing program messages. Lori, fresh out of her undergraduate work and with little teaching-related experience, relied on the immediate, concrete experiences and vision that AUSL provided and that demanded her daily attention. Although she sometimes had her own sense that particular AUSL practices felt uncomfortable or counter to her students' cultural backgrounds, as she said, it was difficult for her to distinguish between her own philosophy and what she was being told to do since "all I really know is what I've been told." Once she was in her first year of teaching and no longer felt the weight of her obligations to AUSL as heavily, she began to reject some of the prescribed and—as she viewed it—fragmented literature curriculum that her AUSL school expected her to teach. Freed of the daily expectations of the AUSL residency, she also created her own reading materials and planned lessons to be more responsive to her students' needs. However, the overarching practices and philosophy of AUSL—particularly as they were expressed through her residency and mentor teacher—continued to serve as her guiding framework.

Abe, meanwhile, with more than an additional decade of experiences under his belt, entered the AUSL–DePaul arrangement with a more developed set of commitments that appeared to be partly responsible for allowing him to pick and choose the aims he espoused with greater agency. Although he understood that he needed to adhere to many of the AUSL practices because he was being evaluated on them, he actively resisted and made sense of these practices in relation to his own set of views, along with what he was learning at DePaul. Once he was in a new school context in his first year of teaching and no longer obligated to AUSL, he was able to further identify the vision and practices that made sense to him—those more aligned with DePaul—and, as he put it, be himself.

Contexts That Shape Residents' Learning

While Abe's and Lori's personal backgrounds certainly shaped their learning-to-teach processes amidst competing programmatic aims, these personal influences were also mediated by the school contexts in which they each learned to teach, the strength of their programmatic influences, and the timing of their AUSL and DePaul learning. Lori had consistency in the school contexts in which she did the majority of her learning, staying at Caraballo through both her residency and first year of teaching, and had a mentor who actively promoted the primary AUSL practices that were central at Caraballo. Such consistency meant that Lori had no real need or opportunity to explore DePaul's philosophy or practices or grapple with their inconsistencies with AUSL's aims, since her contexts demanded only AUSL aims, and these served her well. Abe, on the other hand, began in an AUSL school with a mentor whose modeling of AUSL practices was weak, and went on to a dramatically different, non-AUSL school context. The transition to a non-AUSL school forced Abe to reexamine his own aims in light of his AUSL and DePaul learning, leading him to an active rejection of many AUSL practices.

For these two residents, then, the strength of programmatic influences was quite different. Lori experienced a largely coherent set of priorities from AUSL, given the strong alignment between her mentor's practices, her placement at Caraballo for 2 consecutive years, and the broader AUSL program. With a strong degree of coherence in her AUSL influences and the daily demands of the AUSL portion of the program, weekly DePaul coursework over the course of the residency year played a minimal role for her. For Abe, however, the weaker alignment between his mentor's practices and the AUSL program led to a weaker AUSL programmatic influence. This weaker influence, combined with his transition to a non-AUSL school context and his more developed personal views, created space for DePaul's competing aims to gain traction.

Lori's and Abe's cases also suggest the critical role that timing plays in residencies under partners with competing aims. As Lori noted, attending evening classes at DePaul and teaching 4 days a week was grueling; operating in survival mode did not set up the optimal conditions to learn from DePaul coursework. It is notable that the one specific set of understandings Lori gleaned from DePaul about the effect of poverty on education came from summer coursework, when the AUSL daily teaching portion of the residency had not yet begun. Once the immediacy of the residency began, the learning that happened there eclipsed the much less urgent demands of DePaul coursework. In fact, the DePaul coursework that AUSL residents took was designed for regular master's candidates and intended to be taken across 2 academic years. Condensing this course sequence was a result of AUSL's structural need for candidates to complete their residency year in 1 calendar year. In this way, DePaul's coursework was positioned to be a weaker influence due to the sheer cognitive overload placed on AUSL residents.

CONCLUSIONS AND IMPLICATIONS

In the quotation that begins this chapter, an AUSL resident likens the DePaul–AUSL partnership (or arrangement) to parents who should divorce but are staying together for the sake of their children, given their differing philosophies. Indeed, as Abe's and Lori's cases illustrate, not only were there very real, unreconciled differences in programmatic philosophies between AUSL and DePaul, the differing philosophies of these programmatic "parents" created an additional task for residents: to struggle over these competing aims amidst the already complex task of learning to teach. Lori ultimately sided with the ideas she took from AUSL and mostly abandoned her learning from DePaul, while Abe wrestled more actively, giving DePaul's messages about teaching and learning greater allegiance in the end.

In an age of declining enrollments in teacher preparation, more institutions of higher education are likely to seek partnerships with non-traditional preparation pathways to secure enrollments and funding in exchange for the provision of coursework and access to licensure. What is easily missed in such arrangements that may be viewed as a "win-win" in terms of a financial bottom line is that when programs are vastly incongruent with one another, the ultimate toll falls on the teacher candidate, and (it follows) on his or her students. Although it may be inevitable for programs to have somewhat different aims when brought together under the auspices of a new partnership, we argue that the work of negotiating aims—both stated and expressed—must be the responsibility of the programmatic partners, rather than shifting this burden onto the candidates who are already navigating the complexities inherent in learning to teach.

In the case of DePaul and AUSL, despite sharing deep commitments to social justice and equity, their enacted vision of effective teaching in underserved contexts differed dramatically, thus resulting in disjointed and often confusing learning experiences for teacher candidates. Returning to our parenting metaphor, we contend that it is ultimately the responsibility of the parents to oversee and nurture the development of their child. Programs that are implicitly or explicitly feuding through their enacted aims are causing more than an inconvenience to their candidate; they are detracting from the conceptual and structural program coherence that research suggests is predictive of a candidate's sense of readiness to teach. As preparation pathways continue to face the pressures of enrollment and consider coming together to form an arrangement, the people who lead these arrangements might benefit from interrogating themselves about partnering toward what ends, and at what costs.

NOTE

1. As a point of clarification, DePaul students are required to complete practicum hours prior to their student teaching experiences. Thus, Lori's DePaul classmates had

already participated in field experiences, albeit with less depth and intensity compared with the AUSL residency experience.

REFERENCES

Academy for Urban School Leadership. (2017). *AUSL History*. Retrieved from auslchicago.org/about/ausl-our-history/

Britzman, D. P. (2003). *Practice makes practice: A critical study of learning to teach*. Albany, NY: State University of New York Press.

Danielson, C. (2007). *Enhancing professional practice: A framework for teaching.* Alexandria, VA: ASCD.

DePaul College of Education (2018). *Mission*. Retrieved from education.depaul.edu/about/mission-history/Pages/default.aspx

DePaul Division of Mission and Ministry. (2018). *Mission statement*. Retrieved from offices.depaul.edu/mission-and-values/about/Pages/MissionStatement.aspx

Gatti, L. (2016). *Toward a framework of resources for learning to teach: Rethinking US teacher preparation.* New York: Palgrave Macmillan.

Lemov, D. (2010). *Teach like a champion: 49 techniques that put students on the path to college.* San Francisco: Jossey-Bass.

Newmann, F. M., King, M. B., & Carmichael, D.L. (2007). *Authentic instruction and assessment: Common standards for rigor and relevance in teaching academic subjects*. Des Moines, IA: A report prepared for the Iowa Department of Education.

Sawchuk, S. (2014). Steep drops seen in teacher-prep enrollment numbers. *Education Week*. Retrieved from www.edweek.org/ew/articles/2014/10/22/09enroll.h34.html

Walsh, K., Glaser, D., & Wilcox, D. (May, 2006) *What education schools aren't teaching about reading and what elementary teachers aren't learning.* Washington, DC: National Council on Teacher Quality.

Zeichner, K. (2003). The adequacies and inadequacies of three current strategies to recruit, prepare, and retain the best teachers for all students. *Teachers College Record, 105*(3), 490–515.

Zeichner, K. M., & Gore, J. M. (1990). Teacher socialization. In W. R. Houston (Ed.), *Handbook of research on teacher education* (pp. 329–348). New York, NY: Macmillan.

CHAPTER 8

The Inequitable Impact of Privatization and Marketization of Initial Teacher Preparation in Chile

Carmen Montecinos
and M. Beatriz Fernández

In Chile, a country of 17 million people, there were over 2,153 preservice teacher education programs offered by 70 institutions of higher education in 2012, with an enrollment of nearly 103,682 students (Eyzaguirre & Inostroza, 2014). This number decreased to 76,450 by 2017 (CIAE, 2017). This reduction is not related to labor market demands, but rather to increases in regulation to curb the growth of low-quality programs. It is expected that by 2020 there will be a 55% surplus of teachers in all pre-K–12 curricular areas, except secondary physics and chemistry (Sánchez et al., 2013).

This chapter connects the expansion and (recent) reduction of enrollment in initial teacher education to the implementation of a market model for the provision of educational services over the past 37 years. In the first section we describe general characteristics of the pre-K–12 educational system in Chile. Next, we show how the participation of private providers has impacted the expansion of higher education in general and initial teacher education in particular. The proliferation of low-quality programs has resulted in an inequitable distribution of teachers across schools serving different socioeconomic groups. In the third section, we explore legislative changes introduced in 2016 to address quality concerns associated with this expansion. Maintaining the key features of a quasi-market model, new regulations for initial teacher education speak of a persistent faith in improving quality through increased accountability requirements. Underpinning these changes is policymakers' widely shared assumption that school "failure" in Chile stems from inadequacies in individual teachers' performance.

CHARACTERISTICS OF CHILE'S EDUCATIONAL PRE-K–12 SYSTEM

There are four characteristics of Chile's educational system worth highlighting to understand key challenges in ensuring an equitable distribution of highly qualified teachers. First, the education system consists of two levels of compulsory education: elementary (grades 1–8) and secondary (grades 9–12). Early childhood programs (pre-K to K) are also available in many elementary schools. In secondary schools, for Years 9 and 10 all students follow a college preparatory curriculum. In Years 11 and 12 students choose this track or a technical–vocational track that prepares them to enter the job market. In response to elementary teachers' insufficient disciplinary preparation to address the national curriculum defined for grades 7 and 8, legislation was recently passed making these grades part of secondary education.

As some readers may know, Chile is credited as the cradle of educational policies inspired by the principles of choice and deregulation (Connell, Fawcett, & Meagher, 2009). A number of educational policies implemented beginning in 1981, first under a military dictatorship and later by democratically elected governments, have promoted a market model for the provision of education. In pre-K–12 education these policies have advanced administrative decentralization, accountability, and incentives for the participation of private providers.

This market model has conceptualized parents' right to choose their children's school as a legal right, with the state taking the role of subsidizing demand by providing public funding to schools owned and operated by non-state organizations. Parents can choose among three types of schools: (1) public schools owned and administered by municipal governments funded through an attendance-based state-funded voucher program, (2) private schools funded through the same state-funded voucher program, and (3) private schools fully funded by parents or private organizations.

These alternative options have resulted in an educational system exhibiting a high degree of segregation based on social class (Gonzalez, 2017). Students largely attend school with peers from the same socioeconomic group. In public schools, 80% of the students are from low- or middle low-income background, whereas 20% of the students attending private subsidized schools are from low- or middle-low income socioeconomic groups (García-Huidobro, 2010). Socioeconomic status matters to student outcomes, and this reality is especially prominent in Chile. In fact, in the PISA 2012 testing program, Chile showed one of the highest levels of correlation between a student's home background and attainment on the mathematic test (OECD, 2015).

In a recent analysis of educational policies in Chile, the OECD (2015) identified three educational practices that foster inequity: grade repetition, school choice, and transfer of struggling students from one school to another (see López, Montecinos, Rodríguez, Calderón, & Contreras, 2012). Taking into account that municipal governments cannot afford severance payments given the financial crisis in which many of their schools operate, the evidence also shows that within a municipality, teachers not meeting performance expectations are also transferred among schools (Montecinos, Ahumada, Galdames, Campos, & Leiva, 2015). The dire financial situation in municipal schools is associated with three factors: the insufficient amount of the state voucher; a state voucher based on average daily attendance that provides variable income to schools that have fixed costs; and the steady decrease in enrollment in municipal education. Whereas private providers can charge parents a fee (co-payment), municipal schools, with few exceptions, cannot access this additional income source.

To address the social class segregation that has occurred within this quasi-market educational landscape, the Law for School Inclusion was approved in May 2015. Briefly, private providers receiving a state voucher can no longer select students or charge parents a co-payment, and cannot operate as for-profit businesses (Valenzuela & Montecinos, 2017). The law created three financial incentives, in addition to the state voucher, for schools not charging a co-payment as a way to offset their eventual financial losses. These changes reinforced parental choice and the notion that choice has positive effects on quality improvement as schools compete with each other to recruit students. The finance model based on average daily attendance was maintained, and thus the strain created by a variable income and fixed operating costs was not addressed.

A final characteristic is the high representation of private providers in elementary and secondary education. Public school enrollment has decreased steadily since the 1980s,[1] fueled by the perception that students in private schools outperform students in public schools as well as by parents' belief that private schools leverage more social capital for pupils. In 2011, private voucher schools enrolled 51.8% of students, and private schools fully funded by parents enrolled 8.9% of students, with public schools representing 39.3% (Santiago, Benavides, Danielson, Goe, & Nusche, 2013). By 2015, 38.9% of the students attended a municipal school (Ministry of Education, 2017, cited in OECD, 2017). Public schools suffer a reputational disadvantage and until the passing of the Inclusion Law had become largely the "choice" of families who could not truly choose due to financial (co-payment) or academic (school's selection of students) constraints. The effects of the implementation of the Inclusion Law on public schools' prestige and parents' choices are not yet clear (Valenzuela & Montecinos, 2017).

CHARACTERISTICS OF THE POSTSECONDARY EDUCATION SECTOR BEFORE THE YEAR 2016

Reforms introduced by the military regime in 1981 have shaped the development of higher education over the last 37 years. Uribe and Salamanca (2007) characterize this reform along two axes: expansion and finance mechanisms. The effects of these policies will be first described for the whole system in terms of four indicators: coverage, quality, selectivity, and social class segregation. Later, we describe how these indicators are observed in the context of initial teacher education.

Expansion

Between 1989 and 1991 the system expanded through the partition of the two largest state universities, as well as existing private institutions, into regional universities (from 8 to 25 institutions, known as traditional universities). Additionally, several new private universities entered the system. Between 2000 and 2005, enrollment in private universities grew by more than 900%. This growth is explained by the fact that once private universities became fully licensed by the state, they gained autonomy to open new campuses throughout the country. Traditional universities' enrollments also grew by 160% during this period. A clear outcome of the expansion in the number of postsecondary institutions has been an increase in coverage. In 2003, 70% of university students were the first in their family to enroll in tertiary education, and 38% of people between the ages of 18 and 24 were enrolled at this educational level (Uribe & Salamanca, 2007).

This growth in coverage, however, is in tension with the state's available instruments to guarantee quality. Quality, according to policy, was taken to be an issue of concern to the client (student) and the provider (institution). Students are responsible for making the correct choice by informing themselves about the quality of alternative universities and programs. To inform students' choice, a voluntary accreditation system has been implemented since 2006 for all programs. An evaluative state governance model based on accountability has been the preferred policy to leverage quality improvement (Fernández, 2018; Maroy, 2004). For medicine and for teacher education programs, accreditation was mandatory only for institutions receiving public funding until 2015. By that time, half (51%) of teacher preparation programs were accredited (MINEDUC, 2017a, cited in OECD, 2017).

Finance Mechanisms

Prior to 1981, traditional higher education institutions received funding that allowed students to attend largely tuition-free. Staring in 1981, a considerable part of the cost has been passed on to students and their families. Competitive mechanisms were introduced for universities to obtain state financing. Facing inadequate state funding, and limited in the amount of tuition families could afford, traditional universities developed a number of programs in satellite campuses and side businesses to raise additional cash. Although private and public universities are required to be nonprofit, a number of schemes have been developed to circumvent this provision (a key element in the student movement's platform of 2006 and 2011).[2] Until 2003, new private universities, professional institutes, and technical training centers (covering around 60% of the students in postsecondary programs) were not eligible for state funding, tuition grants, or state-backed student loans. An expansion of the loan system through the participation of banks increased access but also led to a large number of students graduating with high levels of debt.

Selectivity in the University's Admissions Process

Universities admit students through two routes. All traditional universities and some new private universities participate in a consolidated admissions system that sets the minimum entrance score at 450 (out of a maximum of 850) on the national college entrance examination (PSU). Students apply for admission by indicating their preference for a specific program and are ranked with other applicants based on a score that considers high school GPA, the PSU score, and high school rank. Each university program defines how many slots will be available and can admit that number of students.[3] Higher-ranked students are more likely to be admitted into their preferred option, especially if the program is very competitive, thus highly selective. Lower-ranked students will be admitted into their second, third, or fourth option.

Most private universities and professional institutes that are not part of the consolidated system implement the second modality. In this case, each institution sets its own entry requirements. Usually, these are nonselective universities and admit almost anyone who applies as these institutions depend entirely on tuition revenues. In either case, under a legal provision guaranteeing academic freedom, universities define their own programs of studies, as there are no requirements orienting the curriculum or governing graduation with an academic degree or for granting a professional license. Market forces are expected to regulate quality, as better programs will attract better students. Traditional universities have an incentive to attract better-qualified students as the per-student subsidy received from the state is linked to the students' college entrance scores; higher scores bring more state funding.

Studies find a high correlation between students' socioeconomic background and the PSU score (Contreras, Corbalán, & Redondo, 2007). In 2010, the average score on the Spanish subtest in this exam was 471.2 for graduates from a public school, 502.8 for graduates from private subsidized schools, and 605.4 for private school graduates (Universidad de Chile, 2010). This means that a much higher proportion of students graduating from a public high school will not be eligible for admission into a traditional university and their only options will be the nonselective private institutions. In 2005, nationally, 51% of students from public schools, 64% from private subsidized, and 90% of students from private school obtained a PSU score equal to or greater than 450 (Firinguetti & Pavez, 2008).

CHARACTERISTICS OF INITIAL TEACHER EDUCATION BEFORE THE YEAR 2016

University-based programs prepare prospective teachers for one of three educational levels:[4] early childhood (pupils ages 0–5), elementary (grades 1–8), and secondary (grades 9–12). Elementary teachers are prepared as generalists for all subjects covered in the elementary grades, with some programs offering a major in one or two content areas to teach in upper elementary grades. Secondary teachers receive specialized training in one of the disciplines covered in the national curriculum. In addition, universities offer degrees in special education, physical education, and arts to serve students from 1st through 12th grade. The norm is to structure secondary teacher preparation into 8 to 10 semesters, in which pedagogical and disciplinary preparation are concurrent. Elementary as well as early childhood programs are also concurrent, but structured into 8 or 9 semesters. Lately, a number of universities are also offering 12- to 18–month consecutive, secondary teacher preparation programs for people who have previously earned a university degree.

Historically, to teach in a public or private school a teaching degree has been mandatory, although there are special provisions for a temporary license in specific curricular areas. With the General Education Law passed in 2009, a teaching degree or a provisional license is required for early childhood and elementary grades. For secondary schools, university graduates from fields other than teacher education may also be hired for up to 5 years. These graduates must have completed a program of study lasting at least eight semesters at an accredited university.

Expansion of Initial Teacher Education

In 2008 there were 49 institutions offering a degree in elementary teaching; 26 of these were private non-traditional universities, five were professional institutes and 18 were traditional public and private universities (Ministerio de Educación, 2013). In 2011, 850,569 students were enrolled in a university or professional institute (Torre Griggs, 2011) and, of these, 117,245, or 13.8%, were enrolled in a teacher education program (Mizala, Hernández, & Makovec, 2011). Mizala et al. report that from 2000 to 2011 the number of teacher education programs had multiplied by four, with an annual growth of 14%. This growth had been at a higher rate among private non-traditional universities (20% annually) and professional institutes (16%). Cox, Meckes, and Bascope (2010) showed that the highest increase in enrollment was observed among nonselective private universities that offered more loans to their students (566.3% increase from 2000 to 2008). They estimated that in the year 2000 selective universities offered 22.7% of the programs, a percentage that dropped to 9% by 2008.

In addition to the programs offered by these new institutions, a number of traditional, public institutions began offering special programs in small towns and cities throughout the country, with classes taking place on weekends and when schools were in summer recess. These programs enrolled nontraditional students who were not required to take a college entrance examination. Cox et al. (2010) cite two studies showing that 14% of the elementary teaching force in 2005–2006 had graduated from one of these programs. As the funding system for public universities required them to be self-sustaining, these institutions saw in these programs the opportunity to increase their financial resources.

Another explanation for the rising number of students in teacher education is a push for alternative pathways into teaching promoted through the type of educational entrepreneurship that has influenced teacher education policies in the United States (Zeichner & Peña-Sandoval, 2015). Enseña Chile, the local affiliate of Teach For All (the international version of Teach For America), started selecting "outstanding recent college graduates and working professionals from all backgrounds" (Alfonso, Santiago, & Bassi, 2010, p. 3) in 2008 for classroom placement in 2009. Enseña Chile is partly supported by the Inter-American Development Bank (IDB) and "is focusing on placing human capital of the highest quality in the most vulnerable urban and rural schools in the country" (Alfonso et al., p. 3). At the moment, the program is relatively small: 183 current members and 437 alumni (Enseña Chile, 2018).

Enseña Chile's language of "human capital" and "highest quality" to refer to university graduates who did not pursue a teaching degree quite clearly expresses a critique of the quality of teacher education candidates and graduates, using market-oriented language. This critique is often based on linking teacher quality with Chilean students' below-average performance on a number of international testing programs. For example, Chile achieved the best results among participating Latin American countries in PISA 2012, and the second best result after the Autonomous City of Buenos Aires in Argentina in PISA 2015, but lagged behind the average for OECD countries (OECD, 2017; 2018). These results as well as results on the national testing program (SIMCE) frame teachers as individually responsible for the success of the educational system, as does a highly publicized critique of their qualifications as well as of university-based initial teacher education (OPECH, 2015).

When teacher education candidates have participated in international testing programs, results indicate that elementary candidates do not get a strong preparation in the content they will later teach. On the Teacher Education and Development Study in Mathematics (TEDS-M), Chilean candidates' average score placed them 16th among the 17 participating countries (Ávalos & Matus, 2010). On the 2011 INICIA test (national testing of subject matter and pedagogical knowledge for elementary teacher graduates), results showed important gaps. In the test measuring knowledge of Spanish language arts, mathematics, social sciences, and natural sciences, 69% of the novice teachers performed at the "insufficient" level. These findings should be interpreted in light of the fact that these tests have not been subjected to studies of content validity in relationship to curricula taught by the programs, and there is no empirically defined cut-off score or evidence of the relationship between scores on these tests and the quality of these candidates' teaching competencies or performance in the K–8 classroom (Montecinos, 2014).

The expansion of initial teacher education from early 2000 to 2015 relates to social mobility opportunities created by the expansion of tertiary education, to the availability of student loans and scholarships, and to a market for the segment of students who cannot enter traditional universities because of the restrictions outlined earlier. The relative low operating cost of offering a teacher education program in the unregulated higher education sector made these programs an attractive market to providers.

One explanation for the growth of teacher candidates from 2000 to 2015 is an increase in the participation of people who come from lower-performing schools and lower SES. Munita (2010, cited in Mizala et al., 2011) explained that teacher education primarily attracts low-income students who see in teaching a profession that offers job security. On the other hand, students from middle or upper SES groups find teaching less attractive as it is a low status profession. Mizala et al. (2011) examined the characteristics of students enrolled in teacher education programs and found that these students tend to have lower college entrance examination and lower high school GPA rank in comparison to students choosing other university-based programs. Additionally, they tend to come from lower SES backgrounds, more often from public schools, particularly from the technical-vocational high school track. The majority of the students who enter teacher education have opted for this major in their two top preferences in the admissions process. It is unclear if they express this preference because of a vocational interest or because they know their college entry scores are not competitive for admissions into other majors.

Ruffinelli and Guerrero (2009), in the specific case of elementary initial teacher education programs, associate this enrollment increase to the existence of a market. Public and private institutions capitalize on the promise of social mobility associated with a university degree, and with a deregulated system they see an opportunity to offer low-cost programs oriented toward people from the lowest SES quintiles who work and need flexible schedules (Cox et. al, 2010). The growing interest in teaching can also be explained by policies that have increased salary and benefits for teachers, providing job security in public school and greater job opportunities through the expansion of private pre-K–12 schools. This growth may also be associated with an important increase of the government's financial aid program to increase access to higher education, as well as the system of loans created by private, non-traditional universities (Cox et al., 2010).

Selectivity in University Admissions Process

Mizala et al. (2011) compared the college entrance scores of students enrolling in teacher education programs offered by traditional universities with that reported by private nontraditional universities. Findings showed that the average was significantly lower in the latter. It is worth noting that 57% of the teacher education programs offered by nontraditional private universities had not reported their average college entrance examination score either because they did not request that test or because they are not required to inform indicators such as this to the Ministry of Education's higher education office. These findings are similar to those reported in other studies showing that nonselective private higher education institutions have become the choice for public school graduates with PSU scores below 450 (Cox et al., 2010; Ortúzar, Flores, & Milesi, 2012; Rufinelli & Guerrero, 2009).

Segregation by Social Class

Ruffinelli and Guerrero (2009) examined the trajectory followed by 246 novice elementary teachers from high school, to higher education, to place of employment. These participants represented 17 higher education institutions, private and public, from across the selectivity spectrum. Survey findings showed that after graduating from their teacher preparation program, new teachers go to work in the same type of school from which they had graduated. Teacher candidates who graduate from private high schools enter prestigious, selective private and public universities. After they graduate, they teach in private schools like the ones in which they had studied. Teachers graduating from a municipal state-funded high school are more likely to graduate from public and private nonselective institutions or selective public universities. Upon graduation, these teachers are more likely to get a teaching position in a municipal school.

Ruffinelli and Guerrero (2009) found that in nonselective universities, 96% of the candidates came from high schools receiving a state voucher, whereas in selective private universities almost 50% of the students came from private high schools fully funded by parents. Based on these findings, the authors concluded that initial teacher education institutions are adding inequity to the school system. Teachers graduating from nonselective private and public universities were more likely to come from lower SES, be unemployed, and experience worse work conditions and lower initial salaries.

In summary, the studies reviewed showed that increased access to higher education has maintained and reinforced the strong stratification by socioeconomic background already present in elementary and secondary schools (Ruffinelli & Guerrero, 2009). In contrast to pre-K–12 schools in which low-income students concentrate in municipal schools, in higher education we find that low-income students concentrate in private institutions. Private institutions are attracting low-income young adults, largely due to the fact that they are less selective or nonselective compared to traditional institutions and offer more flexible payment options and loans. As low-income students aspire to social mobility via professional preparation, the quality of their secondary school is more likely to constrain their choice, but not the choice of their higher-income peers who have attended private high schools fully funded by their families.

POLICIES TO REGULATE THE QUALITY OF INITIAL TEACHER EDUCATION SINCE THE YEAR 2016

The proliferation of low-quality initial teacher preparation programs across Chile has been the target of public debates and criticism by national and international organizations. Examples of these debates and proposals include the 2004 OECD review of Chile's educational policies, the Expert Panel (Panel de Expertos) for Quality Education summoned in 2010, and the presidential panel in 2012. The legislation *System of Teacher Professional Development* (STPD, Law 20.903) approved in 2016[5] captured several of the changes proposed by these panels. As we show next, underpinning this law is the assumption that market leverage combined with state regulations will result in the improvement of teacher education programs and of the quality of their graduates (Fernández, 2018).

Law 20.903 purports to strengthen the teaching profession by improving work conditions that are critical to efforts to attract, prepare, and retain qualified teachers who can provide better educational opportunities for all students (Valenzuela & Montecinos, 2017). In this section we focus on those provisions aiming to improve the quality of initial teacher education. These are designed to provide more information to prospective students and employers and to increase accountability over teacher education programs. That is, this legislation seeks to strengthen the market model by introducing adjustments over the supply side and some over demand. In what follows we analyze STPD, arguing that while holding on to market principles it fails to adequately address questions of equity and segregation.

Mandatory Accreditation

Until 2016, private for-profit agencies carried out accreditation, with each university choosing the agency. Domínguez and colleagues (2012) reported that only 18 out of 423 programs had failed the accreditation process. Institutions were accredited for a minimum of 2 years and a maximum of 7 years. Domínguez and colleagues point out several weaknesses of this process: too many aspects were left to the discretion of peer evaluators, and there were no standards against which to judge the evidence collected through site visits. Additionally, nonaccredited programs could continue to admit and graduate teachers. Even with nonaccredited degrees, graduates could gain teaching employment.

Law 20.903 established that all teacher education programs must be subject to obligatory, periodic accreditation. In addition, the STPD attempts to address previous shortcomings by making mandatory that teacher education programs be accredited by the state's National Accreditation Council (CNA). Nonaccredited programs cannot accept new students; thus, to survive as providers in the educational market system, these programs must adjust to new accreditation requirements. If a program fails accreditation, it can voluntarily submit an improvement plan and its implementation is supervised by the National Education Council. After the plan is satisfactorily completed, according to the judgment of this council, it must go through the accreditation process.

Evaluation of Prospective Teachers

From 2011 to 2015, teacher education graduates were evaluated by the INICIA test. The introduction of this test highlighted the inequities of the system already revealed by the SIMCE and PSU testing programs. INICIA results showed that highly selective programs outperformed nonselective programs, each enrolling candidates from different socioeconomic groups. The test was voluntary, and in 2012 very few graduates took the test. For example, in 2011, 3,271 graduates took the test, a number that dropped to 1,443 in 2012 (or 14% of the eligible population). Moreover, the correlation between PSU and INICIA was 0.70; therefore, some questioned whether teacher preparation programs add to students' entry knowledge base (Domínguez, Bascopé, Meckes, & San Martín, 2012).

Drawing from the INICIA experience, the STPD established two mandatory tests for prospective teachers. Each university must create and administer a diagnostic test to candidates in their first year in the program. One year before they graduate, prospective teachers must take a second test designed and administered by the Ministry of Education at the national level. Teacher candidates cannot receive their degree if they have not taken the test; thus, it is now a graduation requirement. Teacher education programs are requested to implement improvement plans and remedial actions based on the results achieved by their students. A major concern with the national test is that institutions receive results just 6 months before teacher candidates graduate, making remedial actions unrealistic, and undermining the formative aspects of the test. Also, there is no empirical evidence linking test scores to quality of in-classroom teaching, and it is a paper-and-pencil test rather than a performance assessment.

The national test is based on standards for teacher candidates that have been constructed with little participation by teacher educators. Defining mandatory standards for teacher education is problematic due to the constitutional guarantee that prevents the state from dictating curricular matters to universities. The standards are posited, therefore, as orienting guidelines that universities may or may not choose to follow. The assumption is that the national test will align institutions, as they have self-interest in ensuring the success of their graduates (marketing tool). Additionally, test results are given to the accreditation agency that will take these data into consideration when making accreditation decisions.

Increased Selectivity

Another strategy, also consistent with a market model, is to make prospective teacher candidates and teacher education graduates responsible for their own "quality." The new policy requires a minimum college entrance examination score for admission into teacher education. This score is defined by law and is scheduled to increase each year: a PSU score of 500 in 2017, 525 in 2020, and 550 in 2025 (the minimum for all traditional universities before was a score of 450). This proposal raises a serious equity concern, as we know that students' PSU scores are highly correlated with socioeconomic background. The assumption is that higher scores represent the academic talents of the candidate (individual merit) as opposed to the opportunities to learn candidates were afforded in their high schools, which we know in Chile differ by social class. This is a continuity of the logic of strengthening teaching by "attracting talented students," as when in 2010 the government created a scholarship for candidates scoring above 600 on the PSU test. Through this admission pathway, students graduating from public schools (mostly from low SES) will be much less likely to enter teacher education as compared to their more affluent peers. Will this create a homogeneous teaching force that will be removed from the social and cultural background of low-income students?

An alternative admission pathway into teacher preparation programs has also been outlined by STPD. Low-income students graduating from low-performing high schools who fail to meet the PSU cutoff score can be admitted based on their high school ranking or the satisfactory completion of a 1-year academic enhancement program offered by universities. Despite the advantages of these admission pathways over the PSU criteria, this regulation still places the burden on the individual candidate to come into the program better prepared for academic work.

Moreover, a consequence of the combination of these pathways of admission could be that highly selective programs, which served high SES teacher candidates before the law, are likely to increase their cut-off PSU scores. In contrast, less selective programs will enroll more of their students via the high school ranking or academic enhancement program pathways, concentrating teacher candidates with low PSU scores; this means low-SES teacher candidates. In this way, this strategy could reinforce a highly socially stratified educational system behind what seems to be at first glance, more equitable admissions tools.

CONCLUDING REMARKS

There is widespread national agreement on the need to strengthen initial teacher education in Chile (Ministerio de Educación, 2014; Hochschild, Díaz, Walker, Schiappacasse, & Medeiros, 2014). In 2014, President Bachelet announced a new wave of reforms to strengthen the teaching profession. To this effect, STPD law has introduced measures to increase the rigor of the accreditation process and of the teacher education curriculum through a renewal of national standards and evaluations for teacher candidates, and to increase the selectivity of teacher education programs. Empirical evidence is needed to understand how these strategies are interpreted and enacted by teacher preparation programs and how they affect the provision of initial teacher education.

STPD has not addressed the problem of inequity that comes with choice and selectivity as the key social processes through which a market model proposes to leverage improvement. There is ample evidence at the pre-K–12 educational levels as well as in initial teacher education that the range of choice is linked to students' social class and that selectivity more often relegates low SES students to poor-quality educational institutions. Although STPD creates new measures to incentivize providers to invest greater resources in initial teacher preparation, it is unclear where the funding to make these changes will come from.

Contrary to what neoliberals promised, the participation of private providers in Chile has diminished rather than increased the overall quality of teacher education programs. Policy strategies to regulate teacher quality that are based on entry requirements place the burden of quality on the individual applicants, instead of on the institutions. The political cost of changing the market model to effectively increase universities' investments in quality teacher education programs is apparently too big; it is easier to emphasize pressure on the individuals who apply for admissions by increasing the minimum PSU score. STPD addresses, in part, this unfair burden by placing the consequences of low performance on the national exam on teacher preparation programs, rather than on candidates. Teacher preparation programs are now required to create remedial actions to address weaknesses in prospective teachers' performance on this test. Changing the accreditation requirements does not change the market logic of incentives and fear of punishments as catalyzers for institutional change.

We need the academy, in alliance with social movements, to advocate for alternative forms of accountability that do more than inform consumers' choices. Following Ryan (2005), improvement requires democratic forms of accountability that involve all actors acknowledging their responsibility for discrepancies between what was promised and what was delivered, as well as for the unintended consequences of decisions made by various stakeholders. For example, citizens could demand evidence of validity of the national test for teacher candidates, and timely feedback for institutions. Also, policymakers need to be expected to provide evidence that students with a PSU score below the cut-off score will not be as good, caring, and committed teachers as their peers who score above that cut-off. More importantly, any policy implemented to improve quality must provide prior evidence that it will be equitable and will not have a differential impact on prospective teachers from different socioeconomic groups. In Chile, quality has been pursued without sufficient attention to equity, and that is what needs our immediate attention.

Beyond a reliance on a test that can be corrected for social class or other biases, a more thorough discussion is needed in Chile, and probably elsewhere, about what quality education entails and what quality schools entail. An initial teacher education policy that attempts to fix the "teacher problem," and in some instances the market problem, needs to be developed in the context of responses to larger questions such as "what teachers are need for what *country project?*" For example, teacher education accountability policies from a democratic perspective (Cochran-Smith et al., 2018) are based on democratic values and goals and promote complex conceptions of teaching, teacher education, and learning: a complexity often erased by tests that measure mastery of disciplinary content knowledge. We need a new conversation centered on teachers' well-being and not just their productivity.[6]

NOTES

1. In 1981, 80% of the student population attended a public school (Elacqua, 2012).

2. This changed in 2016 with the introduction of provisions to fully finance tuition for students from the lowest 60% income groups who attend traditional universities and other institutes that meet certain criteria.

3. In 2018 a new higher education law was passed that caps enrollment, program expansion, and tuition for universities that are part of the tuition-free initiative for students in the lowest 60% income groups.

4. Until 2014, professional institutes were also allowed to grant a teaching degree for elementary and early childhood grades. Currently, only accredited universities can offer these degrees.

5. The legislation was highly resisted by the Teachers' Association, leading to the second largest national teacher strike in Chilean history (59 days).

6. This work was funded by CONICYT/FONDECYT INICIACIÓN Grant 11170663. Support from PIA-CONICYT Basal Funds for Centers of Excellence Project FB0003 is gratefully acknowledged.

REFERENCES

Alfonso, M., Santiago, A., & Bassi, M. (2010). *Estimating the impact of placing top university graduates in vulnerable schools in Chile* (Technical Notes No. IDB-TN-230, Inter-American Development Bank Education Division (SCL/EDU)). Retrieved from idbdocs.iadb.org/wsdocs/getdocument.aspx?docnum=35572277

Ávalos, B., & Matus, C. (2010). *La formación inicial docente en Chile desde una óptica internacional: Informe nacional del estudio internacional IEA TEDS-M.* Santiago, Chile: Ministerio de Educación.

CIAE (2017). *Evolución de la matrícula en carreras de formación inicial docente (2005–2017).* Santiago, Chile: Observatorio Formación Docente. Retrieved from www.ciae.uchile.cl/download.php?file=noticias/00_1502132623.pdf

Cochran-Smith, M., Cummings Carney, M., Stringer Keefe, E., Burton, S., Chang, W.C., Fernández, M. B., . . . Baker, M. (2018). *Reclaiming accountability in teacher education*. New York, NY: Teachers College Press.

Connell, R., Fawcett, B., & Meagher, G. (2009). Neoliberalism, new public management and the human service professions: Introduction to the Special Issue. *Journal of Sociology, 45*(4), 331–338.

Contreras, M., Corbalán, F., & Redondo, J. (2007). *Cuando la suerte está echada: estudio cuantitativo de los factores asociados al rendimiento en la PSU*. Retrieved from www.opech.cl/bibliografico/calidad_equidad/Estudio_sobre_la_PSU_Contreras_Corbalan_Redondo.pdf

Cox, C., Meckes, L. y Bascopé, M. (2010). La institucionalidad formadora de profesores en Chile en la década del 2000: Velocidad del Mercado y Parsimonia de las Políticas. *Pensamiento Educativo*, 46–47, 205–245.

Domínguez, M., Bascopé, M., Carrillo, C., Lorca, E., Olave, G., & Pozo, M. A. (2012). Procesos de acreditación de pedagogías: Un estudio del quehacer de las agencias. *Calidad en la Educación, 36*, 53–85.

Domínguez, M., Bascopé, M., Meckes, L., & San Martín, E. (2012). ¿Producen mejores resultados las carreras de pedagogía básica con más años de acreditación? *Estudios Públicos, 128*, 1–59.

Elacqua, G. (2012). The impact of school choice and public policy on segregation: Evidence from Chile. *International Journal of Educational Development, 32*(3), 444–453.

Enseña Chile (2018, July 13). PeCh + Alumni [webpage]. Retrieved from www.ensenachile.cl/quienes-somos/pech-alumni/

Eyzaguirre, S., & Inostroza, D. (2014). Antecedentes para perfeccionar la formación inicial docente. *CEP, 379*, pp. 1–17.

Fernández, M. B. (2018). Framing teacher education: Conceptions of teaching, teacher education, and justice in Chilean national policies. *Education Policy Analysis Archives, 26* (34), 1–37. Retrieved from dx.doi.org/10.14507/epaa.26.2806

Firinguetti, L., & Pavez, R. (2008). Inequidades en la enseñanza media municipalizada: El caso de la provincia de Concepción. *Ultima Decáda, 29*, 49–70.

García-Huidobro, J. E. (2010). Para hacer pública la educación pública. In S. Martinic & G. Elacqua (Eds.), *¿Fin de ciclo? Cambios en la gobernanza del sistema educativo* (pp. 91–110). Santiago, Chile: Facultad de Educación de la Pontificia Universidad Católica de Chile y Oficina Regional para América Latina de UNESCO.

Gonzalez, J. (2017). Putting social rights at risk: Assessing the impact of education market reforms in Chile. In B. S. Ndimande & C. Lubienski (Eds.), *Privatization and the education of marginalized children: Policies, impacts, and global lessons* (pp. 143–160). New York, NY: Routledge.

Hochschild, H., Díaz, F., Walker, J., Schiappacasse, J., & Medeiros, M. P. (2014). El Plan Maestro, diálogos para la profesión docente. *Calidad en la Educación, 41*, 121–135. Retrieved from dx.doi.org/10.4067/S0718-45652014000200005

López, V., Montecinos, C., Rodríguez, J. I., Calderón, A., & Contreras, J. F. (2012). Enacting solidarity to address peer to peer aggression in schools. In C. Sleeter & E. Soriano (Eds.), *Building solidarity across communities of difference in education: International perspectives* (pp. 23–44). New York, NY: Teachers College Press.

Maroy, C. (2004). *Regulation and inequalities in European education systems*. Final Report. Contract n°: HPSE-CT2001-00086. Project n°: SERD-2000-00069. Retrieved from www.uclouvain.be/cps/ucl/doc/girsef/documents/reguleducnetwork_VF_10dec041.pdf

Ministerio de Educación. (2013). *Presentación de resultados evaluación diagnóstica INICIA 2012.* Retrieved from www.cnachile.cl/Biblioteca%20Documentos%20de%20Interes/Informe%20Resultados%20Prueba%20INICIA%202012.pdf

Ministerio de Educación (2014). *Informe final. Sistematización y análisis de diálogos temáticos del plan nacional de participación ciudadana para la reforma educacional.* Santiago, Chile: Ministerio de Educación.

Mizala, A., Hernández, T., & Makovec, M. (2011). *Determinantes de la elección y deserción en la carrera de pedagogía* (Technical Report, Grant FONIDE N° F511059). Retrieved from www.educacion2020.cl/sites/default/files/informe_final-alejandra_mizala-udechile-f511059.pdf

Montecinos, C. (2014). Análisis crítico de las medidas de presión propuestas para mejorar la formación inicial de docentes en Chile por el Panel de Expertos para una Educación de Calidad. *Estudios Pedagógicos, 40,* no. Especial, 285–301.

Montecinos, C., Ahumada, L., Galdames, S., Campos, F. & Leiva, M.V. (2015). Targets, threats and (dis)trust: The managerial troika for public school principals in Chile. *Education Policy Analysis Archives, 23* (87). Retrieved from dx.doi.org/10.14507/epaa.v23.2083

Observatorio Chileno de Políticas Educativas (OPECH). (2015). *Medir y castigar: La "no-pedagogía de la evaluación" en el proyecto de Carrera Profesional Docente.* Retrieved from http://www.opech.cl/_doc/medir_y_castigar_evaluacion_cpd_documento.pdf?fbclid=IwAR3vOWthjmcQE0XpDssbNb8pvdgTy1Gbg7v2_tjJbgHojAUx7_m8f1wIkKo

Organisation for Economic Co-operation and Development (OECD). (2015). "Chile", *Education Policy Outlook 2015: Making Reforms Happen.* Paris, France: OECD Publishing. Retrieved from dx.doi.org/10.1787/9789264225442-19-en.

Organisation for Economic Co-operation and Development (OECD). (2017). *Education in Chile, reviews of national policies for education.* Paris, France: OECD Publishing. Retrieved from dx.doi.org/10.1787/9789264284425-en

Organisation for Economic Co-operation and Development (OECD). (2018). *PISA 2015, Results in Focus.* Paris, France: OECD Publishing.

Ortúzar, S., Flores, C., & Milesi, C. (2012, August). *Distribución de profesores principiantes, jefes UTP y directores en distinto tipo de establecimientos: Variación en sus características educacionales y percepciones.* Paper presented at the Segundo Congreso Interdisciplinario de Investigación en Educación, Santiago, Chile.

Panel de Expertos para una Educación de Calidad. (2010). *Informe Final: Primera Etapa. Propuestas para fortalecer la profesión docente en el sistema escolar chileno.* Santiago, Chile: Ministerio de Educación.

Ruffinelli, A., & Guerrero, A. (2009). Círculo de segmentación del sistema educativo Chileno. *Calidad en la Educación, 31,* 20–44.

Ryan, K. E. (2005). Making educational accountability more democratic. *American Journal of Evaluation, 26*(4), 532–543.

Sánchez, M.J., Gutiérrez, G., Hochschild, H., Medeiros, M.P., Ortiz, M., & Sepúlveda, M.J. (2013). Mercado de profesores en el sistema escolar urbano chileno. *Calidad en la Educación, 39,* 155–194. Retrieved from dx.doi.org/10.4067/S0718-45652013000200006

Santiago, P., Benavides, F., Danielson, C., Goe, L., & Nusche, D. (2013). Teacher evaluation in Chile 2013. *OECD reviews of evaluation and assessment in education.* OECD iLibrary. Retrieved from dx.doi.org/10.1787/9789264172616-en

Torre Griggs, D. (2011). Perspectivas en Educación, N°5. Santiago, Chile: Consejo Nacional de Educación. Retrieved from www.cned.cl/sites/default/files/actas/201112N05.pdf

Universidad de Chile (2010). Compendio estadístico proceso de admisión año académico 2010. Santiago, Chile: Universidad de Chile. Retrieved from psu.demre.cl/estadisticas/documentos/p2010/2010-compendio-estadistico.pdf

Uribe, D., & Salamanca, J. (2007). *Country background report—Chile OECD thematic review of tertiary education*. Santiago, Chile: División de Educación Superior, Ministerio de Educación.

Valenzuela, J. P., & Montecinos, C. (2017). Structural reform and equity in Chilean schools. *Oxford Research Encyclopedia of Education.* Retrieved from oxfordre.com/education/view/10.1093/acrefore/9780190264093.001.0001/acrefore-9780190264093-e-108

Zeichner, K., & Peña-Sandoval, C. (2015). Venture philanthropy and teacher education policy in the U.S: The role of the New Schools Venture Fund. *Teachers College Record, 117*(6), 1–44.

CHAPTER 9

Teach For America, the Education Entrepreneur Network, and the Reshaping of Teacher Preparation

Kerry Kretchmar, Beth Sondel, and Joseph Ferrare

The United States is experiencing a dramatic increase in a particular type of fast-track teacher preparation program that is situated outside of universities, prepares teachers for urban and rural schools, and draws on a technocratic approach to pedagogy. Teach For America (TFA), the best-known fast-track teacher preparation program, currently has over 60,000 alumni and places corps members in classrooms as teachers of record after a 5-week summer institute (Teach For America, 2018a). TFA's influence extends far beyond teacher preparation, and its impact on the educational reform movement has been profound. Since its founding, TFA has asserted a dual mission: preparing individual teachers and building a movement for educational equity (Kopp, 2001). TFA was started with a goal to cultivate leaders who would build a broader educational reform movement (Damast, 2012) and provides a variety of leadership paths for alumni in schools, districts, and politics. In 2018, 3,700 TFA alumni are school level leaders, 471 are school system leaders, and 30,000 are members of Leadership for Educational Equity (LEE), an organization that provides "personalized support for corps members and alumni seeking a career in organizing, policy, advocacy, and elected leadership" (Teach For America, 2018a). In this chapter, we explore TFA's role in the advancement of market-based reforms in teacher education and TFA's contributions to a two-tiered, inequitable system of teacher preparation.

Using social network analysis, we illustrate how TFA is a central node in a network of organizations and stakeholders—defined below as "jurisdictional challengers" (Mehta & Teles, 2012)—that are reshaping teacher education, specifically for teachers being prepared to work in low-income schools that primarily serve students of color. In particular, in this chapter we illustrate how this network provides credentials, supports legislation, and influences public discourse to advance market-based teacher education reforms. Ultimately, we contend that TFA perpetuates a two-tiered system wherein students' demographic characteristics determines the type of training received by their teachers, while shifting commonsense perceptions about what constitutes as effective teaching and to whom that effectiveness applies.

THE LITERATURE ON TFA'S IMPACT ON EDUCATIONAL REFORM

Significant research has examined TFA's influence on educational reform and public debate. Many have contended that TFA has impacted public discourse around teaching by furthering a narrative that teaching can be a 2-year job rather than life-long career (Darling-Hammond, 1994; Labaree, 2010; Vasquez-Heilig & Jez, 2014) and by bolstering the assumption that existing teachers are one of the primary obstacles to educational equity (Teach For America, 2018b). Research has also explored the ways TFA is at the head of market-based educational reforms that use a business lens to promote policies based on valorizing choice, accountability, competition, and efficiency (Kretchmar, Sondel, & Ferrare, 2014; Lahann & Reagan, 2011; Miner, 2010; Pitzer, 2010). TFA alumni are prominent leaders in many educational reform ventures, with a particular proliferation in charter school reform efforts and educational entrepreneurism (Higgins, Hess, Weiner, & Robison, 2011; Kretchmar, Sondel, & Ferrare, 2014). Yet little research has examined the influence of TFA on teacher education policy specifically.

THE CURRENT STATE OF TEACHER EDUCATION

A movement to deregulate teacher education and promote fast-track, non-university-based entry into the teaching profession fits within the larger narrative of public institutions in crisis that has been used to rationalize privatization of schools and market-based reforms (Apple, 2013; Berliner & Glass, 2014; Chubb & Moe, 1990; McShane & Hess, 2014; Saltman, 2010a, 2010b). In recent years, teacher education has increasingly been blamed for educational inequities.

Historically, American schools have faced teacher shortages and have especially struggled to staff schools in low-income communities (Ingersoll & Smith, 2003). University-based teacher education has failed not only to produce enough teachers but also to consistently prepare a workforce of teachers who are able to effectively educate the diverse student needs and backgrounds in the United States (Fraser, 2007). The overall quality of teacher education varies significantly and includes many highly effective programs that skillfully connect theory, clinical practice, and communities (Darling-Hammond, 2006) as well as ineffective and poor teacher preparation programs (Levine, 2006). However, policy and funding efforts have moved away from trying to replicate strong university-based models and, instead, policies and funding have shifted to focus on expanding teacher preparation programs and projects that fit into a market-based vision for educational reform (Zeichner, 2010).

While funding has poured into fast-track preparation programs and charter schools of education (programs that operate independently from university systems financially and through policy), the public universities and colleges that still prepare 70–80% of the nation's teachers have continued to experience dramatic budget cuts (Lyall & Sell, 2006; Newfield, 2018). Between 2008–2013, states cut $16 billion from higher education budgets (Hiltonsmith & Draut, 2014). For teacher education programs who wish to transform and improve, a decreasing investment in universities has significant repercussions and limits the ability to innovate (Zeichner, 2010).

As funding for university-based teacher education programs becomes more limited, programs also face increased state and national reporting demands (Cochran-Smith, Piazza, & Power, 2013). The Obama administration's agenda included the creation of systems of accountability for teacher education programs through the Teacher Preparation Regulations. Overturned by the Senate in 2017, this proposed set of federal regulations included an evaluation and ranking of teacher preparation programs based on their graduates' students' results on standardized assessments. This system included consequences for low-performing and at-risk programs that were not showing improvement. Scholars, educators, and the public have argued that these regulations rely on narrow and fallible measures of teacher and student performance, and ultimately punish programs that prepare teachers for underperforming schools in low-income communities of color (Kumashiro, 2015). While these regulations were rejected at the federal level, many states continue to move forward with elements of these regulations, in particular efforts to evaluate and rank teacher preparation programs based on the test scores of their graduates' students and consequently reward or punish programs.

These increased accountability demands have influenced the operation and structure of teacher education programs (Beyer, 2007; Gatti, 2016; Kumashiro, 2010; Sleeter, 2008; Weiner, 2007). Zeichner (2010) has argued that increasing the required documentation and measurement of all aspects of programs detracts from quality teacher preparation, as teacher educators are forced to focus their energy and effort on rationalizing and reporting every element of their work and program. Relatedly, these accountability pressures can result in narrowing the curriculum and inducing a more technocratic approach to teaching that fails to prepare teachers for the multiple dimensions of the profession (Au, 2007; Darling-Hammond, 2004). While the Trump administration has not yet put forth any policies specifically related to teacher education, Education Secretary Betsy DeVos has a long history supportive of charter school reform, privatization, and other market-based approaches to education that have historically been implemented alongside alternative routes to certification.

FAST TRACK TEACHER PREPARATION

As resources for higher education wane and accountability demands are increased, targeted philanthropic and federal funding has supported the significant growth of teacher certification programs that function independently from universities. Different kinds of programs fall under this umbrella, yet fast-track, market-based teacher preparation programs have experienced the most significant growth and policy support. These programs prepare teachers primarily for schools serving low-income students of color using a teacher-as-technician model and a narrow definition of success as measurable outcomes (Kretchmar & Zeichner, 2016).

Corporate philanthropists, such as the Walton Family, Gates, Dell, and Fischer Foundations, have effectively promoted market-based educational policies through significant contributions (Colvin, 2005; Scott, 2009). These foundations operate under the assumption that educational reform will benefit from the same principles and strategies that have proven successful in the business world, particularly a focus on competition, accountability, and efficiency (Scott, 2009; Tompkins-Stange, 2016). One way philanthropists have promoted these practices is through funding *jurisdictional challengers*. Jurisdictional challengers offer alternatives to educational services (e.g., credentials for teachers and administrators) that have historically been under the administration of traditional institutions such as colleges of education, public school districts, and teachers' unions (Mehta & Teles, 2012). An analysis by Reckhow and Snyder (2014) provided evidence that foundations are increasingly funding jurisdictional challengers. In particular, they found that the top 15 funders of education tend to give money to the same organizations, indicating an overlap in their agenda and policy goals. TFA was supported by 13 of the 15 top funders in 2010 with a total of $44.5 million (Reckhow & Snyder, 2014).

This focused funding of jurisdictional challengers extends beyond foundations to the federal government. For instance, the 2010 Innovation in Education competitive grant program did not fund any university or college proposals. In contrast, the program awarded a $50 million grant to TFA and $20 million grant to The New Teacher Project (TNTP) (Zeichner, 2011). TNTP is another alternative teacher preparation and training organization; it was founded by TFA alumna Michelle Rhee, and is heavily staffed by TFA alumni and utilizes a fast-track training model very similar to TFA's. This focused funding has contributed to the growth of alternative pathways to teaching (Grossman & Loeb, 2008). For example, TFA grew from a program with 500 corps members to more than 5,961 new teachers in 2013, though their expansion has curtailed, with 3,500 new corps members in 2017 (Teach For America, 2017).

In addition to supporting the growth of fast-track teacher training programs, foundations and the federal government have promoted the expansion of charter schools of education that operate independently from university systems. The largest among these is Relay Graduate School of Education, an independent, master's-granting institution that currently has 15 locations and was created in partnership with KIPP, Achievement First, and Uncommon CMOs and TFA. Many other similar programs exist, such as the MATCH Teacher Residency and the YES Prep Teaching Excellence Programs. These programs prepare and license teachers in a variety of ways, but typically use accelerated models that focus on preparing a teacher as technician.

Federal policies have supported the growth of these programs. In 2011, for instance, the GREAT (Growing Achievement Training Academies for Teachers and Principals) Act was introduced in the Senate. Designed by leaders from the NewSchools Venture Fund, Relay, and others, the intention of the bill was to promote teacher and principal preparation programs that could operate independently from universities and also outside of state regulations. This bill was introduced but not enacted in its first iteration; however, language from the GREAT Act was written into a provision of the Every Student Succeeds Act of 2016. This provision allowed states to authorize "teacher preparation academies" and use Title II funding to support their development. Further, states that use funds for teacher preparation academies are required to allow those enrolled in the teacher preparation academies to serve as teachers of record (Zeichner & Peña-Sandoval, 2015).

The movement toward a more competitive, market-oriented educational system in United States has increased accountability measures for all programs. Programs such as TFA and Relay Graduate School of Education (GSE) were designed around intensive accountability metrics that measure teaching effectiveness through standardized assessment data (Foote, 2009). For example, Relay GSE requires that all graduates show at least a year's worth of growth in their students using measurable assessment metrics. These programs rely heavily on standardized proof points to secure philanthropic and federal funding and thus they may not experience the same disconnection between evaluation measures and reporting requirements that is faced by many traditional programs.

Many critics of university-based teacher education have used the growth and ostensible success of these fast-track and charter programs to support the deregulation of teacher education (Mehta & Teles, 2014; Zeichner & Peña-Sandoval, 2015). Members of think tanks and advocacy organizations such as the American Enterprise Institute and National Council on Teacher Quality (NCTQ), among others, have long contended that teacher education would benefit from market-based reforms and alternative pathways into the profession, arguing that these shifts would increase competition among providers and recruit different candidates into the profession (Hess, 2001). Others, such as Wisconsin's former Governor Scott Walker, have argued that anyone with a college degree, a passing score on a content exam, and a clean criminal record should be able to become a teacher (Beck, 2015). In fact, The American Board for Certification in Teacher Excellence (ABCTE), which requires only a bachelor's degree, background check, and certification test, is an approved pathway to becoming a teacher in 13 states (American Board for Certification in Teacher Excellence, 2018). Under a proschool choice Secretary of Education, Betsy DeVos, continued federal support for alternative pathways and deregulated teacher preparation is expected.

While the current landscape of teacher preparation is more complex and variable by state than we can fully describe in the scope of this chapter, generally the expansion of fast-track preparation programs and charter schools of education are providing concentrated preparation of teachers for low-income schools that primarily serve students of color, while schools in middle-class and wealthy communities continue to be staffed by teachers prepared through university-based programs (Kretchmar & Zeichner, 2016). This increasingly bifurcated model of teacher preparation raises important questions about equity in schooling. Although we are not suggesting that TFA is responsible for these trends in entirety, below we illustrate how the organization is a central transmitting node within a network of jurisdictional challengers who are reshaping teacher preparation in the United States.

NETWORKS

Policy networks have served as an important structure that jurisdictional challengers, such as TFA, rely on to influence and, at times, bypass traditional policy structures in education (Kretchmar, Sondel, & Ferrare, 2014; Reckhow & Snyder, 2014). Policy networks are self-organizing sets of interconnected organizations that exchange a wide range of resources, expertise, and reputation to accomplish shared policy objectives (Davies, 2005; Rhodes, 2006). New networks of governance have emerged and are increasingly powerful in shaping educational policy outside of traditional elected governmental structures (Ball, 2012; Ball & Junemann, 2012; Saltman, 2010a; Scott, 2009). Through this, we see "the transfer of power and coordination from bureaucratic structures to informal social networks of private individuals and organizations working to transform public education by constructing new education markets" (Au & Ferrare, 2015, p. 9). Even traditional bureaucratic bodies such as the federal government are increasingly making use of policy networks as a mechanism to mobilize jurisdictional challengers to push policy initiatives at state and local levels (Mehta & Teles, 2012). In this way, policy networks are not only a governance structure but also an explicit strategy of education reform (Rhodes, 2006). Using policy network analysis, scholars have begun examining these new networks of governance in order to understand how they function in policymaking processes (Ball, 2012). In this chapter, we examine the ways TFA utilizes an organizational network of market-oriented reformers to influence teacher preparation policy and narratives.

SOCIAL NETWORK ANALYSIS OF TFA

Our analysis utilizes basic graphing techniques from social network analysis. Social network analysis (SNA) is both a theory and method for examining the structure, process, and composition of ties between actors. In SNA, ties represent pathways between actors through which material and nonmaterial resources flow and create opportunities and constraints for action (Wasserman & Faust, 1994). Thus, a central assumption of SNA is that actors and their actions can only be understood by situating them in the structured sets of relationships in which they are always embedded.

Our primary methodological objective was to use basic network graphs to depict the flow of personnel and alumni from TFA to other organizations engaged in efforts to reform teacher education. We used *ego-centric* graphs to accomplish this task. As the name implies, ego-centric graphs illustrate the ties between a focal actor (TFA in this case) and the alters to whom the actor is tied on some set of relations. Ego-centric networks can be understood in contrast to socio-centric (or whole network) graphs that depict the entire set of ties between all actors in a bounded network (Borgatti, Everett, & Johnson, 2018).

When constructing ego-centric graphs of TFA and their alters, we paid exclusive attention to the transmission of human resources (i.e., alumni, personnel) from TFA to their partners in the teacher preparation policy network. The use of the ego-centric approach in this context means that we focused on the broader teacher preparation policy network from the vantage point of TFA. For example, it is likely the case that the organizations to which TFA directs human resources also create ties between one another and even reciprocate resources back to TFA. While this is no doubt an important feature of the teacher preparation policy network, our primary concern here was to investigate TFA's role as a central transmitter within this context.

Below, we use simple directed graphs to illustrate TFA's transmission of human resources within the teacher preparation policy network. Directed graphs use arcs (←→, →, or ↔) to illustrate the direction of ties, such as "sends money to" or "seeks advice from." In Figure 9.1, for example, we use a directed graph to depict the flow of personnel from TFA to organizations involved in the deregulation of teacher education. It is important to note that our use of directed graphs was for interpretive purposes only. That is, we did not use any formal network measures to describe the structure or composition of TFA's ties to other organizations. While useful in many situations, such measures extend beyond the scope of the primary objectives of this chapter.

In addition to using directed graphs, we analyzed archival documents from the organizations in the network in order to identify the flow of information and influence. Most notably, we analyzed lobbying records and proposed legislation to illustrate how actors in the network utilized resources to influence policy outcomes related to teacher preparation. Even though our use of

Figure 9.1. Teach For America's Connections to Organizations Involved in the Deregulation of Teacher Education

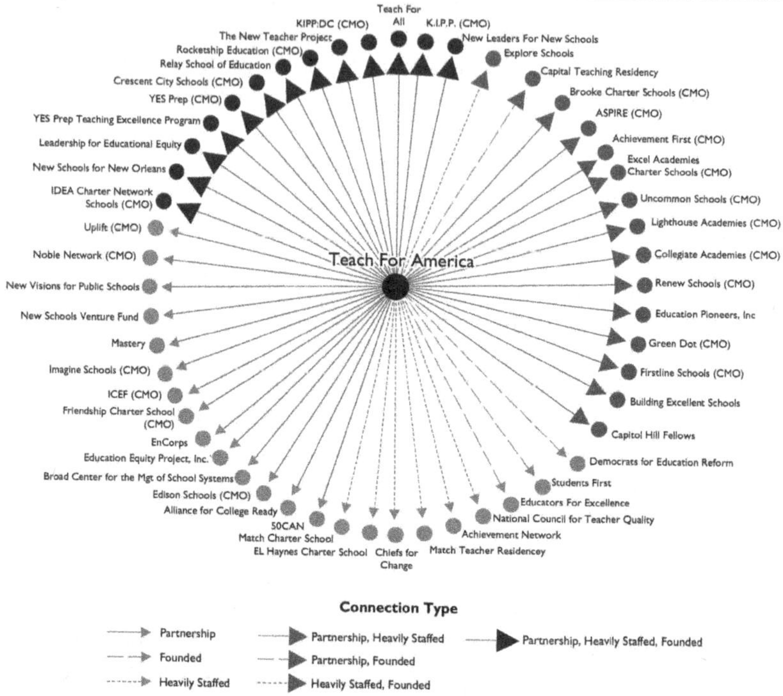

SNA was descriptive, then, we nevertheless have sought to illustrate qualitative evidence of how TFA is able to influence these policy outcomes.

DATA AND ILLUSTRATION OF HUMAN RESOURCES FROM TFA

Our analysis drew upon multiple sources of archival data, such as annual reports, Form 990 tax filings, web content, alumni documents, and marketing materials. In order to illustrate the flow of human resources from TFA to other organizations, we searched for evidence of the following:

- Organizations that were founded by TFA alumni
- Organizations that have formal, documented partnerships with TFA, including CMOs where TFA places corps members
- Organizations with one or more TFA alumni in senior level positions

We then used a directed graph to depict the presence of these criteria. Each tie was given a weight ranging from 1 to 3 to indicate the number of the above criteria present in the tie between TFA and the corresponding organization (i.e., a value of 1 indicates any one of the three conditions above, a 2 indicates any two, and so on).

We used two visualization strategies to illustrate the type of connection between TFA and its alters. First, the arrowheads were weighted to reflect the number of conditions connecting TFA to each organization. The thickest arrowhead indicates that all three conditions were met, while the smallest represents only a single condition. In addition, the type of line represents the specific way in which TFA is connected to each organization. In most cases, SNA analysts use only a single relation at a time in order to appropriately generate network measures (e.g., density). Since our analysis does not utilize formal SNA measures, we include the multiplex relations simultaneously. We acknowledge that there may be quantitative differences within each of the qualitatively different relations. However, our objective was less concerned with measuring the precise amount of resources flowing, and to instead illustrate the range of different resources moving through the network.

TFA AS A CENTRAL TRANSMITTING NODE WITHIN POLICY NETWORKS

TFA states that system-wide transformation is incumbent on preparing their alumni for leadership positions in schools, districts, and communities as well as in political roles at the local, state, and federal level (TFA, 2012). Here we will discuss how TFA is a central transmitting node within a network of jurisdictional challengers. In Figure 9.1 we exhibit the connection between TFA and the jurisdictional challengers who are shifting attitudes about and policies around teacher preparation at multiple levels. Twenty-eight organizations within the network feature arrowheads indicating a Level 2 or 3 connection, which demonstrates that many alumni of TFA's programs are spearheading or engaged with organizations in this network. This network has played a pivotal role in shifting teacher preparation to organizations that exist outside of higher education and further altering the content and delivery model used to educate teachers for the 21st century. In addition to sharing personnel and funders, organizations within the network of jurisdictional challengers subscribe to a similar ideology about effective teaching and teacher preparation. This includes a view of the teacher as a technician and test scores as the primary indication of a teacher's effectiveness (Kretchmar & Zeichner, 2016). Teacher preparation within the network of jurisdictional challengers is presented in opposition to theory and tends to focus heavily on discrete classroom management techniques and measurable outcomes (Stitzlein & West, 2014).

We will now discuss how the network visualized in Figure 9.1 changed the governance of teacher education and affected the policies and rhetoric around it. Specifically, we will describe how the network has influenced teacher preparation by: (1) providing credentials, (2) advancing legislation that challenges the public sector, and (3) shaping the narrative around teaching and teacher preparation.

CREDENTIAL PROVIDERS

Fast-track preparation programs have a long history in the United States, yet the recent expansion of these programs is due in large part to efforts by TFA alumni. Within the network depicted in Figure 9.1 are multiple organizations that supply teacher certifications or master's degrees independent of universities. TNTP, for example, is a national, fast-track alternative certification program modeled in large part on TFA, the primary difference being that TNTP targets career changers as opposed to recent college graduates. Further, TNTP has evolved and serves as a human capital consultant to districts and CMOs and houses a research and policy office. TNTP features the largest arrowhead in Figure 9.1 to denote their connections with TFA on three levels; they were founded by TFA alumna Michelle Rhee, TFA alumni constitute much of their personnel, and they have a formal partnership with TFA. Teach For All provides an example of how this network's influence extends internationally. Originally founded and presently led by Wendy Kopp, Teach For All has created a network of organizations across the globe to create and implement their fast-track alternative certification model (for more on Teach For All, see Friedrich, 2014).

That TFA is a central actor in the proliferation of popular education reforms is not a secret. In fact, TFA openly considers itself a "human capital generator" for many jurisdictional challengers featured in Figure 9.1 (Brinson, Boast, Hassel, & Kingsland, 2012). Most prominent CMOs, such as KIPP, Achievement First, and YES Prep, were founded by TFA alumni and are heavily staffed by TFA alumni or engaged in formal partnership with TFA. An increasing number of TFA alumni and corps members teach in charter schools, and specifically many teach in "no excuses" CMOs (TFA, 2013). Nationally, 33% of KIPP (Knowledge is Power Program) teachers have participated or are participating in TFA (KIPP, 2018). In some regions and schools that percentage is higher. For example, nearly half of the staff at KIPP Minnesota consists of TFA corps members or alumni (KIPP, 2016). TFA has created both the supply and demand within many CMOs, by playing an important role in the expansion of charter organizations through the development of leaders at all levels, and then using TFA corps members and alumni to staff these schools and related organizations (Kretchmar, Sondel, & Ferrare, 2014).

In its inception, TFA was bound by licensure regulations to partner with university-based programs in most states. At most sites, TFA would provide summer institute training, job placement, and mentorship through the organization and then would partner with a university for on-the-job coursework that led to a license and in many cases a master's degree. Yet, as a result of the

Every Child Succeeds Act provision described in detail below and of state regulatory changes, TFA is increasingly able to partner instead with charter teacher education programs that provide teacher licensure and master's degrees, allowing corps members to gain licensure and master's degrees completely outside of a university system. Other CMOs, such as YES Prep and Match, have created their own credentialing programs so they can hire and license teachers in house. As exhibited in Figure 9.1, many of these credential providers, including Relay Graduate School of Education and YES Prep Teaching Excellence Program, are intricately connected to TFA and are heavily staffed and led by TFA alumni. Relay GSE, for example, provides teacher training programs and grants master's degrees. In addition, one of their explicit goals has been to "shake things up a bit" to shift teacher preparation in the United States. In their official literature, they position their faculty against university-based professionals, claiming that they find "exceptional thinkers" who "think outside the box," rather than those who "sit in ivory towers" (Otterman, 2011, in Stitzlein & West, 2014, p. 5).

The approaches promoted in programs like Relay, Match and Yes Prep not only exist outside of the university, but contrast with the research-based practices seen in high-quality, university-based preparation programs that develop teachers as professionals, focus on learner-centered pedagogy, and assess effective teaching through holistic performance assessments (Kretchmar & Zeichner, 2016; Zeichner and Peña-Sandoval, 2015). Relatedly, Stitzlein and West (2014) argue that teachers (at Relay) are trained to implement specific sets of practices largely predetermined by others. Unlike professionals, they are prepared to produce a product without understanding why, how, or even if it should be produced in the first place (p. 9). This "teacher as technician" model prepares candidates to work efficiency and uncritically in the "no excuses" school environment. This approach contrasts with the focus of strong university-based teacher preparation programs, such as Alverno or Stanford's Teacher Education Program, which develop teachers as professionals who learn to utilize complex and varied knowledge, skills, and dispositions related to pedagogy, content, and understanding learners in a social context (Darling-Hammond, 2006). We must continue to question the implications of preparing teachers for marginalized communities as technicians through programs like Relay and Match; they may not be provided with teacher preparation that offers tools for critically analyzing the sometimes repressive practices (Sondel, 2016) of no-excuses models.

Not only are the majority of Relay's incoming students affiliated with TFA, but in 2012, all of their matriculated students worked in no-excuses charter schools (Caperton & Whitmire, 2012). *No-excuses* charters, named in reference to the assertion that we cannot allow poverty to serve as an excuse for low expectations and/or performance (Thernstrom & Thernstrom, 2004), are characterized by an extended school year and school day, an exacting focus on test preparation, a highly ruled and regulated environment, and harsh and dehumanizing discipline policies (Golann, 2015; Golann & Torres, 2018;

Goodman, 2013; Sondel, 2016). While no excuses charters have been lauded for bolstering student test scores (Angrist, Dynarski, Kane, Pathak, & Walters, 2012), they tend to use prescriptive and technocratic approaches to teaching, focus on discrete strategies, and rely on a narrow vision of effective teaching (Kretchmar & Zeichner, 2016; Kronholz, 2012; Stitzlein & West, 2014).

Foundation support extends beyond programmatic funding through tuition subsidies. For example, the full cost of tuition and fees for the Relay Teaching Residency is $35,000, but students' out of pocket tuition cost is $6,500 due to the financial support of foundations (including Gates, NewSchools Venture Fund, JP Morgan, and Credit Suisse) and to the use of AmeriCorps awards (Relay, 2018). Furthermore, Relay's connections within the network illustrated in Figure 9.1 are likely to support the organization's reach. For example, during Cami Anderson's tenure as superintendent of schools in Newark, New Jersey, she developed a partnership between Newark Public Schools and Relay that provided teachers up to $20,000 for completion of a Relay program. This funding was not available for university-based teacher education programs (Braun, 2015; Relay, 2015). This sort of partnership is an example of how particular organizations and pathways are privileged within the network.

This has led to an increasingly two-tiered system in which teachers working primarily in marginalized communities are receiving training that is focused narrowly with a teacher-as-technician model, whereas students in middle-class and majority White communities are in schools staffed by teachers with the broader and more holistic preparation provided by high-quality university-based programs. This preparation has implications for educational equity, as it follows that low-income schools will have a narrow, technical approach to teaching, while schools serving middle- and upper-class students will express a more holistic view of teaching, learning, and effectiveness.

POLICY ADVOCATES

Many organizations within the network have supported or worked to advance legislation promoting the deregulation of teacher education or market-based reforms. In 2015, TFA spent $588,148 on lobbying costs for the following purposes, as stated in their federal Form 990:

> In support of state appropriations for Teach For America's in-state operations through regular state budget processes. In addition, regional staff also worked for the passage of various pieces of legislation which would impact Teach For America's ability to operate in a given community including the passage of alternative certification legislation and legislation permitting Teach For America to be recognized by the state as an alternative pathway to teach [*sic*] licensure. Teach For America has used consultants at the state level to provide lobbying services, such as bill and regulation tracking on matters, including but not limited to: teacher

> certification and state funding at the federal level, Teach For America staff interfaced with members of congress, their personal and committee staff and key members of the president's administration and federal agencies to advocate for legislation and regulations that would support Teach For America and the constituencies we serve. (TFA Form 990, 2015a)

It is worth noting that TFA's lobbying budget has increased significantly since 2010 (Hootnik, 2014). When their explicit lobbying budget and personnel are combined with the indirect legislative support outlined below, the impact of the organization on teacher education policy becomes significant.

TFA wields indirect legislative influence through alumni entering policy and advocacy tracks after completing the program. TFA reports that approximately 1,000 TFA alumni are in government/politics/policy/advocacy careers (TFA, 2017). TFA offers opportunities and extensive support for alumni who wish to pursue careers in politics and advocacy. For example, the Capitol Hill Fellows program is a year-long fellowship open only to TFA alumni with the goal of offering "important voices and perspectives to the legislative branch in Washington, DC" (Capitol Hill Fellows, 2018). Compensated with a $60,000 per year stipend, 15 fellows per year work full time in a House or Senate office or serve on the staff of a congressional committee. Fellows are mentored by a TFA alum on Capitol Hill. This fellowship is paid for in entirety by a venture capitalist, Arthur Rock, who sits on TFA's board and has also made sizable contributions to charter schools (Simon, 2013). In addition, TFA started Leadership for Educational Equity (LEE), which is a "nonpartisan organization dedicated to empowering Teach for America corps members and alumni to grow as leaders." LEE has over 30,000 members and offers resources, fellowships in a variety of leadership areas trainings, and support to develop leaders for policy, advocacy, political, and community leadership roles. LEE has received significant funding and, in 2013 alone, reported over 10.5 million dollars in grant and contribution revenue, compared to 3.85 million in 2012 (Leadership for Educational Equity, 2019).

TFA's direct lobbying as well as indirect influence on alumni leaders trained through LEE, Capitol Hill Fellows program, and other affiliated fellowships impacts not only TFA, but teacher education policy more broadly. TFA's influence on teacher education policy is evident through their efforts to lobby for modifications of the "highly qualified teacher" provisions in federal law (TFA, 2012). The No Child Left Behind Act (NCLB) of 2001 mandated that all students were entitled to a Highly Qualified Teacher (HQT), or a teacher with full certification in the core subject they are teaching. NCLB mandated that districts that did not have enough highly qualified teachers would need to distribute those without certification equally through districts rather than allow them to be concentrated in low-income areas and areas that serve students of color (Zeichner, 2013). TFA and many other organizations in the network successfully lobbied for and publicly supported a HQT provision first passed in 2002 that allowed alternative route teachers "making satisfactory progress toward[s]" completing the requirements for full state certification to be considered highly qualified. This provision allowed teachers entering education through TFA and similar programs to continue to be concentrated in high-needs schools and enabled districts to do this without notifying parents that their child's teacher was not certified. The U.S. Court of Appeals for the Ninth Circuit overturned this provision as unlawful, and yet the HQT amendment has been renewed twice (2010 and 2013) through Congress after being slipped into Budget Repair bills (Zeichner, 2013).

The left-hand column of Table 9.1 highlights those organizations and individuals who have issued written support of these provisions; those in bold are affiliated with the TFA network and so also represented in Figure 9.1. Further, we have highlighted Eli Broad, who is a significant funder of many organizations in the network and is also associated with the Broad Center for the Management of School Systems from Figure 9.1. Their support included the argument that, without HQT, classrooms would be left without teachers. However, the law states that districts could still hire teachers in training, such as TFA recruits and Teaching Fellows, but would need to distribute these teachers equally throughout a district rather than concentrate them in high-poverty schools. In contrast, the right-hand column of Table 9.1 represents the 93 civil rights, community, and education organizations that opposed the HQT amendment. None of these individuals or organizations exist within the network represented in Figure 9.1.

Many members of the network outlined in Figure 9.1 issued public support for the GREAT Act and the proposed Teacher Preparation Regulations, both mentioned above. The GREAT Act advocated for teacher and administration preparation programs to exist outside of state regulations and university oversight (Zeichner & Peña-Sandoval, 2015), allowing programs like those provided by Relay GSE to provide credentials without state approval. The proposed Teacher Preparation Regulations included evaluation and ranking of teacher preparation programs based on standardized test scores of graduates' students. Many of the individuals and organizations in the network, including Democrats for Education Reform, Relay, NCTQ, TNTP, and Uncommon Schools, issued public support of the GREAT Act and the proposed Teacher Preparation Regulations. In TFA's statement on the Teacher Preparation Regulations, they specifically noted their support for evaluating teacher education programs using measures of student achievement growth (TFA, 2015b). These sorts of public statements, combined with lobbying and indirect legislative influence, provide support for advancing market-based teacher preparation legislation.

SHAPING PUBLIC PERCEPTION

Through advertising and think tanks, many of the organizations within the network contribute to public perceptions of teachers and teacher education.

TFA and Relay are consistently cited by think tanks such as the American Enterprise Institute, Manhattan Institute, and Fordham Foundation as evidence that a deregulated market and alternative programs should be expanded (Hess & DuPre, 2015; Higgins et al., 2011). This discourse further has been used to advocate for the entry of for-profit companies, such as University of Phoenix and Kaplan into the business of teacher education (Zeichner, 2010).

The National Council on Teacher Quality (NCTQ) has been an important force in shaping the narrative on teacher preparation. NCTQ's stated mission is to "provide an alternative national voice to existing teacher organizations and to build the case for a comprehensive reform agenda that would challenge the current structure and regulation of the profession" (National Council on Teacher Quality, 2011). According to their website, NCTQ's aim is to serve as a warehouse of data to inform the teacher training marketplace to create pressure on leaders to shift policy in favor of market-based alternatives to teacher preparation. In 2012, NCTQ conducted their first evaluation of university-based programs through an analysis of syllabi, selectivity metrics, and clinical experiences, expressing a technocratic and assessment-based understanding of what it takes to develop as a teacher. This evaluation ranked four out of 1,200 Elementary and Secondary Education preparation as four out of four stars and 163 programs as one star. Schools of education have criticized NCTQ's reports for their lack of transparency and weak methodology. As a result, many states and institutions refuse to participate in the evaluations (Sawchuk, 2011) yet their rankings continue to be published by *U.S. News and World Report*. The president of NCTQ, Kate Walsh, has long been an advocate of alternative certification, and two members of the NCTQ leadership team are TFA alumni (NCTQ, 2018). Past advisory board members have included Wendy Kopp and Colorado State Senator and unsuccessful gubernatorial candidate Michael Johnston, a TFA alum.

CONCLUSION

Governance is increasingly driven by networks of resources, expertise, and reputation that exist outside of traditional elected systems (Grabher & Powell, 2005). In this chapter, we have demonstrated that TFA is a central node in a network of jurisdictional challengers who have advanced an agenda to deregulate teacher education. TFA is situated centrally in a network has been able to impact policy in profound ways, through first advancing a narrative about a broken teacher education system and then providing solutions undergirded by market-based principles, such as fast-track alternative preparation programs and charter schools of education (Ball, 2012). As we have outlined, TFA's network presents bold, negative characterizations of teacher education programs, through organizations such as NCTQ and in collaborative advocacy efforts for legislation like the Highly Qualified Teacher Amendment and the GREAT Act. Finally, they provide both the supply and the demand for these alternative credentials. This network is operating on multiple levels to advance market-based teacher preparation reforms in the United States and has effectively shifted the landscape of teacher education.

University-based teacher education programs have an important role to play in the fight for equitable education, and we must work to promote the practices of strong programs and transform those that are less effective, rather than permit the elimination traditional pathways to teaching (Zeichner & Peña-Sandoval, 2015). Equitable education requires a fight for the types of schools and teaching force that TFA staff, alumni, and corps members would want for their own children, not a system that promotes a narrow, teacher-as-technician model of training for educators of low-income students of color and a holistic and complex approach to teacher preparation for educators of middle- and upper-class students.

Table 9.1. Supporters and Opponents of the Highly Qualified Teacher Provision

Supporters of Highly Qualified Teacher (HQT) amendment	
50CAN: The 50-State Campaign for Achievement Now	Preston Smith, President, Rocketship Education
Achieve Hartford!	Students for Education Reform
Achievement First	StudentsFirst
Aspire Public Schools	**Teach For America**
Eli Broad, Founder, The Broad Foundations	**Teach For America Regions**
	Alabama
Building Excellent Schools	**Appalachia**
Cynthia Brown, Vice President for Education Policy, Center for American Progress Action Fund	**Baltimore**
	Bay Area
Chiefs for Change:	**Charlotte**
Janet Barresi	**Chicago**
Tony Bennett	**Colorado**
Stephen Bowen	**Connecticut**
Chris Cerf	**D.C. Region**
Deborah A. Gist	**Dallas-Ft Worth**
Kevin Huffman	**Delaware**
Paul Pastorek	**Detroit**
Gerard Robinson	**Eastern North Carolina**
Hanna Skandera	**Greater Nashville**
Eric Smith	**Greater New Orleans**

Supporters of Highly Qualified Teacher (HQT) amendment	
John White	**Teach For America Regions (continued)**
Chicago Public Schools	**Greater Newark**
ConnCAN: The Connecticut Coalition for Achievement Now	**Greater Philadelphia**
Connecticut Council for Education Reform	**Hawai'i**
Council of the Great City Schools	**Houston**
Democracy Prep Public Schools	**Indianapolis**
Democrats for Education Reform	**Jacksonville**
E.L. Haynes Public Charter School	**Kansas City**
Excel Bridgeport	**Las Vegas Valley**
Green Dot Public Schools	**Massachusetts**
Dr. Jane Hannaway	**Memphis**
The Thomas B. Fordham Institute	**Metro Atlanta**
IDEA Public Schools	**Miami-Dade**
Jason Kamras, 2005 National Teacher of the Year, Chief of Human Capital, DC Public Schools	**Milwaukee**
KIPP Public Charter Schools	**Mississippi Delta**
MarylandCAN: The Maryland Campaign for Achievement Now	**New Mexico**
Match Teacher Residency	**New York**
MinnCAN: The Minnesota Campaign for Achievement Now	**Northeast Ohio Oklahoma**
National Alliance for Public Charter Schools National Center for Alternative Certification	**Phoenix**
National Council on Teacher Quality	**Rhode Island**
New Leaders	**Rio Grande Valley**
New Schools for New Orleans	**Sacramento**
NewSchools Venture Fund	**San Antonio**
NYCAN: The New York Campaign for Achievement Now	**Seattle-Tacoma**
The Parents' Campaign	**South Carolina**
	South Dakota
	South Louisiana
	Southwest Ohio
	St. Louis
	Twin Cities
	TNTP
	Uncommon Schools

Supporters of Highly Qualified Teacher (HQT) amendment	
PennCAN: The Pennsylvania Campaign for Achievement Now	The University of Chicago Urban Education Institute
Relay Graduate School of Education	Urban Teacher Residency United
RI-CAN: The Rhode Island Campaign for Achievement Now	

Opposition to HQT amendment (Coalition for Teacher Quality)	
Alliance for Multilingual Multicultural Education	National Disability Rights Network
American Council on Education	National Down Syndrome Congress
American Association of Colleges for Teacher Education	National Down Syndrome Society
American Association of People with Disabilities	National Education Association
American Association of State Colleges and Universities	National Indian Education Association
American Council for School Social Work	National Latino Education Research & Policy Project National Opportunity to Learn Campaign
Association of University Centers on Disabilities	National PTA
ASPIRA Association	National Urban League
Autistic Self Advocacy Network	Opportunity Action
Autism National Committee	Parents Across America
Center for Teaching Quality	Partnership for 21st Century Skills
Citizens for Effective Schools	Public Advocates Inc.
Communities for Excellent Public Schools	Public Advocacy for Kids
Council for Exceptional Children	Rural School and Community Trust
Council of Parent Attorneys and Advocates	School Social Work Association of America
Disability Policy Collaboration, A Partnership of The Arc and UCP	SEDL
Disability Rights Education and Defense Fund Inc	South East Asia Resource Action Center
Easter Seals	TASH—Equity, Opportunity, and Inclusion for People with Disabilities
Education Law Center	Teacher Education Division of the Council for Exceptional Children
FairTest, The National Center for Fair & Open Testing	TESOL International Association

Opposition to HQT amendment (Coalition for Teacher Quality)
First Focus Campaign for Children
Gamaliel Foundation
Helen Keller National Center
Higher Education Consortium for Special Education
Hispanic Association of Colleges and Universities
Latino Elected and Appointed Officials National Taskforce on Education
Lawyers' Committee for Civil Rights Under Law
League of United Latin American Citizens
Learning Disabilities Association of America
Movement Strategy Center
NAACP
NAACP Legal Defense and Educational Fund, Inc.
National Alliance of Black School Educators
National Association of Elementary School Principals
National Association of School Psychologists
National Association of Secondary School Principals
National Association of State Directors of Special Education
National Center for Learning Disabilities
National Consortium on Deaf-Blindness
National Council for Educating Black Children
National Council of Teachers of English
United Church of Christ Justice & Witness Ministries
State and Local Organizations:
Abbott Leadership Institute
Action Now—Illinois
Action Now—North Carolina
ACTION United
Alliance of Californians for Community Empowerment (ACCE)
Arkansas Community Organizations
Bay Area Parent Leadership Action Network
Brighton Park Neighborhood Council
California Association for Bilingual Education
Californians for Justice
Californians Together
California Latino School Boards Association
Campaign for Quality Education
Center for the Future of Teaching and Learning Coalition for Educational Justice
Delawareans for Social and Economic Justice
Educate Our State
Grow Your Own Illinois
Inner City Struggle
Justice Matters
Legal Advocates for Children and Youth
Montgomery County Education Forum
Parent-U-Turn

Opposition to HQT amendment (**Coalition for Teacher Quality**)	
National Council of Teachers of Mathematics	Parents for Unity
	RYSE Center
	San Francisco Teacher Residency
	Texas Association of Chicanos in Higher Education
	Young Voices—Providence
	Youth On Board—Massachusetts
	Youth Together

REFERENCES

American Board for the Certification in Teacher Excellence. (2018). *How to become a teacher*. Retrieved from www.americanboard.org/

Angrist, J. D., Dynarski, S. M., Kane, T. J., Pathak, P. A., & Walters, C. R. (2012). Who benefits from KIPP? *Journal of Policy Analysis and Management*, *31*, 837–860.

Apple, M. W. (2013). *Education and power.* New York, NY: Routledge.

Au, W. (2007). High-stakes testing and curricular control: A qualitative metasynthesis. *Educational Researcher*, *36*(5), 258–267.

Au, W., & Ferrare, J. J. (Eds.). (2015). *Mapping corporate education reform: Power and policy networks in the neoliberal state*. New York, NY: Routledge.

Ball, S. J. (2012). *Global Education Inc: New policy networks and the neo-liberal imaginary.* London, UK: Routledge.

Ball, S. J., & Junemann, C. (2012). *Networks, new governance and education*. Bristol, UK: Policy Press.

Beck, M. (2015). Scott Walker proposes way for "real life experience" to qualify as teaching license. *Wisconsin State Journal*. Retrieved from host.madison.com/news/local/education/local_schools/scott-walker-proposes-way-for-real-lifeexperience-to-qualify/article_776203a9-87e1-5c30-80e7-cbbcf70d0a42.html

Berliner, D. C., & Glass, G. V. (Eds.). (2014). *50 myths and lies that threaten America's public schools: The real crisis in education.* New York, NY: Teachers College Press.

Beyer, L. (2007). Teacher education and the new professionalism: The case of the USA. In J. Freeman-Moir & A. Scott (Eds.), *Shaping the future: Critical essays on teacher education* (pp. 25–42). Rotterdam, The Netherlands: Sense.

Borgatti, S. P., Everett, M. G., and Johnson, J. C. (2018). *Analyzing social networks* (2nd ed.). London, UK: Sage.

Braun, B. (2015, March 8). Look out Rutgers and Seton Hall—Cami's "Relay-GSE" is out to eat your lunch. *Bob Braun's Ledger*. Retrieved from www.bobbraunsledger.com/look-out-rutgers-and-seton-hall-camis-relay-gse-is-out-to-eatyour-lunch/

Brinson, D., Boast, L., Hassel, B. C., & Kingsland, N. (2012). *New Orleans-style education reform: A guide for cities–lessons learned 2004–2010.* Chapel Hill, NC: Public Impact.

Caperton, G., & Whitmire, R. (2012). *The achievable dream.* New York, NY: The College Board.

Capitol Hill Fellows. (2018). Capitol Hill Fellows program. Retrieved from www.teachforamerica.org/life-as-an-alum/alumni-resources/capitol-hill-fellows

Chubb, J. E., & Moe, T. M. (1990). *Politics, markets, and America's schools.* Washington, DC: Brookings Institution Press.

Cochran-Smith, M., Piazza, P., & Power, C. (2013, January). The politics of accountability: Assessing teacher education in the United States. *The Educational Forum*, *77*(1), 6–27.

Colvin, R. L. (2005). A new generation of philanthropists and their great ambitions. In F. M. Hess (Ed.), *With the best of intentions: How philanthropy is reshaping K–12 education* (pp. 21–48). Cambridge, MA: Harvard Education Press.

Damast, A. (2012, March). Q&A: Teach for America's Wendy Kopp. *Bloomberg Business*. Retrieved from www.bloomberg.com/news/articles/2012-03-26/q-and-a-teach-for-americas-wendy-kopp

Darling-Hammond, L. (1994). Who will speak for the children. *Phi Delta Kappan*, *76*(1), 21–34.

Darling-Hammond, L. (2004). Inequality and the right to learn: Access to qualified teachers in California's public schools. *Teachers College Record, 106*, 1936–1966.

Darling-Hammond, L. (2006). *Powerful teacher education: Lessons from exemplary programs.* San Francisco, CA: John Wiley & Sons.

Davies, J. S. (2005). Local governance and the dialectics of hierarchy, market and network. *Policy Studies,* 26, 311–335.

Foote, D. (2009). *Relentless pursuit: A year in the trenches with Teach For America.* New York, NY: Vintage Books.

Fraser, J. W. (2007). *Preparing America's teachers: A history*. New York, NY: Teachers College Press.

Friedrich, D. S. (2014). Global microlending in education reform: Enseñá por Argentina and the neoliberalization of the grassroots. *Comparative Education Review, 58*, 296–321.

Gatti, L. (2016). *Towards a framework of resources for learning to teach: Rethinking US teacher preparation.* New York, NY: Palgrave Macmillan.

Golann, J. W. (2015). The paradox of success at a no-excuses school. *Sociology of Education, 88*, 103–119.

Goodman, J. F. (2013). Charter management organizations and the regulated environment: Is it worth the price? *Educational Researcher*, *42*, 89–96.

Grabher, G., & Powell, W. (2005). *Networks: Critical studies in economic institutions* (Vol. 1). Camberley, UK: Edward Elgar.

Grossman, P., & Loeb, S. (Eds.). (2008). *Taking stock: An examination of alternative certification.* Cambridge, MA: Harvard Education Press.

Hess, F. M. (2001). *Tear down the wall: The case for a radical overhaul of teacher certification.* Washington, DC: The Progressive Policy Institute.

Hess, F. M., & DuPre, S. (2015, February 11). The crazy campus crusade against Teach For America. *National Review*. Retrieved from www.nationalreview.com/article/398347/crazy-campus-crusade-against-teach-america-frederick-m-hess-sarah-dupre

Hess, F. M., & Finn, C. (2007). What innovators can, and cannot do. *Education Next*, *7*(2), 48–56.

Higgins, M., Hess, F., Weiner, J., & Robison, W. (2011). Creating a corps of change agents. *Education Next, 11*(3), 15–21.

Hiltonsmith, R., & Draut, T. (2014). The Great Cost Shift Continues. *Demos*. Retrieved on April 15, 2019 from www.demos.org/sites/default/files/publications/TheGreatCostShift2014-Brief_0.pdf

Hootnik, A. (2014, May). Teachers are losing their jobs and Teach For America's expanding: What's wrong with that? *The Nation*. Retrieved from www.thenation.com/article/179363/teachers-are-losing-their-jobs-teach-americas-expanding-whats-wrong?page=0,1

Ingersoll, R. M., & Smith, T. (2003). The wrong solution to the teacher shortage. *Educational Leadership, 60*(8), 30–33.

Knowledge is Power Program. (2016). Teach For America: A Local Partner in Addressing the Teacher Diversity Gap. Retrieved on April 18, 2019 from www.kipp.org/news/minneapolis-post-teach-for-america-a-local-partner-in-addressing-the-teacher-diversity-gap/

Knowledge Is Power Program. (2018). Retrieved on June 1 from www.kipp.org.

Kopp, W. (2001). *One day, all children: The unlikely triumph of Teach For America and what I learned along the way.* New York, NY: Public Affairs.

Kretchmar, K., Sondel, B., & Ferrare, J. (2014). Mapping the terrain: Teach For America, charter school reform, and corporate sponsorship. *Journal of Education Policy, 29*(6), 742–759.

Kretchmar, K., & Zeichner, K. (2016). Teacher prep 3.0: A vision for teacher education to impact social transformation. *Journal of Education for Teaching, 42*(4), 417–433.

Kronholz, J. (2012). A new type of ed school. *Education Next, 12*(4). 42–49

Kumashiro, K. (2010). Seeing the bigger picture: Troubling movements to end teacher education. *Journal of Teacher Education, 61*, 56–65.

Kumashiro, K. (2015, January 12). Review of proposed 2015 federal teacher preparation regulations. National Education Policy Center. Retrieved from nepc.colorado.edu/thinktank/review-proposed-teacher-preparation

Labaree, D. (2010). Teach For America and teacher ed: Heads they win, tails we lose. *Journal of Teacher Education, 61*(1–2), 48–55.

Lahann, R., & Reagan, E. M. (2011). Teach For America and the politics of progressive neoliberalism. *Teacher Education Quarterly, 38*(1), 7–27.

Leadership for Educational Equity. (2019). Who We Are? Retrieved on April 17, 2019: educationalequity.org/who-we-are

Levine, A. (2006). *Educating school teachers*. Washington, DC: The Education Schools Project.

Lyall, K. C., & Sell, K. R. (2006). The de facto privatization of American public higher education. *Change: The Magazine of Higher Learning, 38*(1), 6–13.

McShane, M. Q., & Hess, F. M. (2014). The politics of entrepreneurship and innovation. In B. S. Cooper, J. G. Cibulka, & L. D. Fusarelli (Eds.), *Handbook of education politics and policy* (2nd ed.), p. 304–322. New York, NY: Routledge.

Mehta, J., & Teles, S. (2012). Jurisdictional politics: A new federal role in education. In F. M. Hess & A. P. Kelly (Eds.), *Carrots, sticks, and the bully pulpit: Lessons from a half century of federal efforts to improve America's schools* (pp. 197–216). Cambridge, MA: Harvard Education Press.

Mehta, J., & Teles, S. (2014). Professionalization 2.0: The case for plural professionalism in education. In M. McShane & F. Hess (Eds,), *Teacher Quality 2.0: Will Today's Reforms Hold Back Tomorrow's Schools?* Cambridge, MA: Harvard Education Press.

Miner, B. (2010, March 24). Looking past the spin: Teach For America. *Rethinking Schools*. Retrieved from www.rethinkingschools.org/archive/24_03/24_03_tfa.shtml

National Council on Teacher Quality. (2011). Building better teachers: National review of teacher preparation programs. Retrieved from www.nwosu.edu/uploads//education/nctq.pdf

National Council on Teacher Quality. (2018). About. Retrieved from www.nctq.org/about/

Newfield, C. (2018). Have we wrecked public universities? The case of the American decline cycle. *The British Journal of Sociology*, *69*(2), 484–493.

Otterman, S. (2011, July 21). Ed schools' pedagogical puzzle. *The New York Times.* Retrieved from www.nytimes.com/2011/07/24/education/edlife/edl-24teacher-t.html

Pitzer, H. K. (2010). "What's best for kids" vs. teacher unions: How Teach For America blames teacher unions for the problems of urban schools. *Workplace: A Journal for Academic Labor*, *17*, 61–74.

Reckhow, S., & Snyder, J. W. (2014). The expanding role of philanthropy in education politics. *Educational Researcher*, *43*, 186–195.

Relay Graduate School of Education. (2015). Relay Newark announces NPS program [Blog post]. Retrieved from www.relay.edu/blog-entry/relay-newark-announces-nps-program

Relay Graduate School of Education. (2016a). Our institution. Retrieved from www.relay.edu/about/institution

Relay Graduate School of Education. (2016b). Our approach. Retrieved from relay.edu/about-us/approach

Relay Graduate School (2018). *Relay teaching residency.* Retrieved from relay.edu/aspiring-teachers/relay-teaching-residency/program-overview-relay-teaching-residency

Rhodes, R. A. W. (2006). Policy network analysis. In M. Moran, M. Rein, & R. E. Goodin (Eds.), *The Oxford handbook of public policy* (pp. 423–445). Oxford, UK: Oxford University Press.

Rich, M. (2015, February 5). Fewer top graduates want to join Teach For America. *The New York Times.* Retrieved from www.nytimes.com/2015/02/06/education/fewer-top-graduates-want-to-join-teach-for-america.html

Saltman, K. J. (2010a). *The gift of education: Public education and venture philanthropy.* London, UK: Palgrave Macmillan.

Saltman, K. J. (Ed.). (2010b). *Schooling and the politics of disaster.* New York, NY: Routledge.

Sawchuk, S. (2011). States' Ed. Schools backing out of NCTQ review. *Education Week.* [Blog post]. Retrieved from blogs.edweek.org/edweek/teacherbeat/2011/04/states_ed_schools_peel_off_nct.html

Scott, J. (2009). The politics of venture philanthropy in charter school policy and advocacy. *Educational Policy*, *23*, 106–136.

Simon, S. (2013). Teach For America rises as political powerhouse. *Politico Pro Education.* Retrieved from www.politico.com/story/2013/10/teach-for-america-rises-as-political-powerhouse-098586

Sleeter, C. E. (2008). Equity, democracy, and neoliberal assaults on teacher education. *Teaching and Teacher Education*, *54*, 1947–1957.

Sondel, B. (2016). "No excuses" in New Orleans: The silent passivity of neoliberal schooling. *The Educational Forum-Kappa Delta Pi, 80*(2), 171–188.

Stitzlein, S. M., & West, C. K. (2014). New forms of teacher education: Connections to charter schools and their approaches. *Democracy and Education*, *22*(2), 1–10.

Teach For America 990 Form. (2012). *Internal Revenue Service Form 990.* Retrieved from www.guidestar.org/

Teach For America. (2013). *Teach For America annual letter 2012–2013*. Retrieved from www.teachforamerica.org/sites/default/files/teach_for_america_fy12-13_annual_letter.pdf

Teach For America 990 Form. (2015a). *Internal Revenue Service Form 990*. Retrieved from www.guidestar.org/

Teach For America. (2015b). Teach For America statement on Obama administration forthcoming release of teacher preparation regulations. Retrieved from www.teachforamerica.org/

Teach For America. (2016c). TFA and the teaching workforce: What the numbers tell us. Retrieved from www.teachforamerica.org

Teach For America. (2017). Teach For America Releases its 2017 corps profile. Retrieved from teachforamerica.org/top-stories/teach-america-releases-its-2017-corps-profile

Teach For America. (2018a). What we do. Retrieved from www.teachforamerica.org/what-we-do

Teach For America. (2018b). What the research says. Retrieved from www.teachforamerica.org/sites/default/files/what-the-research-says.pdf

Thernstrom, A., & Thernstrom, S. (2004). *No excuses: Closing the racial gap in learning*. New York, NY: Simon & Schuster.

Tompkins-Stange, M. E. (2016). *Policy patrons: Philanthropy, education reform, and the politics of influence*. Cambridge, MA: Harvard Education Press.

Vasquez-Heilig, J. V., & Jez, S. J. (2014). Teach For America: A return to the evidence. Retrieved from nepc.colorado.edu/publication/teach-for-america

Wasserman, S., & Faust, K. (1994). *Social network analysis: Methods and applications*. New York, NY: Cambridge University Press.

Weiner, L. (2007). A lethal threat to U.S. teacher education. *Journal of Teacher Education, 58*, 274–286.

Zeichner, K. (2010). Competition, economic rationalization, increased surveillance, and attacks on diversity: Neo-liberalism and the transformation of teacher education in the U.S. *Teaching and Teacher Education, 26*, 1544–1552.

Zeichner, K. (2011). Improving teacher education in the United States. *American Educational Research Association Essays*. Retrieved from duckduckgo.com/l/?kh=-1&uddg=https%3A%2F%2Flarrycuban.files.wordpress.com%2F2011%2F07%2Fzeichner_aera_essay-1b.pdf

Zeichner, K., & Peña-Sandoval, C. (2015). Venture philanthropy and teacher education policy in the U.S.: The role of the new schools venture fund. *Teachers College Record, 117*(6), 1–44.

Zingg, L. (2018, February 20). Kickstart your career in public leadership. Retrieved from www.teachforamerica.org/stories/kickstart-your-career-in-public-leadership

CHAPTER 10

Academic Achievement of Students Taught by Teachers from Differing Preparation Programs

Denise K. Whitford, Dake Zhang, and Antonis Katsiyannis

Since the 1980s there has been controversy surrounding the alternative preparation of teachers in the United States. On one side of the debate, there are those who are strong supporters of traditional preparation programs and critical of alternative preparation programs, while on the other side of the debate, there are those who are strong supporters of alternative programs that fill gaps in the teaching workforce. In this chapter we will (1) discuss the pros and cons of traditional and alternative teacher preparation, (2) outline this protracted controversy over teacher preparation, (3) review current findings regarding student achievement, and (4) provide recommendations to improve and sustain student achievement regardless of the preparation program of their teachers.

For context regarding trends in teaching demographics, in the 2015–16 school year, there were an estimated 3,827,100 teachers in public elementary and secondary schools in the United States; about 80% of all public school teachers were White, 9% were Hispanic/Latinx, 7% were Black, and 2% were Asian. Among public school teachers, 77% were female and 23% were male. Females were more likely to teach in elementary schools (89%), versus middle schools (73%) and high schools (59%) (Taie & Goldring, 2017). The American Association of Colleges for Teacher Education (AACTE, 2018) released a report outlining the decline in undergraduate education degrees awarded from nearly 200,000 in the early 1970s to less than 100,000 in 2018. AACTE (2018) also noted an increase in master's education degrees from the mid-1980s until 2010. However, the number of master's education degrees have declined by 14% since 2010. Theories for this decline in education degrees awarded include low pay, poor working conditions, fewer undergraduate degree programs in education, removal of reimbursement policies by school districts for higher education course work, and an increase in access to other fields of study for women, who make up the majority of education degree holders (AACTE, 2018).

TEACHER PREPARATION PROGRAMS

Traditional Teacher Preparation Programs

The two primary sectors of teacher preparation are traditional teacher preparation programs and alternative teacher preparation programs. Definitions of traditional and alternative programs have become fluid over the last several years. However, in most common usage, traditional teacher preparation programs are those in which undergraduate bachelor's students major in education, have a specific content area focus (e.g., math, English, social studies, science), and are trained as an early childhood, secondary education, or special education teacher. In 2014, there were 2,171 teacher preparation providers in the U.S.; 1,497 (69%) were classified as traditional teacher preparation providers. These university-based programs provide education to preservice teachers who have no prior teaching or work experience and their degree generally leads to at least a bachelor's degree, but may also lead to a teaching credential without a degree (Boyd, Goldhaber, Lankford, & Wyckoff, 2007; Shuls & Trivitt, 2015; U.S. Department of Education, Office of Postsecondary Education, 2016). Teachers prepared in traditional programs tend to have supervised teaching experiences through their programs (Boyd et al., 2007; Shuls & Trivitt, 2015).

The three most commonly reported requirements for admission into traditional undergraduate teacher preparation programs are minimum GPA, transcript, and minimum number of courses completed. Traditional programs include coursework on social foundations, pedagogy, subject content, pedagogical methods specific to content areas, child development and educational psychology, special education, and on teaching English Learners and/or students with special education needs (Roth & Swail, 2000). In 2014, the average number of hours of field-based experiences expected by these programs was 100; the average number of student teaching hours was 600. Over 89% (447,116 individuals) of preservice teachers were enrolled in traditional teacher preparation programs. Teachers in traditional preparation programs tend to be female (76%) and White (73%); 11% were Hispanic/Latinx and 10% Black (U.S. Department of Education, Office of Postsecondary Education, 2016).

In summary, traditional preparation programs attract candidates who are predominantly White and female. These programs enroll the vast majority of teacher candidates and allow for extensive coursework in pedagogy and supervised field-based experiences. Unfortunately, in light of increasingly severe teacher shortages, traditional preparation programs are often perceived as unnecessarily rigid and as having limited enrollment rates in content areas such science and mathematics. In addition, traditional preparation programs appear to be less competitive in attracting the best qualified candidates, in relation to other majors (see, e.g., Darling-Hammond, 1990).

Alternative Preparation Programs

As for alternative teacher preparation programs, they tend to attract individuals switching careers, who hold at least a bachelor's degree in a non-education field, and who currently hold an emergency/temporary license. These uncertified inservice teachers participate in accelerated programs that fast-track them through teaching preparation as they work toward licensure. This fast-tracking is a desirable characteristic in districts that are hardest hit by the national teaching shortage, particularly in STEM-related positions and special education positions (Learning Policy Institute, 2017). In rural and high-poverty schools, turnover is rapid and fast-track programs offer a stream of new candidates. Special education teachers, in particular, often have varied and demanding responsibilities, including intervention planning and case management, in addition to teaching and other school roles (Creighton-Martin & Hauth, 2015). This workload in conjunction with a general lack of resources leaves special education teachers vulnerable to burnout; in turn, districts experience high turnover rates. These issues are further exacerbated in rural school districts and high-poverty areas, as they are most likely to have underqualified teachers and less resources for teachers to meet job demands (Ludlow, Conner, & Schechter, 2005).

The duration of programs and their requirements vary by individual states (Boyd et al., 2007; Shuls & Trivitt, 2015; U.S. Department of Education, Office of Postsecondary Education, 2016). Compared to the long period of supervised student teaching in traditional programs, alternative preparation programs often put teachers in training into their own classrooms with minimal supervision (Boyd et al., 2007; Shuls & Trivitt, 2015). The positive aspect of this type of preparation is that teachers have full-time on-the-job training that traditional preparation programs tend to lack. However, although one can argue that this approach may be appropriate for those with a natural ability to teach well, others often experience negative academic and behavioral consequences associated with unsupervised exploration of teaching. Research has yet to determine who does and does not have a natural ability to teach well and because "you don't know what you don't know," such situations can be detrimental to the growth of students who are saddled with teachers who do not possess natural abilities to teach well, lack a foundational understanding of classroom management, or lack knowledge about the nuances of working with culturally and linguistically diverse students and families.

In 2014, 47 states, the District of Columbia, Puerto Rico, and the Virgin Islands reported having approved alternative routes to a teaching credential (U.S. Department of Education, Office of Postsecondary Education, 2016). Alternative preparation programs can be housed at Institutes of Higher Education (IHEs) or non-IHE organizations. In 2014, 473 (22%) alternative teacher preparation program providers were within IHEs, and 201 (19%) were in non-IHEs.

Out of just under 500,000 total teachers in training during the 2012–2013 academic year, over 5% were enrolled in alternative programs at IHEs, and almost 6% were enrolled in alternative programs at non-IHEs. Alternative programs enrolled a more diverse pool of individuals (e.g., 18% of individuals enrolled in non-IHEs were Black, and 18% were Hispanic/Latinx; U.S. Department of Education, Office of Postsecondary Education, 2016). Furthermore, alternative IHE programs and non-IHE programs were more likely to have completers in special education, mathematics, and general science. Traditional preparation programs trained 7% of teachers in mathematics whereas the proportion of math teachers was 8% in alternative IHE programs and 12% in alternative non-IHE programs (U.S. Department of Education, Office of Innovation and Improvement, 2004). Attrition rates, however, among alternative preparation teachers were double the rate of traditional preparation teachers; among Teach For America (TFA) teachers (considered to be the nation's most prestigious alternative preparation program) attrition was even higher. By the fourth year of teaching, more than 50% of alternative preparation teachers overall and 85% of TFA teachers leave the field, compared to 37% of traditionally prepared teachers (Boyd et al., 2007; see also, Darling-Hammond, Holtzman, Gatlin, & Heilig, 2005; Kane, Rockoff, & Staiger, 2008).

In summary, although teachers from alternative preparation programs often fill positions in critical subject areas, particularly in science and mathematics, and represent a more diverse pool of teachers and second career individuals, attrition rates are high. Specifically, attrition rates among alternatively prepared teachers were double the rate of traditionally prepared teachers; among TFA teachers, rates were even higher. Although teacher turnover has historically been linked to poor student outcomes, recent research indicates there are several losses that can contribute to poor student outcomes. First, the loss of experienced teachers does not necessarily mean a loss of good teachers; second, financial losses that go into finding new teachers and time taken away from good teachers to train and mentor new teachers may be just as likely contributing to poor student outcomes (Ronfeldt, Loeb, & Wyckoff, 2013). Researchers also indicate that the link between teacher turnover and student achievement may be in part dependent on school climate, as teachers are more likely to remain and students excel in schools with positive climates (Kraft, Marinell, & Shen-Wei Yee, 2016).

THE CONTROVERSY IN TEACHER PREPARATION

Traditional versus Alternative Teacher Preparation Programs

Alternative preparation programs can be traced even earlier than the early 1980s when states officially endorsed alternative teacher preparation, and it was common practice in the 19th century for school districts to hire and certify their own teachers (Darling-Hammond, 1990). The State of Virginia initiated the first modern alternative preparation program in 1982, followed by New Jersey, Texas, and California (Dill, 1996; Feistritzer, 1998). The issue of alternative teacher preparation programs has been one of the most controversial and confusing topics in the discourse about U.S. teacher education since the 1980s when alternatively prepared teachers started entering classrooms in greater numbers (Zeichner & Schulte, 2001). Alternative teacher preparation programs were created to diversify and increase the teaching force by allowing those without certification to switch careers and expedite entry into K–12 classrooms (Boyd et al., 2007; Shuls & Trivitt, 2015).

The background factors that caused the movement toward alternative preparation mainly included critical teacher shortages, the poor quality of individuals entering the teaching profession, and growing criticism of traditional teacher education practices (Dill, 1996; Feistritzer, 1998; Kopp, 1989; Stoddart & Floden, 1995). Subject areas such as mathematics education, science education, and special education have reported chronic teacher shortages since the 1980s (Darling-Hammond, Hudson, & Kirby, 1989; Learning Policy Institute, 2017). Alternative preparation programs have made it possible for many scientists and mathematicians interested in teaching to smoothly enter the education field (Dill, 1996). Alternative preparation programs have also made it easier for teachers of color to enter the teaching field without completing the traditional college education programs (Middleton, Mason, Stilwell, & Parker, 1988).

In the early 1980s, studies showed that many high-ability college students were not interested in pursuing an education degree, and some research shows that undergraduate students enrolled in education majors were among the least academically competent students of all college students (Stoddart & Floden, 1995), based on their American College Testing (ACT) and Graduate Record Examinations (GRE) scores (Darling-Hammond, 1990). The resulting call for recruiting "high-ability individuals" into the education workforce has also led to growing support for alternative teacher certification (Feistritzer, 1998).

However, these practical reasons that aimed to create a convenient shortcut for non-education majors to get into the field have raised extensive concerns. One common argument against alternative preparation reflects cases where the standards are lower than those required in traditional college and university teacher preparation. Alternative teacher preparation programs have been viewed as weakening teaching as a profession, because these programs ignore the need for professional knowledge and focus primarily on direct classroom experience (Zumwalt, 1991). Consequently, these less-qualified teachers, certified in alternative preparation programs with lowered standards, brought disadvantages to students of color and students from low socioeconomic backgrounds, because teachers without full certification are more likely to be hired by large urban school districts, and there are high percentages of low-income students of color attending schools in these districts (Darling-Hammond, 1990).

Another criticism against the initial motivation to recruit mathematicians and scientists to teaching careers is that alternative preparation programs do not prepare these professionals with adequate educational foundational knowledge and appropriate pedagogical methodology. An assumption underlying alternative preparation programs is that subject matter preparation is the most critical factor for teaching, while educational philosophy and pedagogical skills can be learned with brief on-the-job training. However, this intuitive assumption may not be true because supervision does not always materialize for alternatively prepared trainees (Darling-Hammond, 1990). The lengthy traditional teacher preparation programs typically include a considerable number of courses in educational foundations (e.g., child development, learning philosophy and theories, etc.) and instructional methods (e.g., inclusive teaching, classroom organization and management, reading/math instruction methods, etc.). In addition, intensely supervised internships or student teaching experiences of either a semester or full year are typically required to complete a traditional teacher education program, but are not required for alternatively prepared trainees.

These misgivings toward alternative preparation programs result in questions about the quality and effectiveness of alternatively prepared teachers. Substantial research has examined the teaching effectiveness of alternatively prepared teachers. It is not an uncommon opinion among observers that alternative certification is generally negatively related to student achievement and that full certification is positively related to student achievement (Betts, Zau, & Rice, 2003; Goldhaber & Brewer, 2000). Studies conducted during the previous shortage era concluded that teachers trained by traditional routes are generally more highly rated and more successful than teachers prepared through alternative preparation programs, including in fields where many people assume teachers' content knowledge is essential, such as science education and vocational education (Darling-Hammond, 1990). Teachers trained in alternative programs appear to demonstrate even more difficulties during the early teaching career phases (Adams, Hutchinson, & Martray, 1980; Glassberg, 1980), as they appear to have greater difficulty with curriculum development, pedagogical knowledge, addressing individual students' special needs, adjusting to students' differential learning styles, classroom management, and student motivation (Feiman-Nemser & Parker, 1990; Grossman, 1989; Lenk, 1989; Mitchell, 1987).

There have also been research presenting positive findings about alternative teacher preparation programs and their effectiveness. Although alternative teacher preparation programs have been criticized for lack of strong pedagogy-related coursework and limited field-based experiences, traditional teacher preparation programs have also been under recent criticism for lacking content-specific expert guidance during candidate training (Feuer, Floden,

Chudowsky, & Ahn, 2013). Advocates of alternative certification argue that alternative programs will actually enhance the status of the teaching profession by bringing academically competent individuals into teaching who would not otherwise have entered into the profession (Schaefer, 1999).

Alternative certification does not automatically mean poor student outcomes. Constantine et al. (2009) used a random assignment procedure to compare alternatively certified teachers to traditionally trained teachers and found no differences between the two groups in comparable elementary classrooms. Further research reported that teachers prepared via alternative programs seem to yield very different teaching effectiveness at different grade levels and for different subjects. For example, Henry and colleagues (2014) compared the academic achievement of students from traditionally prepared teachers in North Carolina public universities to those from out-of-state and alternative preparation program backgrounds. They found that teachers trained by out-of-state traditional teacher preparation programs were less effective in elementary grades and high school, and alternatively trained teachers were less effective in high school. Sass (2015) examined three groups of early-career, alternatively certified teachers who received different types of alternative training in Florida. Using testing data for students in grades 4–10, he found the performance of some types of alternative certification better than others, and some worse than traditionally certified teachers, depending on the specific program, sample size, subject, type of test, and specification.

The complexity of what is considered an alternative program has also been widely discussed. There is a huge heterogeneity within alternative programs, and teaching effectiveness varies significantly within this range of program types. A single definition of what constitutes alternative certification has not been settled (Humphrey & Wechsler, 2007; Wilson, Floden, & Ferrini-Mundy, 2001, 2002), though these programs do typically encompass attaining certification outside the traditional four- or five-year undergraduate program. Different states have their own variation with alternative programs, and the programs vary upon each state's certification standards, and also upon who is certifying what. As Henry et al. (2014) stated,

> there is more variation in teacher effectiveness within preparation/certification categories than between them, which has been taken to mean that variables other than preparation may have greater effects on a teacher's classroom success. (p. 9)

Some national programs, such as TFA and Troops to Teachers, that recruit candidates into teaching and provide support, but whose participants must also complete other certification programs, make the alternative teacher preparation program category even more heterogeneous. Like other alternative certification programs, TFA recruits people who typically do not have an education degree or other formal training in education. However, TFA distinguishes itself from typical alternative programs or traditional certification programs with (1) much more selective standards and screening procedures, (2) a 5-week intensive training before TFA teachers start their first teaching job, and (3) ongoing mentoring and support during their contracted 2 years of teaching (TFA, 2016). Henry et al. (2014) reported that TFA corps members were more effective in teaching science, technology, engineering, and mathematics subjects than teachers trained by other alternative preparation programs. These encouraging results suggest the possibility of building an effective system of recruiting non-education majors to teach for students in schools with high needs.

Research on Teacher Effectiveness Based on Preparation

Research on teacher effectiveness, based on traditional versus alternative routes in preparation, has been mixed and there is a paucity of data-based studies linking preparation to student achievement (see National Research Council, Committee on the Study of Teacher Preparation Programs in the United States, 2010; Whitford, Zhang, & Katsiyannis, 2017). Caution, however, should be exercised in considering alternative preparation programs together, as they are quite diverse (see Sass, 2015). For example, Henry and colleagues (2014) reported that mathematics scores at all school levels and science scores in high schools were higher among students with TFA teachers, while Clark and colleagues (2013) found higher math scores among 6th- through 12th-graders with TFA teachers. Similarly, Glazerman, Mayer, and Decker (2006) found TFA teachers to be more effective regarding math achievement (though not in reading) than traditionally prepared teachers (see also Xu, Hannaway, & Taylor, 2011). Further, Sass (2015) concluded that alternative preparation teachers had stronger preservice academic skills than traditionally prepared teachers (e.g., higher initial pass rates on certification exams and higher college entrance exam scores) and made a favorable impact in student achievement in Florida.

Some studies reported no differences between traditional and alternative programs in student performance while others reported either traditional programs or alternative programs (particularly TFA and involving math and science) having positive differential effects on student performance. Constantine and colleagues (2009) found no significant differences in effectiveness between alternative and traditionally prepared teachers; Uriegas, Kupczynski, and Mundy (2014) found no differences in managing behavior. Boyd, Lankford, Loeb, Rockoff, and Wyckoff (2008), however, found that students of traditionally prepared teachers achieved significantly higher test scores in 4th and 5th grade than students of teachers from alternative route programs (i.e., TFA, New York Teaching Fellows) in New York. Similarly, Wilson et al. (2002) reported that preservice teacher subject-matter preparation and pedagogical coursework had a positive impact on student achievement.

TEACHER PREPARATION PROGRAMS AND STUDENT OUTCOMES

In the age of accountability, the teaching profession has gotten increased scrutiny (NCLB, 2002; ESSA, 2015). The role of public schooling is to educate children and adolescents so that they in turn can become productive citizens. The education landscape has been changing and schools are now starting to move away from strictly academic rigor and move into vocational training and talent developments. Regardless, basic academic skills are still essential in everyday life—skills like literacy and general knowledge of mathematics, science, and history. Laws like the Individuals with Disabilities Education Act (IDEA), No Child Left Behind (NCLB), and the Every Student Succeeds Act (ESSA) center teacher accountability for the transference of these academic skills to children and adolescents, based on a teacher's ability to improve academic outcomes for all students. These laws have pushed for the preparation of highly skilled teachers, otherwise known as "highly qualified." The teacher preparation debate often turns to the qualifications and ability of "fast-tracked" teachers to improve the academic achievement of their students, particularly in comparison to teachers who spent more time learning and perfecting their craft before testing it out on vulnerable populations of students.

In a recent meta-analysis, Whitford and colleagues (2017) identified 12 studies from 1998 to 2015 with 118 independent effect sizes regarding academic achievement for students taught by teachers in traditional and alternative preparation programs. The purpose of the study was to determine the impact that teachers from traditional and alternative preparation programs had on the achievement of their students. The first key finding was that only 12 studies in an 18-year period provided enough quantitative information to conduct a meta-analysis. This limited number of studies was surprising, considering the long-standing debate on this topic and the policy decisions created based around this debate. The second finding was that, in general, there was not much of a difference between the academic performance of students who were taught by traditional preparation teachers and of students taught by their alternative preparation counterparts; students of alternative preparation teachers did slightly better overall ($g = 0.03$; 95% $CI = 0.01, 0.04$, $p = 0.001$). Differences, although small, were observed, however, based on school level (i.e., elementary school, middle school, or high school), academic subject area, and type of alternative preparation program (see Table 10.1 for statistically significant results by content area, grade level, and preparation program).

The studies showed (1) positive results for the achievement of students with alternative teachers at the elementary and middle school level ($g = 0.03$ and 0.09, respectively), (2) general positive effects for students with teachers from alternative programs (g ranged from 0.04 to 0.12), and (3) greater increases in effect specifically for the TFA alternative preparation program.

Table 10.1. Content Area Academic Achievement by Preparation Grade Level and Preparation Program

	EFFECT SIZE						HETEROGENEITY		
	k	*g*	*SE*	*p*	*CI*		*Q*	*p*	I^2
Elementary School									
TFA vs. TTP Mathematics	6	0.08	0.02	<0.001	0.04,	0.01	5.69	0.337	12.14
ATP & TFA vs. TTP Mathematics	13	0.04	0.02	0.006	0.00,	0.08	33.79	0.001	64.48
Middle School									
ATP vs. TTP English/ELA/Reading	12	0.53	0.21	0.011	0.12,	0.93	99.57	<0.001	88.95
ATP & TFA vs. TTP English/ELA/ Reading	13	0.11	0.04	0.015	0.02,	0.19	103.91	<0.001	88.45
ATP & TFA vs. TTP Mathematics	29	0.12	0.05	0.022	0.02,	0.22	110.41	<0.001	74.64
High School									
ATP vs. TTP Science	6	–0.14	0.07	0.046	–0.28,	0.00	8.05	0.153	37.92
TFA vs. TTP Science	9	0.05	0.02	0.026	0.01,	0.10	327.22	<0.001	97.56
All School Levels Combined									
ATP vs. TTP Science	10	–0.03	0.01	0.005	–0.06,	–0.01	9.33	0.408	3.49
TFA vs. TTP Mathematics	14	0.08	0.02	0.002	0.03,	0.12	418.21	<0.001	96.89
TFA vs. TTP Science	11	0.06	0.02	0.006	0.02,	0.10	342.15	<0.001	97.08
ATP and TFA vs. TTP Mathematics	59	0.04	0.02	0.021	0.01,	0.08	749.53	<0.001	92.62

Note. Statistically significant findings from analyses with more than one study in Whitford, Zhang, & Katsiyannis (2017); ATP is alternative teacher preparation; TTP is traditional teacher preparation; TFA is Teach For America.

At face value, alternative preparation programs appear to take the "least qualified" people and place them in the highest need areas. However, Whitford and colleagues (2017) reported that those entering alternative preparation teachers are not necessarily the least qualified compared to traditionally prepared teachers. Specifically, findings indicated higher academic performances of students taught by teachers from TFA than of those taught by teachers prepared through traditional programs, but found less of a distinction between students taught by teachers from other alternative preparation programs and teachers taught by traditional preparation teachers. A plausible reason for the differences between general alternative preparation programs and TFA may be the rigorous standards set by TFA for applicants admitted into the program. The value of this approach is that students potentially have a higher likelihood of being taught by teachers who have strong content knowledge and may possibly teach in more creative ways than those exhibited by traditionally prepared teachers. Alternative teacher preparation programs, on the other hand, have a reputation for being a catch-all alternative for those switching careers, potentially looking for what may inaccurately be perceived as an easier job. However, these non-traditional teachers may also bring fresh ideas and creative methods for reaching our most vulnerable students in terms of representation in the academic achievement gap.

RECOMMENDATIONS

Teachers and teacher preparation are under criticism and therefore policymakers are interested in expanding the pool and quality of teachers coming into the profession (NCTQ, 2010; Rock et al., 2016). Preparation programs, even in well-known universities, often accept students who lack the skills to complete other, more rigorous, academic programs on campus. Moreover, critical teacher shortages across the United States have led to an influx of personnel who may not be as qualified as expected in preparation programs and classrooms. As previously mentioned, low pay, poor working conditions, fewer undergraduate degree programs in education, removal of reimbursement policies by school districts for higher education course work, and an increase in access to other fields of study for women, who make up the majority of education degree holders (AACTE, 2018), may have the greatest influences on teaching as a viable career. Preparation programs are expected to increase or maintain enrollments or risk losing their programs altogether, leading to a mentality favoring quantity over quality. Unfortunately, these factors can filter into preparation courses and cause a watering down of the curriculum and a lower threshold of knowledge and skills than what should really be acceptable measures of a quality teacher.

Despite the current teacher shortage, stakeholders must advocate for stricter admissions decisions in teacher preparation programs, insist on high standards for teacher preparation, and follow through on rigorous expectations. Furthermore, preparation programs, traditional and alternative, must improve the content area knowledge of teachers, in combination with pedagogical skills. For example, all future teachers should earn, at a minimum, a bachelor's degree from an accredited institution of higher education in their desired content area (e.g., English, mathematics, science, social studies). After the bachelor's is obtained, teacher candidates would then attend a rigorous and selective, extended or expedited, certification program that focuses on highly effective pedagogy and interventions in elementary, secondary, special education, and/or gifted education settings. These proposals will likely make the teacher shortage worse, but if we want to improve the quality of teachers and the student achievement they produce, these recommendations are critical. Such ambitious goals, however, will necessitate that legislators and policymakers make teacher preparation a high priority and ensure that financial incentives are readily available to attract qualified applicants, that high-quality professional development is available, and that practicing teachers are competitively compensated.

REFERENCES

Adams, R. D., Hutchinson, S. & Martray, C. (1980). A developmental study of teacher concerns across time. Paper presented at the American Educational Research Association (AERA) Annual Meeting. Boston, MA.

American Association of Colleges for Teacher Education [AACTE]. (2018). Colleges of education: A national portrait executive summary. Retrieved from secure.aacte.org/apps/rl/res_get.php?fid=4178&ref=rl

Betts, J. R., Zau, A. C., & Rice, L. A. (2003). *Determinants of student achievement: New evidence from San Diego*. San Francisco, CA: Public Policy Institute of California.

Boyd, D., Goldhaber, D., Lankford, H., & Wyckoff, J. (2007). The effect of certification and preparation on teacher quality. *The Future of Children, 17*, 45–68.

Boyd, D., Lankford, H., Loeb, S., Rockoff, J., & Wyckoff, J. (2008). The narrowing gap in New York City teacher qualifications and its implications for student achievement in high-poverty schools. *Journal of Policy Analysis and Management, 27*(4), 793–818. doi:10.1002/pam.20377

Clark, M. A., Chiang, H. S., Silva, T., McConnell, S., Sonnenfeld, K., Erbe, A., & Puma, M. (2013). *The effectiveness of secondary math teachers from Teach for America and the Teaching Fellows programs* (NCEE 2013-4015). Washington, DC: National Center for Education and Regional Assistance, Institute of Education Sciences, U.S. Department of Education. Retrieved from ies.ed.gov/ncee/pubs/20134015/pdf/20134015.pdf

Constantine, J., Player, D., Silva, T., Hallgren, K., Grider, M., & Deke, J. (2009). *An evaluation of teachers trained through different routes to certification*. NCEE 2009-4043. Washington, DC: U.S. Department of Education. Retrieved from ies.ed.gov/ncee/pubs/20094043/pdf/20094043.pdf

Creighton-Martin, C. & Hauth, C. (2015). *The survival guide for new special education teachers* (2nd Ed.). Arlington, VA: Council for Exceptional Children.

Darling-Hammond, L. (1990). Teaching and knowledge: Policy issues posed by alternate certification for teachers. *Peabody Journal of Education, 67*(3), 123–154.

Darling-Hammond, L., Holtzman, D., Gatlin, S. J., & Heilig, J. V. (2005). Does teacher preparation matter? Evidence about teacher certification, Teach For America, and teacher effectiveness. *Education Policy Analysis Archives, 13*(42). Retrieved from epaa.asu.edu/epaa/v13n42

Darling-Hammond, L., Hudson, L., & Kirby, S. N. (1989). *Redesigning teacher education: Opening the door for new recruits to science and mathematics teaching.* Santa Monica, CA: RAND.

Dill, V. S. (1996). *Alternative teacher certification.* In J. Sikula (Ed.), *Handbook of research on teacher education* (2nd ed., pp. 932–960). New York, NY: Macmillan.

Every Student Succeeds Act (ESSA) of 2015, Pub. L. No. 114-95, § 20 U.S.C., 70 (2015).

Feiman-Nemser, S., & Parker, M. B. (1990). Making subject matter part of the conversation in learning to teach. *Journal of Teacher Education, 41*(3), 32–43. doi:10.1177/002248719004100305

Feistritzer, C. E. (1998). *Teacher preparation and classroom size reduction.* Formal Testimony before the House Committee on Education and the Workforce, February 24, 1998.

Feuer, M. J., Floden, R. E., Chudowsky, N., & Ahn, J. (2013). *Evaluation of teacher preparation programs: Purposes, methods, and policy options.* Washington, DC: National Academy of Education.

Glassberg, S. (1980). A view of the beginning teacher from a developmental perspective. Paper presented at the American Educational Research Association (AERA) Annual Meeting. Boston, MA.

Glazerman, S., Mayer, D., & Decker, P. (2006). Alternative routes to teaching: The impacts of Teach for America on student achievement and other outcomes. *Journal of Policy Analysis and Management, 25,* 75–96.

Goldhaber, D. D., & Brewer, D. J. (2000). Does teacher certification matter? High school teacher certification status and student achievement. *Educational Evaluation and Policy Analysis, 22,* 129–145. doi:10.3102/01623737022002129

Grossman, P. (1989). Learning to teach without teacher education. *Teacher College Record, 91*(2), 191–208.

Henry, G. T., Bastian, K. C., Fortner, C. K., Kershaw, D. C., Purtell, K. M., Thompson, C. L., & Zulli, R. A. (2014). Teacher preparation policies and their effects on student achievement. *Education Finance and Policy, 9*(3), 264–303.

Humphrey, D., & Wechsler, M. (2007). Insights into alternative certification: Initial findings from a national study. *Teachers College Record, 109*(3), 483–530.

Kane, T. J., Rockoff, J. E., & Staiger, D. O. (2008). What does certification tell us about teacher effectiveness? Evidence from New York City. *Economics of Education Review, 27,* 615–631.

Kopp, W. (1989). *An argument and plan for the creation of the teacher corps.* (Bachelor's thesis). Princeton, NJ: Princeton University.

Kraft, M. A., Marinell, W. H., & Shen-Wei Yee, D. (2016). School organizational contexts, teacher turnover, and student achievement: Evidence from panel data. *American Educational Research Journal, 53*(5), 1411–1449. doi:10.3102/0002831216667478

Learning Policy Institute. (2017). Where have all the teachers gone? New study finds that tackling teacher turnover is critical step in ending U.S. teacher shortage. Retrieved from learningpolicyinstitute.org/press-release/where-have-all-teachers-gone

Lenk, H. A. (1989). A Case Study: The Induction of Two Alternate Route Social Studies Teachers. Unpublished doctoral dissertation. Teachers College, Columbia University.

Ludlow, B. L., Conner, D., & Schechter, J. (2005). Low incidence disabilities and personnel preparation for rural areas: Current status and future trends. *Rural Special Education Quarterly, 24*(3), 15–24.

Middleton, E. J., Mason, E. J., Stilwell, W. E., & Parker, W. C. (1988). A model for recruitment and retention of minority students in teacher preparation programs. *Journal of Teacher Education, 39,* 14-18. doi:10.1177/002248718803900104

Mitchell, N. (1987). Interim Evaluation Report of the Alternative Certification Program (REA87-027-2). Dallas, TX: DISD Department of Planning, Evaluation, and Testing.

National Council on Teacher Quality (NCTQ). (2010). *2009 state teacher policy yearbook: National summary.* Washington, DC: Author.

National Research Council, Committee on the Study of Teacher Preparation Programs in the United States. (2010). *Preparing teachers: Building evidence for sound policy.* [Summary]. Washington, DC: The National Academies Press. Retrieved from www.nsf.gov/attachments/117803/public/2b--Preparing_Teachers.pdf

No Child Left Behind (NCLB) Act of 2001, Pub. L. No. 107-110, § 115, Stat. 1425 (2002).

Rock, M. L., Spooner, F., Nagro, S., Vasquez, E., Dunn, C., Leko, M., . . . Jones, J. J. (2016). 21st century change drivers: Considerations for constructing transformative models of special education teacher development. *Teacher Education and Special Education, 39(2),* 98–120. doi:10.1177/0888406416640634

Ronfeldt, M., Loeb, S., & Wyckoff, J. (2013). How teacher turnover harms student achievement. *American Educational Research Journal, 50,* 4–36. doi: 10.3102/0002831212463813

Roth, D., & Swail, S. (2000). *Certification and teacher preparation in the United States.* Honolulu, HI: Pacific Resources for Education and Learning. Retrieved from www.educationalpolicy.org/pdf/PREL%20Certification.pdf

Sass, T. R. (2015). Licensure and worker quality: A comparison of alternative routes to teaching. *Journal of Law and Economics,* 58, 1–35.

Schaefer, N. (1999). Traditional and alternative certification: A view from the trenches. In M. Kanstoroom & C. Finn (Eds.), *Better teachers, better schools* (pp. 137–162). Washington, DC: Thomas Fordham Foundation.

Shuls, J. V., & Trivitt, J. R. (2015). Teacher effectiveness: An analysis of licensure screens. *Educational Policy, 29(4),* 645–675. doi:10.1177/0895904813510777

Stoddart, T., & Floden, R. E. (1995). *Traditional and alternate routes to teacher certification: Issues, assumptions, and misconceptions.* National Center for Research on Teacher Learning. East Lansing, MI: Michigan State University. Retrieved from files.eric.ed.gov/fulltext/ED383697.pdf.

Taie, S., & Goldring, R. (2017). *Characteristics of public elementary and secondary school teachers in the United States: Results from the 2015–16 National Teacher and Principal Survey First Look (NCES 2017- 072).* U.S. Department of Education. Washington, DC: National Center for Education Statistics. Retrieved from nces.ed.gov/pubsearch/pubsinfo.asp?pubid=2017072

Teach For America [TFA]. (2016). Retrieved from www.teachforamerica.org/

Uriegas, B., Kupczynski, L., & Mundy, M. (2014). A comparison of traditional and alternative certification routes on classroom management. *SAGE Open,* 1–6. doi:10.1177/2158244014553599

U.S. Department of Education, Office of Innovation and Improvement. (2004). *Innovations in Education: Alternative Routes to Teacher Certification.* Washington, DC: Author.

U.S. Department of Education, Office of Postsecondary Education. (2016). *Preparing and credentialing the nation's teachers: The Secretary's 10th Report on Teacher Quality*, Washington, DC: Author. Retrieved from title2.ed.gov/Public/TitleIIReport16.pdf

Whitford, D., Zhang, D., & Katsiyannis, A. (2017). Traditional versus alternative teacher preparation programs: A meta-analysis. *Journal of Child and Family Studies, 27*(3), 671–685. doi:10.1007/s10826-017-0932-0

Wilson, S. M., Floden, R. E., & Ferrini-Mundy, J. (2001, February). *Teacher preparation research: current knowledge, gaps, and recommendations.* [Research report]. Document R-01-3. Center for the Study of Teaching and Policy, University of Washington. Retrieved from www.education.uw.edu/ctp/sites/default/files/ctpmail/PDFs/TeacherPrep-WFFM-02-2001.pdf

Wilson, S. M., Floden, R. E., & Ferrini-Mundy, J. (2002). Teacher preparation research: An insider's view from the outside. *Journal of Teacher Education, 53*(3), 190–204.

Xu, Z., Hannaway, J., & Taylor, C. (2011). Making a difference? The effects of Teach for America in high school. *Journal of Policy Analysis and Management, 30*, 447–469.

Zeichner, K. M., & Schulte, A. K. (2001). What we know and don't know from peer-reviewed research about alternative teacher certification programs. *Journal of Teacher Education, 52(4)*, 266–282.

Zumwalt, K. (1991). Alternative routes to teaching: Three alternative approaches. *Journal of Teacher Education, 42(2)*, 83–92.

About the Editors and Contributors

Christopher A. Lubienski is a professor of education policy at Indiana University. His research centers on the political economy of education policy and research use in policymaking.

T. Jameson Brewer is an assistant professor of social foundations of education in the Teacher Education Department at the University of North Georgia. His research focuses on the impact of privatization in education.

Jamie C. Atkinson is an assistant professor in the Department of Reading, Foundations, and Technology in the College of Education at Missouri State University.

Deron Boyles is professor of philosophy of education in the Department of Educational Policy Studies at Georgia State University.

Jim Burns is an assistant professor of curriculum and instruction in the Teaching and Learning department at Florida International University.

Anthony Cody is a National Board–certified teacher and co-founder of the Network for Public Education.

Hilary Conklin is an associate professor of teacher education at DePaul University.

Brian W. Dotts is a clinical associate professor of social foundations at the University of Georgia.

M. Beatriz Fernández is an assistant professor in the Instituto de Estudios Avanzados en Educación at the Universidad de Chile.

Joseph J. Ferrare is an assistant professor in the Department of Educational Policy Studies & Evaluation at the University of Kentucky, where he also holds appointments in the Department of Sociology and Martin School of Public Policy & Administration.

Lauren Gatti is an associate professor in Teaching, Learning and Teacher Education at the University of Nebraska–Lincoln.

Antonis Katsiyannis is Alumni Distinguished Professor in the College of Education at Clemson University.

Kerry Kretchmar is an associate professor in the Department of Education at Carroll University (Waukesha, WI). Her research interests include examining the way market-based reforms are impacting teachers, teaching, and teacher education.

Priya Goel La Londe is an assistant professor at The University of Hong Kong.

Warren Mark Liew is an assistant professor at the National Institute of Education, Nanyang Technological University in Singapore.

Kavita Kapadia Matsko is an associate professor at the School of Education and Social Policy at Northwestern University.

Carmen Montecinos is a professor of psychology and director of the Leadership Center for School Improvement at the Pontificia Universidad Católica de Valparaíso.

Dario Sforza, EdD, is Superintendent of the Carlstadt–East Rutherford (New Jersey) Regional School District.

Beth Sondel is an assistant professor of education at University of Pittsburgh. Her research partners critical theory and qualitative methods to investigate the sociopolitical context of teaching.

Christopher H. Tienken is an associate professor in the Department of Education Leadership, Management, and Policy at Seton Hall University.

Westry Whitaker is an assistant professor of middle and secondary education in the Teacher Education Department at the University of North Georgia.

Denise K. Whitford is an assistant professor of special education at Purdue University.

Dake Zhang is an associate professor at the Rutgers University Graduate School of Education.

Index